P9-CEV-532

ITALY

A Culinary Journey

PASCHALE·CICONIA·VENETIAR
DVCE·ANNO·CHRISTI·MDXCI
VRBIS·CONDITAE·MCLXX
CVRANTIBVS
ALOYSIO·GEORGIO·PROC·M·ANTONIO·BARBARO
EQ·ET·PROC·IACOBO·FOSCARENO·EQ·ET·PROC

Vino

ITALY

A Culinary Journey

CollinsPublishersSanFrancisco

A Division of HarperCollinsPublishers

First published in USA 1991
by Collins Publishers San Francisco

Produced by Weldon Owen Pty Limited
43 Victoria Street, McMahons Point, NSW 2060, Australia
Telex AA23038; Fax (02) 929 8352
Weldon Owen Inc.
90 Gold Street, San Francisco, CA 94133, USA
Fax (415) 291 8841
Member of the Weldon International Group of Companies
Sydney • San Francisco • Chicago • London • Paris

President: John Owen
General Manager: Stuart Laurence
Publisher: Wendely Harvey
Foreign Editions Editor: Derek Barton
Editor: Gillian Hewitt
Assistant Editor: Vanessa Finney
Editorial Assistant: Tristan Phillips
Indexer: Susan Leipa, Comsearch Information Services
Picture Researcher: Brigitte Zinsinger
Designer: John Bull, The Book Design Company
Production Director: Mick Bagnato
Maps and Illustrations: Oliver Williams
Map Maker's Assistant: Allyson Smith
Jacket Artwork: John Bull, The Book Design Company
Food Styling: Janice Baker
Food Photography: Peter Johnson

Library of Congress
Cataloging-in-Publication data:

Italy, a culinary journey.
p. cm.
"Produced by Weldon Owen Pty Limited"--T.p. verso.
Includes index.
ISBN 0-00-21560-0 : $45.00
1. Cookery, Italian. 2. Cookery--Italy. I. Weldon Owen Pty Limited.
TX723.I92 1991
641.5945--dc20
91-9943
CIP

Typeset by Letter Perfect, Sydney, Australia
Produced by Mandarin Offset, Hong Kong

A Weldon Owen Production

Enjoying the sun in Nesso on Lake Como, Lombardia
LEO MEIER

Page 1: Deep-Fried Mushrooms, Jerusalem Artichokes with Onions, Swiss Chard with Butter, Broad Beans and Bacon (recipes page 70)
PETER JOHNSON

Pages 2-3: The Rialto Bridge, Venezia
JENNIFER FRY/BRUCE COLEMAN LIMITED

Pages 4-5: Tomato Soup, Salad of Raw Vegetables and Bread, Chicken Liver Croutons, Spaghetti with Garlic, Oil, and Hot Chili Peppers (recipes pages 137-8)
PETER JOHNSON

CONTRIBUTORS

Antony Luciano
Consulting Editor, writer and producer of television programs on Italian food and wine

Gianna Batzella
Native of Sardegna, writer and academic in Italian studies

Don Andrea Scirè Borghese
Descendant of the noble Italian Borghese family, chef, and restaurant owner

Donna Marisa Borghese
Native Roman, catering and hospitality specialist, and restaurant owner

Anna Teresa Callen
New York-based food specialist of Italian descent, author of numerous books on cooking, and owner of a cooking school

Antonio Carluccio
London-based chef and restaurant owner, television broadcaster, and author of *An Invitation to Italian Cooking*

Vincenzo J. Cincotta
Professor in Italian studies, and author of a number of literary works on Sicilia

Mary Beth Clark
Owner of the International Cooking School of Italian Food and Wine in Bologna, international food consultant, and writer

Maria Teresa Corino
Native of Piemonte, chef, and freelance writer

Franca Corino
Native of Piemonte, chef, and expert on northern Italian cooking

Vilma Pesciallo Garabaghi
Native of Liguria, based with the Italian Consulate General in New Orleans

Mimmetta Lo Monte
Regional Italian cooking specialist and author of *La Bella Cucina* and *Mimmetta Lo Monte's Classic Sicilian Cooking*

Gaetano Rando
Native Roman, writer, and academic in Italian studies

Rita Rando
Native of the Aeolian Islands, radio broadcaster and freelance writer

Tiny St Johann's church stands in the Villnöss Valley, high in the Dolomites, near the Austrian border.
DALLAS AND JOHN HEATON/SCOOPIX

CONTENTS

CONTENTS

GERMANIA
AUSTRIA
UNGHE
SVIZZERA
VALLE D'AOSTA
Aosta
Bolzano
TRENTINO ALTO ADIGE
LOMBARDIA
Milano
Torino
PIEMONTE
VENETO
Venezia
FRIULI-VENEZIA GIULIA
Trieste
Golfo di Venezia
LIGURIA
Genova
EMILIA-ROMAGNA
Bologna
MONACO
Firenze
TOSCANA
ISOLA D'ELBA
MARCHE
Ancona
UMBRIA
Perugia
LAZIO
Roma
L'Aquila
ABRUZZO
MOLISE
Campobasso
CORSICA
SARDEGNA
Cagliari
Mare Adriatico
Mare Tirreno
CAMPANIA
Napoli
M. VESUVIO
ISOLA D'ISCHIA
ISOLA DI CAPRI
PUGLIA
Bari
Potenza
BASILICATA
Golfo di Taranto
CALABRIA
ITALIA
ISOLE EOLIE
ISOLE EGADI
Palermo
SICILIA
M. ETNA
Reggio di Calabria
Mare Mediterraneo
ALGERIA
TUNISIA

INTRODUCTION

Much of Italy's history is reflected in its cooking, the origins of which can be traced to the ancient Greeks and Etruscans, with subsequent Byzantine and oriental influences. The Greeks brought with them their knowledge of the sea and its produce; the Etruscans their farming skills.

Initial culinary refinements took place in the imperial kitchens of ancient Rome, where cooks drew on the exotic and extravagant to please the jaded palates of the emperor and the city's elite. Peacocks, puppies, doormice, and elephant's trunk were among the more outlandish dishes served at banquets of the time. Eating was a fashionable pastime and the affluent regarded themselves as epicures. However, the principal food of the citizens of the time was *pulmentum*, a simple porridge-like polenta made from cereal grain, cheese, some pork, and mutton, served with boiled greens, usually wild grasses.

With the disintegration of the Roman Empire the art of cooking fell into obscurity until the Middle Ages, only surviving in the monasteries, where the best recipes were recorded by the monks. Only through their diligence have many early recipes survived. A valuable record also remains in the form of a cookbook attributed to the Roman gastronome Apicus, written in the first century AD.

Although spices and condiments were prominent in the cooking of ancient Rome, their use ended when the Empire collapsed, the supply routes ceasing to operate. A basic rural kitchen replaced the exotic, and it was not until the return of the Crusaders from the Holy Land, and the Saracen conquests in the south, that spices were reintroduced.

By the thirteenth century the Republic of Venezia extended as far east as Syria and Turkey, and in time it became one of the world's richest maritime powers, its ships carrying spices to Europe's markets. With the exotic new ingredients that were found on these voyages, Venetian cooking grew in sophistication, its culinary innovations spreading throughout Europe. It was in Venezia that forks, napkins, and fine glassware were first introduced as a measure of wealth and refinement.

With the Renaissance came a resurgence of interest in early Greek and Roman recipes and, prompted by various illustrious Florentine patrons, menus became more varied. Traditional food underwent new methods of preparation and presentation and new dishes emerged, the emphasis on heavy spicing diminishing in favor of refined, lighter flavors. Led by the Florentines, Italian cooking became the first fully developed cuisine in Europe, and by the end of the sixteenth century it had largely taken its current form.

Italy today comprises twenty regions, each offering its own individual kitchen developed through a combination of geographical and historical circumstances.

In the ninth and tenth centuries the Islamic invasion brought to Italy a new culture, with its foods, flavorings, and techniques. It was the Saracens who introduced the Sicilians to nougat, marzipan, and other rich desserts, now famous worldwide. *Cascà*, or *couscous*, is part of Sardegna's Arab gastronomic legacy.

Calabria's simple cooking has eggplant, chili, and bell peppers amongst its staples. The Moors brought the eggplant to Italy in the fifteenth century; chili and bell peppers came from South America with returning explorers and missionaries. Maize, too, came from the New World, first brought to Venezia in the sixteenth century. In time it became the basis for polenta, a staple of northern Italy to this day and at one time often the only food available to the poorest.

Genova's sailors, like those of Venezia, also traveled the world, returning with their ships filled with spices such as pepper, cinnamon, and cloves, but once they were home the sailors preferred more delicate flavorings. Few spices are used today in Ligurian cooking, although herbs are popular, basil forming the heart of the region's ubiquitous *pesto* sauce.

There is some debate over who introduced rice to Italy, its cultivation starting in the fifteenth century in Lombardia. In the north it is eaten widely, the country's most famous rice dish being the golden *risotto alla milanese,* containing saffron, a spice used by the ancient Greeks and Romans. But the greatest culinary influence in Lombardia came from the French invasion in the nineteenth century. Butter became the favored cooking base and by the end of the century French-style cooking was more common in Milano than Italian.

The Austrian influence is prominent in the north, where stews and boiled meats are common. *Speck* and *Knödel* are found in Trentino-Alto Adige, where in many areas German remains the principal language. Marche's elaborate lasagne-style dish known as *vincisgrassi* is derived from a dish created for Prince Windisch-Graetz, once a commander of Austrian forces in the region.

Just over a century ago, in 1860, Garibaldi united the country politically. Together with the victorious march of the Garibaldini it is said that the tomato also made its conquest of the peninsula, northern volunteers leaving home rice eaters and returning converted to the *spaghetti al pomodoro.* The tomato came from South America, reaching Italy in the sixteenth century. With consummate dedication, southern Italians, particularly the people of Napoli, grew it everywhere they could. It soon became a favored topping on pizza, a pie that has been popular since Roman times.

Today the Roman kitchen has a reputation for fine, simple peasant-style dishes, many utilizing animal offcuts and offal, once eaten mainly by servants and slaves. Bologna is regarded as the country's culinary capital. It is the principal city of Emilia-Romagna and the focal point for the agricultural produce of the Po Valley, the country's most fertile region. It is here that the richest dishes can be found, the finest bread, and the best dairy products, crowned by the incomparable Parmigiano-Reggiano, Parmesan cheese. Little outside influence is evident in the region's cooking: over generations it has evolved at peasant level, a combination of local ingredients and dedicated home-style preparation.

So while methods and ingredients vary throughout the country, all dishes are prepared to the same, broad, basic premise: recipes are simple, and are made with the finest, freshest ingredients available. The best cooking takes place in the home, where the meal is a traditional family ritual, to be enjoyed as the highlight of the day.

Antony Luciano

Vernazza, one of the five villages collectively known as Cinque Terre, five lands, that nestle in the cliffs in eastern Liguria.

STREICHAN/ZEFA

S V I Z Z E R A
Formazza
Lago Maggiore
Domodossola
MATTERHORN
MONTE ROSA
Breuil-Cervinia
Valtournanche
Verbania
Omegna
Stresa
Courmayeur
MONTE BIANCO
Aosta
Gressoney
VALLE D'AOSTA
ALPI PENNINE
VAL DI GRESSONEY
Lago d'Orta
Arona
Verres
Dora
Valgrisanche
PARCO NAZIONALE GRAN PARADISO
Biella
Ivrea
Novara
Santhia
Locana
Baltea
Vercelli
PIEMONTE
Cirie
Chivasso
Trino
Casale Monferrato
Susa
Bardonecchia
Torino
Rivoli
Moncalvo
Sestriere
ALPI COZIE
Moncalieri
Chieri
MONFERRATO
Valenza
Alessandria
Asti
Pinerolo
Tanaro
Tortona
Racconigi
Novi Ligure
Saluzzo
Bra
Alba
Savigliano
Acqui Terme
LANGHE
Fossano
APPENNINO LIGURE
Busca
Cuneo
Mondovi
ALPI MARITTIME
FRANCIA
LIGURIA
Golfo di Genova

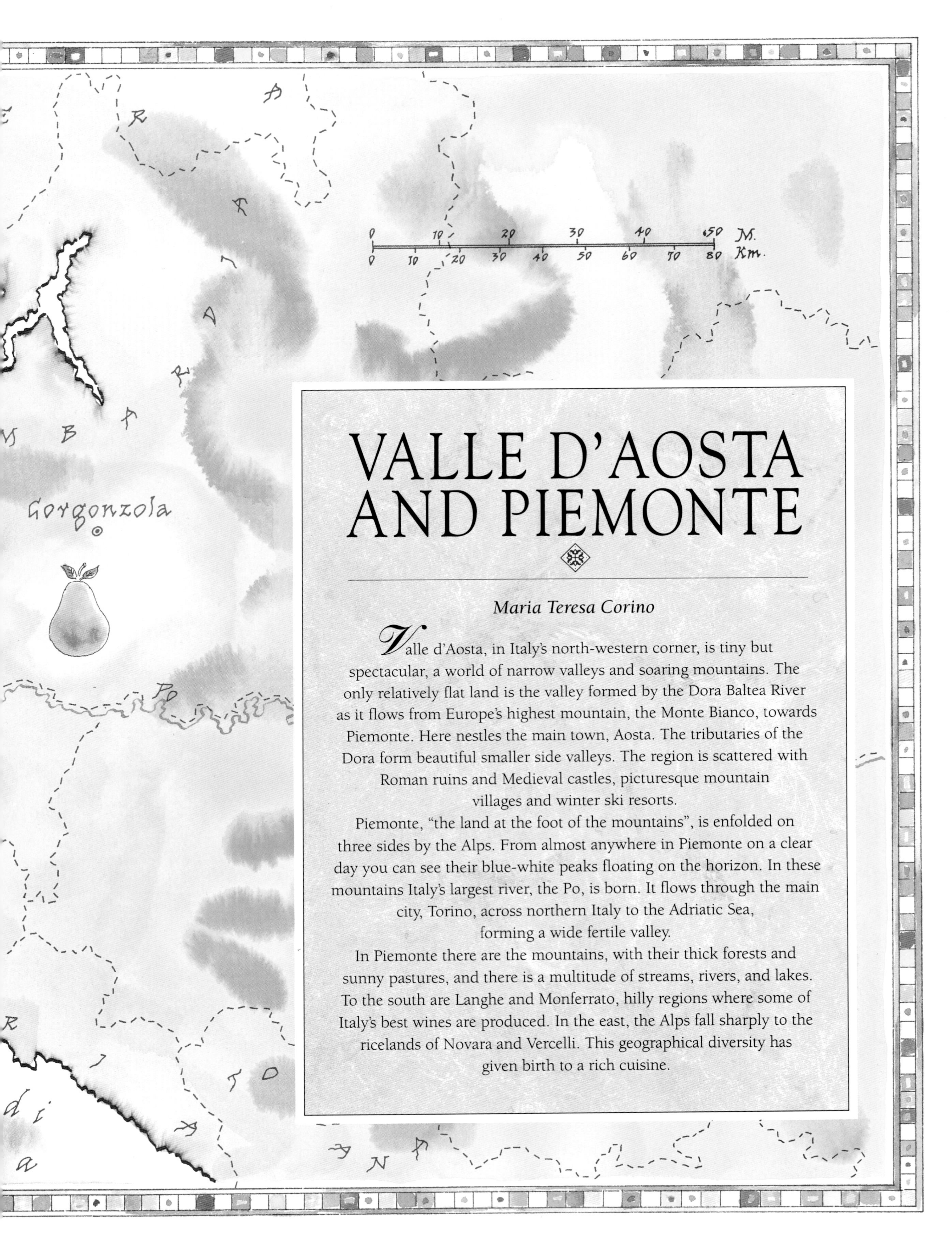

VALLE D'AOSTA AND PIEMONTE

Maria Teresa Corino

Valle d'Aosta, in Italy's north-western corner, is tiny but spectacular, a world of narrow valleys and soaring mountains. The only relatively flat land is the valley formed by the Dora Baltea River as it flows from Europe's highest mountain, the Monte Bianco, towards Piemonte. Here nestles the main town, Aosta. The tributaries of the Dora form beautiful smaller side valleys. The region is scattered with Roman ruins and Medieval castles, picturesque mountain villages and winter ski resorts.

Piemonte, "the land at the foot of the mountains", is enfolded on three sides by the Alps. From almost anywhere in Piemonte on a clear day you can see their blue-white peaks floating on the horizon. In these mountains Italy's largest river, the Po, is born. It flows through the main city, Torino, across northern Italy to the Adriatic Sea, forming a wide fertile valley.

In Piemonte there are the mountains, with their thick forests and sunny pastures, and there is a multitude of streams, rivers, and lakes. To the south are Langhe and Monferrato, hilly regions where some of Italy's best wines are produced. In the east, the Alps fall sharply to the ricelands of Novara and Vercelli. This geographical diversity has given birth to a rich cuisine.

DUSCHER/BRUCE COLEMAN LTD

VALLE D'AOSTA

This tiny region is a land of narrow valleys, forests, and green pastures, dominated by sharp peaks of ice and rock, including the four highest mountains in the Alps. It has more in common with the adjoining mountainous areas in Switzerland and France than with the rest of Italy.

Valle d'Aosta is a beautiful, harsh place and its people are tough, hard, and reserved. Valgrisenche is called "a man's paradise, a woman's purgatory, a mule's hell". The original inhabitants of this area, the Salassi, kept the Roman armies at bay for some time, until a massive campaign practically exterminated them. The Romans colonized the central valley, established Aosta, built a road through the Alps, and left many acqueducts and bridges throughout the region. From the sixth century, the region was mainly under French political and cultural dominance. The inhabitants speak Italian, French, and the local patois, a Franco-Provençale dialect, which varies from valley to valley.

JOHN G. ROSS/SUSAN GRIGGS AGENCY

Golden corncobs by the hundred hang drying in the sun on a Valle d'Aosta farm. Cornmeal is used for making polenta, one of the regional staples.

The traditional economy is based on subsistence agriculture and dairying. Cattle are taken to graze on high pastures in summer and brought back to warm stables during the winter months. The region's most famous product is *fontina*, a mild but flavorful cheese, thanks to the herbs in the pastures. There are also delicious soft fresh *toma* cheeses, and milk, butter, and cream which taste like you've always suspected they should.

Valle d'Aosta's food is rich and hearty, to warm you up and give you the energy to climb mountains. Soups are thick, including many versions of *zuppa alla valdostana*, a rich vegetable soup, and soups made with ingredients such as chestnuts, bread, potatoes, nettles, onions, rye flour, cabbage, and cheese. The local variety of polenta is roughly stone-milled and darker than usual because the normal cornmeal is mixed with flour from a local high altitude corn. Dark bread is also common, made from hardy rye. The higher slopes are covered with chestnut woods: try chestnuts boiled, roasted, or in the sweet *monte bianco* with cream. Even the poorest villagers have a pig, and sausages keep well in winter, so there are many pork specialties, especially *saucisses*, small pork and beef sausages, and *boudin*, a sort of black pudding made with pig's blood, potatoes, lard, and spices.

A large area of the forest is now protected by the magnificent national park of Gran Paradiso. However, you can still find wild boar, deer, mountain goat, and particularly chamois on local restaurant tables. One of Valle d'Aosta's most delicious products is *mocetta*, lean chamois meat that has been marinated in brine, garlic, sage, rosemary, and bay leaves and then air dried. It is similar to prosciutto, but much tastier and leaner.

Sweet snacks and desserts usually feature fruit, imagination being used to create *leccornie*, delicious things from simple ingredients: apples with breadcrumbs, pears in wine or cream, blueberries with fresh creamy cheese, and countless short pastry fruit tarts.

FROM VALLEY TO VALLEY

While many of the beautiful lateral valleys of the Valle d'Aosta remain unspoiled, there are those that have been recklessly built up because of extensive tourism in the region, which accounts for 60 per cent of the area's income.

If you want to ski here, you can join the *beau monde* in Courmayeur, one of Italy's oldest and most famous ski resorts, dominated by the Monte Bianco. It has

Once a royal hunting ground, Gran Paradiso National Park is still home to a multitude of wildlife, such as chamois, marmots, martens, polecats, royal eagles, and ibex. Many rare alpine plants can also be found in the park.

been popular since the 1600s for its mineral waters and mountain climbing. In Breuil-Cervinia you can ski all year round on the glacier. Or stay right in Aosta and be on the ski fields in eighteen minutes, thanks to a new cable car. Aosta is rich in Roman ruins and there are some fine Medieval palaces and churches. It is a great place to simply wander about. As this is the region's major market center, it has some of the best restaurants, and food and craft shops.

The Gressoney Valley is Valle d'Aosta's Teutonic pocket. The Walser people migrated here from Switzerland in the Middle Ages and thanks to the isolation of these valleys, their language and traditions have survived. Their cuisine includes specialties such as *speck und knolle*, a soup of cornmeal gnocchi, lard, sausages, and black pudding; prized local potatoes; and particularly high-quality cheeses in a land of cheese, especially *tome* and *fontina*. This is one of the best places to try *polenta grassa*, polenta enriched with butter and cheese.

PIEMONTE

Piemonte is landlocked, embraced by mountains on three sides, and has long, cold winters, with plenty of rain, snow, and thick fog. The people tend to be closed and hard-working. Tourism is a major industry, but it is mainly confined to the mountain resorts and the lakes.

Until the sixteenth century Piemonte was a region of warring duchies, principalities and city-states. Food for the masses was a matter of grabbing the little available—gruels, wild plants, and the local lord's leftovers. Torino, now the region's capital, was still a rough frontier town in 1563 when it became the capital of the Kingdom of Savoia. Gradually people from all over Piemonte were attracted to the new capital—rough, humorous country people whose idea of heaven was to eat, drink, and dance. But the tiny independent kingdom had to fight to survive, and the no-nonsense house of Savoia wanted "every man to be a soldier". So they became what they are today, a hard-working and serious people. Even the nobility was restrained in its habits, a rare characteristic.

An expectant pig at feeding time. Pork and pork products are common ingredients in the cooking of northern Italy and almost every farm has at least one pig.

JULIAN NIEMAN/SUSAN GRIGGS AGENCY

Much of the countryside was divided into small isolated farms where people ate what they could raise themselves, supplemented with a few preserved goods exchanged for farm produce on occasional trips to the market. Every farm would have its chickens, rabbits, and pig, and maybe ducks, geese, turkeys, and guinea hens. The chickens guaranteed a constant supply of eggs which, especially in summer, were turned into thick omelettes or *sformati*, vegetable flans. They were also used for many desserts, creams, and soups, golden *tagliatelle,* and ravioli.

The vegetable garden provided herbs, especially rosemary, sage, and parsley, and a variety of vegetables: garlic, onions, cardoons, spinach, bell peppers, tomatoes, celery, asparagus, pumpkins, beans, leeks, eggplant, beets. These were also grown in larger quantities in the moist valleys and flatlands.

One of the year's most festive days was the day the pig was killed. It always involved a big meal, as every part which could not be preserved as sausages, salami, or *pancetta* had to be eaten within two or three days. In the old days the best cuts went to the lord, so inventive recipes were developed using parts such as the blood (a savory cake and lasagne with blood), the trotters (boiled with flavorful ingredients and then fried) and the liver (minced patties flavored with juniper and bay). The brains, heart, sweetbreads, and lungs, with many other parts of the pig and a variety of vegetables, became the local *fritto misto.*

Other feast days in the countryside were the day the wine was drawn off, celebrated with a huge *bagna cauda* and large amounts of wine, and the day the wheat was threshed, when the workers would be served rivers of Barbera and *bati il gran* ("beat the wheat") soup, a thick beef broth with tomatoes, pasta, sautéed chicken livers, or tiny meat balls.

The connoisseurs' dish in Piemonte is *bollito misto*, a selection of boiled beef cuts with just enough fat to make them tender. It is one of those totally simple dishes which rely on superlative ingredients. The same cows that supply fine beef also give milk of the highest quality, and many delicious cheeses are made here. Butter is used in cooking rather than oil.

The rivers and lakes used to be full of fish, and even prawns, but many have now disappeared through the combined effects of pollution and overfishing. Trout can still be found in the mountain streams, though, and carp lower down, and hopeful fishermen still line the banks.

The woods are also a rich source of food. Game is popular, particularly pheasant and hare, and is often cooked in local full-bodied red wines. In the fall, gathering the many varieties of wild mushrooms is a popular pastime, while in summer there are delicious tiny strawberries. The most precious fruit of the woods is one of the hallmarks of Piemontese cooking—the white truffle. However, only a few men and their specially trained dogs know how to find this underground treasure.

You cannot travel around Piemonte without becoming aware of the importance of the grape: in many areas the hills are completely covered in vineyards. Easy and cheap to produce, in the past wine was considered essential, not a luxury, providing merriment and escape to people who lived a hard life. It is still mostly made by small producers.

As in most of northern Italy, one of the major staples is polenta. Unfortunately, in the past in many areas it was at times practically the only food, and people would often die or go crazy from acute lack of vitamins. In Piemonte there was always a little something to go with it, if only an anchovy hanging from the ceiling, against which everyone would rub their polenta slice. In the mountains there was milk to accompany it, which has now become the rich *polenta concia* with butter and cheese. Lower down, herbs, vegetables, and chicken liver, or salted cod from Liguria with herbs, garlic, or onions were used. A little of these tasty dishes had to go a long way—just enough to flavor the polenta. Today polenta is used as a mellow companion for game, roasts, cod, and the dish which is probably most Piemontese of all, *bagna cauda,* a hot mixture of anchovies, garlic, and oil into which raw vegetables are dipped.

THE GREAT RICELANDS

The area surrounding Novara and Vercelli is a fertile plain, with straight roads intersecting fields of rice divided by rows of poplars and embankments. There is a feeling of space, especially in spring when the rice fields are flooded and mirror the mountains floating on the horizon.

Most of Europe's rice is produced here, mainly high-quality rice which is perfect for risotto. Rice has been grown in Piemonte for 500 years, but only for the last hundred so extensively, after major works transformed swamps into fertile fields. This cereal was at first considered food for sick people; it then came to be

SWEET THINGS

Sweets are one of the main glories of Piemonte's cooking and are bewildering in their variety and richness. Soft choux pastries filled with cream or *zabaione*, and topped with powdered or caramelized sugar; *baci di dama* ("lady's kisses") round nutty cookie and chocolate sandwiches; small meringues; *brut e bon* ("ugly and good") lumpy nut cookies; chocolate truffles; and *amaretti* cookies.

From Torino come two sweets named after Gianduia, the merry Carnevale character. *Gianduiotti* are triangular hazelnut chocolates and *torta Gianduia* a sinful cake made with hazelnuts, chocolate, cream, cognac, and apricot jelly. In Cuneo you must try *cuneesi al rum*, small meringues soaked in spirit and covered with chocolate.

In the alta Langa you can find a delicious hazelnut cake that is made without flour. Around Alba there is *torrone*, a tooth-breaking hazelnut and honey nougat. Also popular in the hills of Langhe and Monferrato are simple dishes made with fresh fruit, and *panna cotta*, a cream and caramel pudding.

However, Piemonte's best known dessert is the golden, creamy *zabaione*. It can be quickly whipped up for guests and family, using ingredients easily available on the farm—eggs, sugar, and Moscato wine, or, more commonly, Marsala imported from the south.

OTTO ECK/HORIZON

VITTORIA
HOTEL
10

Preceding pages: Boats lie still on Lake Maggiore. In fine weather it is said that the waters of the lake are green in the south and a clear brilliant blue in the north.

seen as an exotic, refined food for the bourgeoisie. Rice enjoyed a great boom in Torino in the mid-1800s and a great list of risotti was born, made from the most varied ingredients from duck to champagne and prawns. Most of these have been recreated in recent times by a number of the city's fine restaurants.

Many delicious dishes come from the rice areas. Novara's gastronomic symbol is the *paniscia*, a hearty Sunday dish of rice, vegetables, beans, lard, pork-liver salame, and wine. The area around Novara produces the creamy blue cheese, Gorgonzola. Widely eaten as a table cheese, it is also served in risotto and in a cream sauce with gnocchi.

Around Vercelli the most traditional dish is rice and beans. A must to try is rice with frogs, which abound in the rice fields. In Vercelli's frog market they are kept alive and cleaned in front of the customer, to ensure their freshness. The frogs in Piemonte are very small and tender and are best just before the fall, when they are at their fattest. They are delicious fried crunchy and golden, or *in guazzetto* with tomato, parsley, white wine, and lemon.

Snails are also harvested in the moist fields. Snails *al cartune*, cart-man style, is named after the men who used to criss-cross the region with horse and cart. Apparently they were very partial to snails, and used horse-shoe nails to extract them from their shells.

The Lakes and Mountains

Lake Maggiore and Lake Orta, in north-eastern Piemonte, have inspired poets and writers who have come to see their tranquil beauty over the centuries. Stendhal in 1800 said "When perchance you have a heart and a shirt, you must sell the shirt to see Lake Maggiore". There are palaces buried among trees and gardens, old churches, and villages that take you back to the Middle Ages. To please the stomach, there are the fast-disappearing perch of Lake Maggiore, frogs, snails, mushrooms, light red wines, and spritzy whites.

Mountains cover almost half of Piemonte and, as in Valle d'Aosta, each valley has a distinct character. The staple foods are polenta, dairy foods, and chestnuts. For those who looked after the herds, food during the summer on the high pastures was of necessity simple, and a careless marmot was coveted prey.

The chapel on the Little St Bernard Pass, high in the Alps of Valle d'Aosta. Even in summer the slopes are still snow covered.

MARTINI/BRUCE COLEMAN LTD

Piemonte's Capital

Torino today is mostly known as an industrial town, dominated by FIAT, Italy's largest car manufacturer. The first part of the country to become industrialized, it attracted massive migration, especially from the south. Large dormitory suburbs now surround the center, turning a series of once separate towns into a city of over one million people.

But the center of Torino remains a quietly beautiful place. Still retaining the Roman grid pattern of streets, it was mostly built in the seventeenth and eighteenth centuries, in elegant Piedmontese Baroque style. The inhabitants place a high value on restraint, good breeding, and work, but they still spend time in the beautiful old cafés, gossiping and watching the world go by. Stroll under the porticos of via Roma, the center's main thoroughfare, lined with elegant shops, then stop in one of the cafés in piazza San Carlo or piazza Castello, and join the *Torino-bene*, the well-dressed members of old Torinesi families, for a hot chocolate, an ice cream, or a vermouth.

Here the pastry shops look like jewellers' stores, with huge antique windows framed in black and gold wood, lights shining on delicate masterpieces of candied fruit and flowers, cream puffs, and chocolates. Vermouth was born in Torino, following an ancient tradition of macerating herbs in wine for their taste and medicinal properties. Also Torinesi are the thin breadsticks, *grissini*, which you'll find on every Italian restaurant table.

For another view of Torino, in fine weather go up to the hills, from where you can see the city and much of Piemonte, as far as the ever-present Alps. Here there are *osterie* where you can eat outside, under leafy pergolas. If the day is grey, stay in town and look for the old *trattorie* around porta Palazzo or between via Po and corso Vittorio, or go to the gilded Cambio, the place for important dinners since the nineteenth century.

Langhe and Monferrato: The Hills

This is southern Piemonte, hills from which come most of the region's great wines and its most traditional, distinctive country cooking.

The Langhe is a range of hills in the province of Cuneo surrounding the market center of Alba. In the "low Langa" the hills are almost totally covered with vineyards. Small towns, castles, and towers perch on the crests, reminders of a troubled feudal past. Further south, as the "high Langa" climbs towards the mountains, vineyards give way to pastures and woodland. Ancient games and dances are preserved here, and still enjoyed in the town squares, though the lure of city life is emptying the highest hills, where hard manual labor is needed to wrest a living from the steep slopes.

The hills of the Monferrato are lower and gentler. They stretch from the outskirts of Torino to Alessandria, from the Po River south to the mountains which divide Piemonte and Liguria. Vineyards dominate the slopes, giving way here and there to luscious vegetable gardens and orchards, or thick woods which shelter mushrooms and wild fruit. The valleys are patchworks of fields and meadows. The cooking here shows some Ligurian influence, such as a greater use of herbs and olive oil. Merchants would take the local wine southwards over the "salt roads" and return with salt, oil, salted anchovies, and cod.

Tartufi

The people of Alba are not needlessly modest. They think they have the best wines in the world and the foremost gastronomic delicacy—white truffles. The price of truffles is nearly as inebriating as their perfume, but it doesn't stop addicts, who can spend hours merely sniffing them and planning their fate. Some people actually sleep with truffles under their pillows. White truffles are used in wafer-thin slices, cut with a special metal tool, the *tagliatartufi*, which is also very good for slivering Parmesan. They are mostly added as a finishing touch on *fonduta, tagliatelle*, risotto, game, and perhaps best of all, on fried eggs.

The *trifolau*, the truffle men, are a secretive breed. They search for their subterranean treasures in the dead of night, in spots known only to themselves and their specially trained truffle dogs. They say that only mongrel dogs are suited to this task, and these often ugly little animals are prized more than the greatest champion show dog.

MILAN HORACEK/BILDERBERG

The Wines of Piemonte and Valle d'Aosta

Piemonte produces some of Italy's best wines, first among them the powerful red Barolo, from the Langhe, a full-bodied, long-lived wine to be drunk with roasts, game, or strong cheeses. From a different part of the Langhe comes Barbaresco, Barolo's more approachable (some say more feminine) partner. This is an elegant wine of full body and flavor, suited to game birds and delicately flavored roasts.

La Barbera, the only wine commonly taking the feminine article, is by far the most widely drunk wine in Piemonte. It is made almost everywhere, but its character changes from zone to zone. It is the people's wine, "the wine which is bread"—red, of course. Some Barbera can age well, but it is usually drunk young.

Another popular light red is Dolcetto. Grown throughout southern Piemonte, it changes from hill to hill but everywhere it is a beloved everyday wine, young, fragrant, and ruby red. Other wonderful reds come from the northern hills, in the shadow of the Alps. Many are made with the Nebbiolo grape which is used for Barolo and Barbaresco, but the rocky soil and mountain air give them a very distinct character. Look out for Carema, Gattinara, and Ghemme.

Some lovely whites are also made in this land of red wine drinkers. The light and dry Cortese from the Monferrato is great with freshwater fish. From Caluso north of Torino comes Erbaluce, which is made into an elegant, perfumed dry white, or two sweet wines, Passito and Passito Liquoroso.

Moscato is a grape from around Asti which is both delicious to eat fresh and the source of Asti Spumante, the most popular sparkling wine in the world, and Moscato Naturale, a still white, most of which is drunk locally. Moscato Naturale is fairly hard to find these days, and those who get the opportunity should try it, even if they do not normally like sweet wines. Gentle enough for children to have a taste, it brings to life in the glass the flavor of the best sun-ripened grapes. "Spumante" sold overseas often has little taste and is just an unpleasantly sweet bubbly. Here, made with care from the right grapes, it is highly perfumed and delicate.

MARY EVANS PICTURE LIBRARY

An illustration from a 1932 issue of the magazine La Domenica del Corriere. *It shows the procession of floats at the wine and truffle festival which is still held annually in Alba.*

The best way to find and enjoy these and the many other wines of Piemonte, many of which are made in minute quantities, is to go into the country and have them with the food which they have partnered for centuries. The Piemonte region has marked out a series of "wine roads" to help people do this. "*Le strade del vino*" take you off the main highways onto tortuous hilly roads, and point out wineries where wines can be tasted and purchased, wine and rural museums, as well as places to eat, from formal restaurants to individual farms.

Valle d'Aosta also has an ancient tradition of winemaking, though the amounts produced are tiny. The locals affectionately call them "*nos petits grands vins*", "our great little wines". Many have an ethereal quality claimed to be derived from the heat reflected from the rocks and the rarified air of some of the highest vineyards in Europe. As in Piemonte, most of the wines are reds, but some dry whites of intense bouquet are also produced. Grappa, a powerful spirit distilled from the marc, is also very popular in Piemonte and Valle d'Aosta. A small glass is often offered after the dessert to complete a meal.

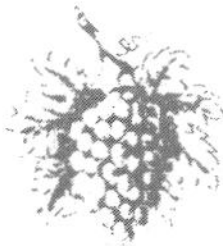

VALLE D'AOSTA AND PIEMONTE

DOC Wines

4. *Asti Spumante*
4. *Barbera d'Alba*
8. *Barbera d'Asti*
7. *Barbera del Monferrato*
1. *Carema*
3. *Colli Tortonesi*
9. *Cortese dell'Alto Monferrato*
4. *Dolcetto d'Acqui*
4. *Dolcetto d'Alba*
4. *Dolcetto di Diano d'Alba*
5. *Dolcetto di Dogliani*
9. *Dolcetto di Ovada*
1. *Erbaluce di Caluso*
2. *Fara*
8. *Freisa d'Asti*
6. *Freisa di Chieri*
2. *Gattinara*
2. *Ghemme*
2. *Grignolino d'Asti*
7. *Grignolino del Monferrato Casalese*
2. *Lessona*
6. *Malvasia di Casorzo d'Asti*
6. *Malvasia di Castelnuovo Don Bosco*
4. *Moscato*
5. *Nebbiolo d'Alba*
8. *Roero*
7. *Rubino di Cantavenna*
2. *Sizzano*
10. *Valle d'Aosta*

DOCG Wines

4. *Barbaresco*
4. *Barolo*

DOC AND DOCG

Any wine that carries the designation DOC (*denominazione di origine controllata*) belongs to a select category of quality wines that comprises about 10 per cent of national production. The designation DOCG (*denominazione di origine controllata e garantita*) is used to guarantee the authenticity of certain elite DOC wines.

RECIPES OF VALLE D'AOSTA AND PIEMONTE

Franca Corino

PETER JOHNSON

PETER JOHNSON

Fondue with Truffles

Fonduta con Tartufi

Fondue with Truffles

This delicate, elegant dish is probably the best showcase for Alba's aromatic truffles.

2 lb (1 kg) fontina *cheese, in small cubes*
4 cups (2 pt/1 l) milk
3 oz (90 g) butter
10 egg yolks
7 oz (220 g) Alba white truffles

Place the *fontina* in a narrow, high container. Cover with milk and leave for a few hours.

Place the butter and egg yolks in a double boiler then add the *fontina* with all the soaking milk. Heat over simmering water, stirring energetically with a wooden spoon. Initially the *fontina* will melt, becoming more and more liquid, then it will tend to condense again.

When the mixture is like thick cream, pour into a heated dish and serve, very hot, sprinkled with thinly sliced truffles and accompanied by fingers of toast.

SERVES: 10

Eggs and Zucchini in Vinegar, Ravioli with Roast Juices, Chestnut Soup

Carpione di Zucchine e Uova

Eggs and Zucchini in Vinegar

Small portions of this dish serve as an *antipasto*, while more generous portions make a light main course.

$1\frac{1}{4}$ lb (625 g) small zucchini (courgettes), cut in 4 lengthwise
olive oil for frying
4 eggs
3 garlic cloves
12 fresh sage leaves or 2 tablespoons dried sage
$\frac{1}{2}$ cup (4 fl oz/125 ml) red wine vinegar
salt
$\frac{1}{2}$ cup (4 fl oz/125 ml) dry white wine, or sufficient to cover the eggs and zucchini

Fry the zucchini, a few at a time, in a little oil on high heat until golden brown on the outside and soft inside. Place the zucchini in a lidded bowl (it should not be metal or plastic). In a separate skillet, fry the eggs in a little oil. Place them on top of the zucchini.

Fry the garlic and sage in oil on moderate heat. When the garlic is golden, remove from heat and add vinegar and salt to taste. Bring the mixture to a boil, add the wine, allow to boil for 1 to 2 minutes, pour over the zucchini and eggs and cover with the lid. This dish will keep for several days outside the fridge.

This marinade can also be used for small trout or carp, about 6 oz (200 g) each, floured and fried in a little oil.

SERVES: 4

Minestra di Castagne

Chestnut Soup

This is a dish to make in the fall, when chestnuts are plentiful and you feel the need for a hearty dish.

2 oz (60 g) butter
3 onions, finely chopped
1 carrot, chopped
3 leeks, chopped
1 garlic clove, finely chopped
2 cloves
6 cups (3 pt/1.5 l) water
2 lb (1 kg) chestnuts

Heat butter until golden. Over low heat, cook the onions, carrot, leeks, garlic and cloves until soft and golden, being careful not to burn them. Add water, bring to a boil and simmer for 1 hour. Add salt to taste and sieve the broth.

Meanwhile, peel the chestnuts, then shake them over high heat on the stove, or over wood coals for extra flavor, until the thin skin can be removed. Ideally this is done using a special chestnut pan with holes in the bottom, but a heavy-bottomed skillet can be used.

Simmer the chestnuts in the broth until they are very soft and fall apart when squeezed with a fork. Purée the chestnuts, using a sieve, and return them to the broth. Serve very hot with small croutons that have been toasted in a 350°F (180°C) oven for 10 minutes.

SERVES: 4

Agnolotti al Sugo di Arrosto

Ravioli with Roast Juices

This labor-intensive dish is a holiday favorite and the center of festive meals, especially at Christmas.

A variety of other sauces can be used, like a fresh tomato sauce, or butter and Parmesan, but this one is the most traditional.

Filling:
8 oz (250 g) juicy lean pork
8 oz (250 g) round of beef or veal
3 oz (90 g) butter
3 to 4 tablespoons olive oil
1 fresh rosemary sprig
2 garlic cloves
1 lb (500 g) spinach or silverbeet, all stalks removed
½ cup (2 oz/60 g) freshly grated Parmesan cheese
4 egg whites
salt and freshly ground pepper
pinch of nutmeg
Pasta:
10 egg yolks
3¼ cups (13 oz/410 g) all purpose (plain) flour

For the filling: Cut the pieces of pork and beef into 4 or 5 pieces. Brown them well in about 1 oz (30 g) butter and the oil with the rosemary sprig and the garlic. Cover and cook for about 1 hour over low heat. Remove the rosemary and garlic. Retaining the pan juices, chop the meat finely. Set aside.

Steam the spinach, squeeze out any excess water, chop finely and sauté briefly in a little butter to dry it out. In a bowl, mix together the chopped meat, spinach, Parmesan, egg whites, and a pinch each of salt, pepper and nutmeg. Blend the mixture well with a wooden spoon. Set aside.

For the pasta: Knead the egg yolks with the flour to make a smooth dough.Cut the dough into a number of pieces and roll out into thin 4-in (10-cm) wide strips using a pasta machine or rolling pin. Make sure you do not allow the dough to dry out.

To make the *agnolotti:* Place a row of tablespoon-sized heaps of filling on each strip of dough, about 1 in (2 cm) apart and to one side of the center of the strip. Fold the other half of the strip over to cover them, pressing firmly with your fingers around each mound in order to seal the filling in. Cut between each of the mounds with a pasta cutter or sharp knife, in order to form small squares.

If you need to keep the *agnolotti* for a little while before cooking, place them, so that they are not touching, on lightly floured tea towels.

Cook the *agnolotti* in plenty of boiling salted water for a few minutes until *al dente* and drain well.

Melt about 2 oz (60 g) of butter with the meat juices, pour over the *agnolotti* and serve immediately.

SERVES: 4

Peperoni con Bagna Cauda

Bell Peppers with Bagna Cauda

Bagna cauda is probably the most distinctive of all Piemonte dishes. A popular *antipasto*, it is also often served as the central dish at informal gatherings. On such occasions it is placed in the center of the table over a small spirit stove, so that it is kept warm, and used as a dip for raw vegetables, traditionally cardoons and bell peppers.

2 garlic bulbs
1¼ cups (10 fl oz/310 ml) olive oil
12 anchovy fillets, chopped
2 oz (60 g) butter
4 thick red or yellow bell peppers (capsicums)

Crush 4 or 5 garlic cloves, slice thinly another 20, and place them in a small saucepan with ⅔ of the oil and the anchovies. Cook over low heat, being careful not to burn the garlic, for 2 hours. Add the butter and the remaining oil. When the butter has melted the *bagna cauda* can be kept warm in a bain-marie until it is needed.

Broil (grill) the bell peppers under high heat, turning them often until the skins are brown/black all over. Cool, then peel. Cut them in half lengthwise and discard the core and seeds.

Place the halved bell peppers on a hot serving plate. Cover with the bagna cauda, reheated until very hot, and serve immediately. Polenta makes a good accompaniment.

SERVES: 4

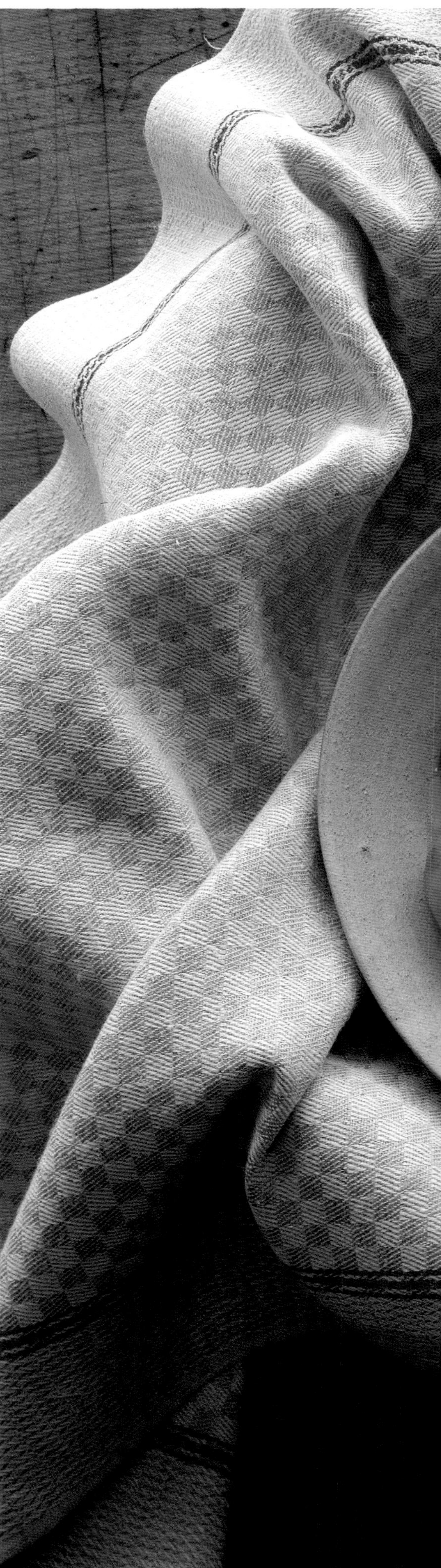

Bell Peppers with Bagna Cauda

PETER JOHNSON

PETER JOHNSON

Cheese Gnocchi

Gnocchi alla Bava

Cheese Gnocchi

You may have to experiment a few times with gnocchi: too much flour and they are hard, too much potato and they fall apart. They should melt in the mouth but keep their shape. Try them also with a simple tomato sauce.

Gnocchi:
2 lb (1 kg) potatoes
1 egg
6 oz (185 g) all purpose (plain) flour

Sauce:
3 oz (90 g) butter
1/3 cup (3 fl oz/90 ml) cream
6 oz (185 g) fontina *or a mild semi-soft cheese, cubed*
3/4 cup (3 oz/90 g) freshly grated Parmesan cheese

For the gnocchi: Boil the potatoes, peel them while they are hot and purée. Knead the potato purée with egg and flour using your hands, floured, on a floured board. Be gentle and knead only until the mixture is well mixed and smooth. Don't be tempted to add more flour or the gnocchi will be too hard.

Take small handfuls of the dough and knead into short segments. Dust the segments with flour and roll each one on the concave side of a fork, pressing lightly with your thumb in a quick flicking movement. They should have an indentation on one side and the imprint of the fork's prongs on the other. Keep separated on a floured board.

For the sauce: Simmer the butter, cream and *fontina* in a double boiler until the cheese melts.

Bring a large pot of salted water to the boil. Add the gnocchi, a few at a time. Cover and cook only until they rise to the surface—2 to 3 minutes. Lift them out with a slotted spoon and place on a heated serving dish.

Pour the cheese sauce over the gnocchi, sprinkle with Parmesan and serve immediately.

SERVES: 6

Fiori di Zucca o di Zucchine Fritti

Fried Pumpkin or Zucchini Flowers

This is the simplest and lightest method for cooking these flowers, but they can also be stuffed with a precooked meat and vegetable filling and cooked in the same way.

1 cup (4 oz/125 g) all purpose (plain) flour
oil for deep frying
30 tightly closed pumpkin or zucchini (courgette) flowers, just picked, cleaned, with the bases cut off
salt to taste

Make a light but not too liquid batter with water and flour and let it stand for 2 hours.

Heat plenty of oil until it is smoking. Dip the flowers one at a time in the batter (holding them closed between your fingers so that the batter doesn't fill them but only covers them) and deep-fry for a few seconds only over high heat, until crunchy. Salt them and serve at once.

SERVES: 6

Fried Pumpkin Flowers

PETER JOHNSON

PETER JOHNSON

Trota alla Salvia

Trout with Sage

This basic method, often using just butter, or simply butter and sage, is the most popular way of cooking trout.

4 trout, 7 to 8 oz (200 to 250 g) each
all purpose (plain) flour for dusting
3 oz (90 g) butter
4 bay leaves
8 to 10 sage leaves, or 1½ teaspoons dried sage
¼ cup (2 fl oz/60 ml) dry white wine
¼ cup (2 fl oz/60 ml) brandy

Wash the trout and pat dry. Lightly coat with flour. Place the butter, bay leaves and sage in a skillet over high heat. Sauté until butter is a golden brown then add the trout. Fry over high heat, turning only once, until the skins are crunchy and golden. Add the wine and brandy, cooking for a further 5 minutes over moderate heat.

Serve immediately on heated plates, garnished with the sage and bay leaves, which by now will be crunchy and tasty.

SERVES: 4

Il Gran Bui

The Great Boiled Dinner

A connoisseur's dish, this is the Piemontese version of *bollito misto.*

1 lb (500 g) yearling beef tail (oxtail)
1 lb (500 g) yearling beef cheek
1 lb (500 g) yearling beef shin
1 lb (500 g) yearling beef shoulder
1lb (500 g) yearling beef rump
2 tablespoons chopped parsley
2 celery stalks, chopped
1 large carrot, chopped
1 onion, chopped
1 fresh rosemary sprig

Place the meat, whole, in a large pot together with the remaining ingredients and more water than is necessary to cover. (The water must cover them all the time they are cooking.) Bring to a boil, then simmer for 2 to 3 hours.

Serve meat and vegetables very hot with the following sauces, or any others that provide strong contrasting flavors. A popular accompaniment in Piemonte is a fruit jelly known as *cognà.*

Trout with Sage

PETER JOHNSON

The Great Boiled Dinner

Bagnet Ross (Red Sauce):
2 lb (1 kg) tomatoes, peeled and seeded
1 onion
3 tablespoons chopped basil
3 tablespoons chopped parsley
1 fresh rosemary sprig
2 garlic cloves
1 small hot red chili pepper
1 carrot
1 small red bell pepper (capsicum)
1 celery stalk
¼ cup (2 fl oz/60 ml) oil
salt and freshly ground pepper

Cook all the ingredients except the oil and salt and pepper over moderate to low heat, uncovered, for about 2 hours until the sauce is thick. Pass through a sieve and return to the pan, adding the oil and salt and pepper to taste. Bring to a boil and serve hot in a sauce boat. Any leftovers are good cold, and will keep in the fridge for several days.

Bagnet Verd (Green Sauce):
3 white bread slices
¼ cup (2 fl oz/60 ml) red wine vinegar
4 tablespoons parsley chopped
1 tablespoon chopped fresh basil
1 garlic clove, chopped
2 yolks from hard cooked eggs
4 anchovy fillets, or 2 salted anchovies
10 capers, drained
¼ cup (2 fl oz/60 ml) oil, approximately

Remove crusts from the bread and soak the bread in the vinegar until soft. Squeeze out the excess vinegar with your hands. (You should be left with about a handful of moist bread.) Chop with all other ingredients except the oil and place in a bowl. Add salt to taste and enough oil to make a fairly thick sauce.

This is much better prepared a few hours before it is needed. The sauce can be kept in the fridge for several days.

SERVES: 6

PETER JOHNSON

PETER JOHNSON

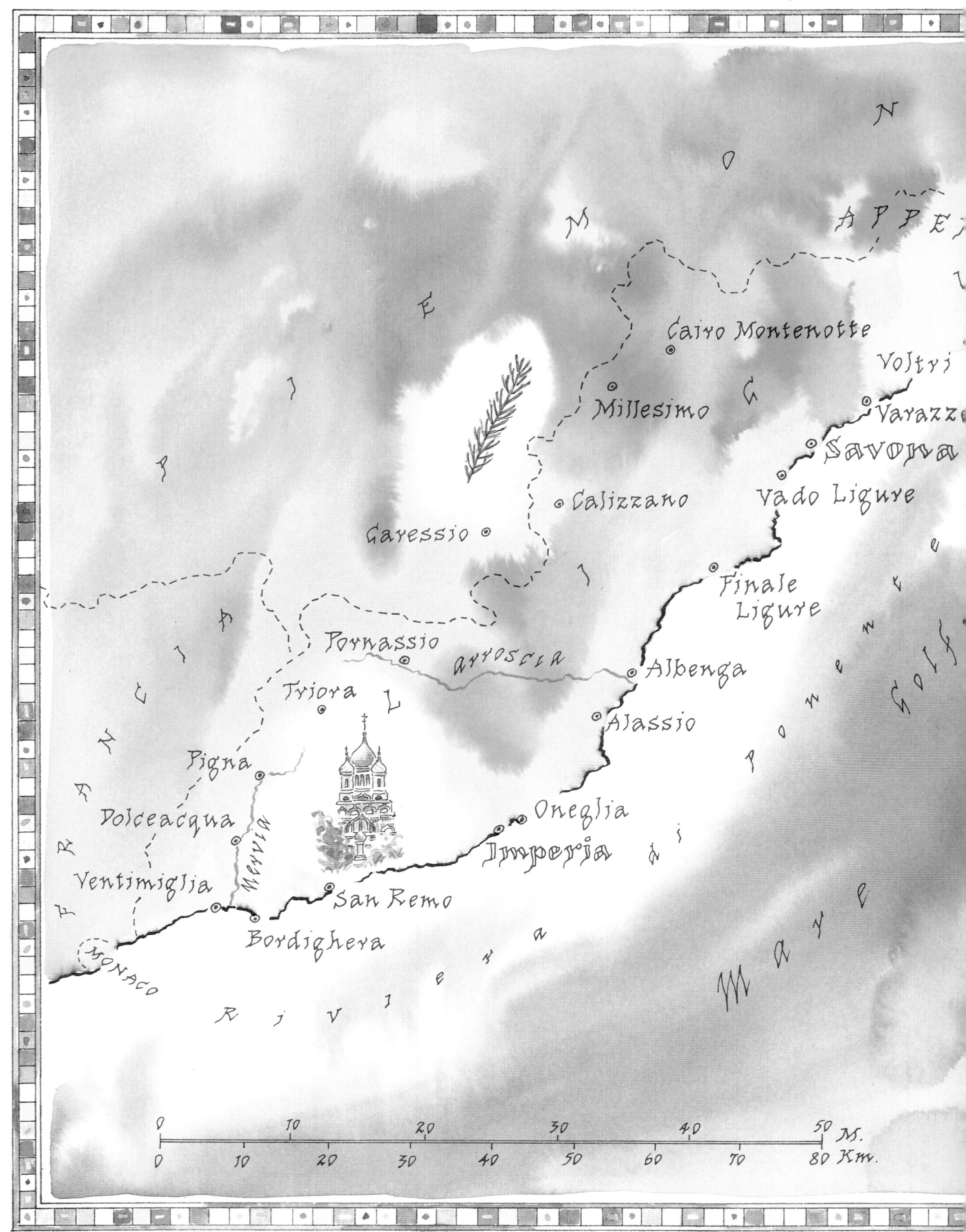

Cairo Montenotte
Voltri
Millesimo
Savona
Vado Ligure
Calizzano
Garessio
Finale Ligure
Pornassio
Arroscia
Albenga
Triora
Alassio
Pigna
Oneglia
Dolceacqua
Imperia
Nervia
Ventimiglia
San Remo
Bordighera
MONACO
FRANCIA
Riviera di Ponente
Mare
M.
Km.

LIGURIA

Vilma Pesciallo Garabaghi

A rocky crescent stretching along the Mediterranean from France to Toscana, Liguria is one of Italy's smallest regions. In many places the mountains drop almost vertically to the sea, with fishing villages built on outcrops or nestling on tiny bays between the promontories. Maritime pines dot the coast and bright patches of bougainvillea are everywhere, while a few miles inland there are some of the greenest hills in all Italy.

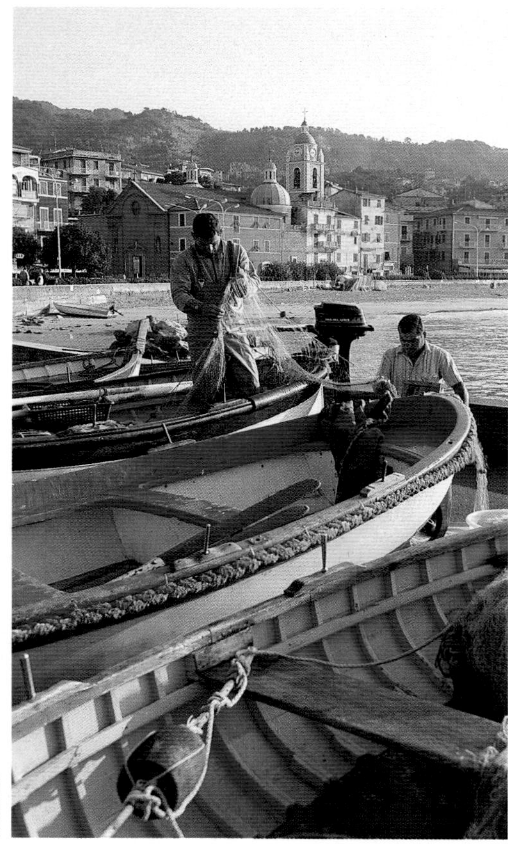
LEO MEIER

Fishermen busy with their nets at San Terenzo, not far from La Spezia. Fishing is a major industry for the Ligurians.

Men of the Sea

The Ligurians have always thought the sea more hospitable than the land, and many great sailors were born in this tiny region. Christopher Columbus is Liguria's best known native son, her men having sailed the world since ancient times. Genova's wealth, like that of Venezia, grew from bringing the East's spices to the markets of Europe. Marco Polo reports having met a number of Ligurian travelers on his journey to China.

Liguria comprises four provinces: from west to east they are Imperia, Savona, Genova, and La Spezia. Today it is one of the most prosperous and industrious regions of Italy and is a major tourist center. Its industry continues to be largely maritime-based, and the ports are active and modern. The harshness of the terrain means that agriculture is of no great importance, although at one time Liguria produced more olive oil that any other Italian region. Now bright carpets of flowers grow where olive trees once stood. Technology and service industries have made this region rich, and lack of land has made the Ligurians daring: they carve up their mountains to claim space from the sea, building commercial centers and airports with the same spirit and audacity shown by their sailor ancestors.

The Riviera di Ponente

West from the French Riviera lies Liguria's Riviera di Ponente. Here, at the Balzi Rossi caves near Ventimiglia, tombs, stone implements, and rock engravings dating from the late Paleolithic age provide an introduction to this ancient land. If you can, stop for a meal at Ponte Ludovico. Here, overlooking the sea and the rocky coastline, you can savor your first Ligurian meal, and discover in it a strong Provençale influence. While the cuisine becomes creamier and more delicate to the east, everywhere you will find exquisite extra virgin olive oils and fragrant basil, rosemary, and thyme—the herbs that grow all over the hills. The main dishes will often be of fish, rabbit, and chicken and the diet of many locals is largely vegetarian, called *di magro*. In this rugged country wedged between sea and mountains there is little land for grazing, so beef, pork, and lamb have never had a prominent place in the local cooking. Instead there are numerous kitchen gardens on the terraced hillsides, providing fruit and vegetables.

Growing grapes in the valleys behind the coastal resort towns of the Riviera di Ponente is a great challenge; the terrain is rocky and steep and has been patiently terraced over the centuries. Excellence rather than quantity is religiously sought after by the wine producers here. A drive along the Valle Nervia leads to the small town of Dolceacqua. In this area, one of the best red wines of northern Italy is produced—the Rossese di Dolceacqua—said to have been a favorite of Napoleon's. In a local wine cellar, you can sit with farmers and sip a glass of Rossese, or sample eel and trout from the River Nervia at a *trattoria*. If you happen to be in this area during the first week of August, you can wander through vineyards and chestnut woods to Pigna for the festival of vernacular poetry.

Along the coast there are fields and fields of cultivated flowers. The charming old towns of Bordighera and San Remo are large centers for the cultivation and worldwide exportation of millions of carnations. In the many elegant restaurants and charming *trattorie* of these towns the daily catch of fish—some anchovies perhaps, or sardines—is served with dry white Pigato and Vermentino wines.

HORIZON/ANTHONY BLAKE

Some of the brightly painted houses that line the waterfront at Portovenere were built in the twelfth century, and were once fortified by the Genovese.

These crisp, pale-gold wines, together with fine reds such as Ormeasco and Rossese di Albenga, are produced in the area extending from Imperia to Genova.

Traveling east along the coast one comes to Oneglia, a Medieval town and resort which is also an important industrial center. Here the crushing of olives into exquisite oils has long been an art. The steep-sided valleys inland from the town are patterned by silvery olive groves, narrow terraces, and the ruins of ancient walls. Not far from Oneglia, in the town of Pontedassio, there is the Museo degli Spaghetti, a spaghetti museum set up by the Agnesi family, the renowned pasta producers. In the rural areas of Liguria, a plate of spaghetti dribbled with fine extra virgin olive oil is considered a suitable remedy for almost any ailment. It could be said to be the local version of chicken soup.

It is tempting to stop in each town on the coast and to explore every valley. There is not a town or village without its history, traditions, and attractions. In the humblest place, be it an inn or a farmhouse kitchen, a rustic bowl of minestrone enriched perhaps by a spoonful of *pesto*, or a boiled octopus dribbled with some fine local olive oil, can be, in its simplicity, perfection itself.

LEO MEIER

A village woman sits plucking a chicken.

Palms line the foreshore at the fishing village of Noli on the Riviera di Ponente.

As you travel eastwards, leaving Provence behind, you will begin to taste the difference at the table. The *pesto* will have become a little lighter in flavor and color. You will find it served on *trenette,* a local variety of ribbon pasta, lasagne, and *trofie. Trofie* are delightful home-made twisted pasta, tapered at the end. Like *trenette*, they are served exclusively with *pesto,* occasionally garnished with beans.

Further east, the loveliness of the surroundings begins to fade. The towns of Voltri, Pegli, Pra, Sestri Ponente, and Cornigliano chaotically follow one another, brutally announcing the advent of the industrial world. Cement has overwhelmed the hills, chimneys belch polluting smoke, and the traffic is unrelenting.

Yet, on these hills decrepit, faded villas can still be seen, corners of ancient gardens with branches of bougainvillea draping the old walls, and lines of maritime pines which must, once, have marked the boundaries of estates. Cornigliano was once a charming sea resort, a town of mariners and fishermen and also of farmers who cultivated the surrounding hills. Now it is the site of one of the largest industrial complexes in Europe. Fortunately, the wine once produced in these hills has not entirely disappeared. Local wine growers have, in recent years, with great tenacity and courage, revived the production of the famous Bianco di Coronata, an exceptional wine with a light sulfurous flavor.

INTERNATIONAL PHOTOGRAPHIC LIBRARY

Genova "La Superba"

Genova, Liguria's proud capital, has been a maritime and commercial center since its earliest days. It is the Mediterranean's largest port and Switzerland's outlet to the sea. While it sprawls into the valleys behind, building ever further up precipitous hills, the city's heart is in its waterfront, with its numerous bars and boarding houses, and its restaurants of every kind. Parts of the city are strikingly modern and the high-tech airport is built on land claimed from the sea. Like the rest of Liguria, Genova is full of contrasts and surprises. There is a marvelous Medieval section of the city remaining, with a maze of ancient alleys, the famous *caruggi,* so intricate as to discourage all but the most daring visitor. Here old trades, some of them rather more respectable than others, are still energetically pursued. In this area, especially under the old archways of Sottorpia, there are typical eateries called *torte e farinata* which seem to have always been there. You are bound to be tempted to taste the Ligurian form of polenta, *farinata,* made with a chickpea paste cooked with oil in a wood-burning oven.

In Genova, there are numerous groups and guilds for the preservation of historic traditions. Even the *pesto* has its own academy dedicated to the preservation of the original recipe.

It is easy to be delighted by Genovese food. It can be an ice cream (try the *pacciugo*) eaten sitting on the keel of an old fishing boat in the little cove of Boccadasse, or a rustic dinner at a *trattoria* just across from the tumultuous fish market, where you can order crunchy fried *frisceu*, fritters of dried and salted cod or a bowl of delicious *ciuppin,* fish soup, made with fish of every variety available from the catch.

A sophisticated local dish which you will find in the city's finest restaurants is *cima alla genovese.* Stuffed breast or shoulder of veal, it is filled with brains, sweetbreads, peas, herbs, pistachios, garlic, and grated cheese, with hard-cooked eggs in the middle. It is boiled for two hours, placed under weights for some time in a cool place, and then served sliced. Another Ligurian specialty is *cappon magro,* an extraordinarily elaborate fish and vegetable salad, served in a pyramid.

Mention, too, must be made of ravioli, a dish of Genovese origin that is known worldwide. It is said that on board ship the Genovese sailors would chop up leftovers and use them as a pasta filling for the next meal, frugality being essential at sea. *Ravioli alla genovese*, however, have a filling that is anything but simple, containing veal, brains, sweetbreads, egg, breadcrumbs, chard, borage, and grated Parmesan cheese. There are many other fillings, including a delicate one made from ricotta and Parmesan. *Ravioli magri* have a vegetable filling. Ravioli in Liguria are generally eaten *in brodo* (in a soup), with a sauce—perhaps a mushroom sauce—or with butter and grated cheese alone. *Ravioli dolci* are little sweet egg-dough envelopes containing ricotta, candied peel, and chocolate.

Ligurian desserts are often forms of sweet bread. For instance there is a sweet *focaccia*, called *focaccia castelnovese,* made with pine nuts that is eaten mainly at Christmas and Easter, and *pandolce genovese,* the most typical of Genovese cakes, is a bread flavored with candied peel, seedless raisins, pine nuts, pistachio nuts, and Marsala. All over Liguria ring-shaped pastries called *canestrelli* can be bought from *panetterie*, making an excellent mid-morning or afternoon snack. A delightful dish of the region when stone fruit is in season is *pesche ripiene al forno,* baked peaches stuffed with crumbled macaroons.

The Ubiquitous Pesto

Pesto is to Liguria what pizza is to Napoli. It appears on the menus of elegant restaurants and rustic *trattorie* alike and, most often, is served over a plate of piping hot *trenette,* the local variety of ribbon pasta. It is also quite frequently served with gnocchi.

Pesto may be creamier in the east and more rustic in the west of Liguria, but the ingredients are essentially the same: just a touch of garlic, pine nuts or walnuts, grated Parmesan cheese, and *pecorino sardo,* and small, fresh basil leaves. Ideally *pesto* should be crushed in a marble mortar with a boxwood pestle; metal utensils should never be used.

There are some peculiarities in the way *pesto* is served in the various kitchens of Liguria. Don't be surprised if on a plate of *trenette al pesto* you find a few slices of potato. A small amount of *pesto* diluted in cream is often stirred into minestrone, just before serving, and a spoonful may even appear on top of a dish of green beans. Little variations such as these would be considered unorthodox on the coast but are absolutely acceptable in the inland hamlets where the scarcity of ingredients serves to stimulate the cook's imagination.

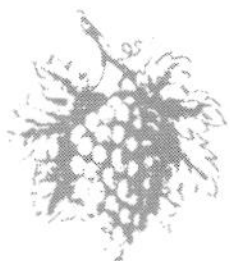

LIGURIA

DOC WINES

Cinque Terre
Riviera Ligure di Ponente (Ormeasco, Pigato, Vermentino)
Rossese di Dolceacqua
Sciacchetrà

OTHER WINES

Rossese di Albenga
Coronata

THE RIVIERA DI LEVANTE

From Genova eastwards the coastline is known as the Riviera di Levante. Here the winding highway is carved into the mountainside, its many overpasses crossing the roofs of the towns and hamlets clinging to the rocky coast. Wherever you stop to take a stroll along the waterfront and breathe in the sea air, a snack to sample is the famous *focaccia,* a savory bread flavored with sage and dribbled with oil, sometimes filled with cheese. The crisp, gold fragrant *focaccia* made in Recco is second to none.

If you can, try to get a lift on a boat so that you can reach the town of Camogli from the sea. It will appear as a fantastic stage set: a tall wall of brightly painted houses dotted by a hundred windows. Camogli, meaning "house of the wives", refers to the sailors' wives, who would often have looked out from these windows for signs of the return of their men. And then you'll reach Portofino, chic and rustic at the same time, stretched along its colorful bay, sheltered by olive groves. Following along the coast, you come first to Santa Margherita, then San Michele di Pagana, and Rapallo. There are luxurious hotels in which to stay where you can taste dishes of great elegance, such as exquisite fish with fine sauces of cream and walnuts.

Many festivals and celebrations take place along the coast during the summer months. In Camogli, tons of fish are fried in a huge pan and served to the crowd. In Lavagna, the historic past of the Fieschi family is lavishly celebrated in August. Often the regional celebrations have an intimate nature, in keeping with the Ligurian spirit. Prizes tend to be given to the most daring fishermen or to the person who has brought Liguria the most honor.

Between the towns of Levanto and Portovenere in the district of La Spezia lie five villages—Riomaggiore, Manarola, Corniglia, Vernazza, and Monterosso—known as Cinque Terre, five lands. It is in these delightful villages nestled in the cliffs that the most famous wines of Liguria are produced. Petrarch described these vines as "growing under the blond sun, preferred by Bacchus". The terraced vineyards in some places are barely out of range of the Mediterranean breakers. The rocky cliffs which cut the villages off from the rest of the region provide protection from the north wind and exposure to the southern sun. The wines produced here are made from Albarola, Bosco, and Vermentino grapes—all white, dry, and delicate—which harmonize well with the local fish, *gamberoni,* large shrimp, and *datteri di mare*, literally "sea dates", mussels that are pried from their hiding places in amongst the rocks.

At the eastern limit of Liguria lies the Gulf of La Spezia, flanked by the sparkling towns of Portovenere and Lerici on its opposing shores. The view from Portovenere is spectacular. On the tip of the promontory there is the thirteenth century church of San Pietro with its striped walls characteristic of Genova, to which the town has been faithful over the centuries. On the eastern side Lerici, with its castle, dominates the coast.

A specialty of La Spezia is *scabeccio,* pickled fried mullet with rosemary and sage, and in this region they also eat *storni in salmi,* a traditional dish of starling with a sauce of vegetables, herbs, olives, and olive oil. The dish *lattuga ripiena,* lettuce cooked in beef broth, is generally served at Easter.

The trip down the Ligurian crescent ends here. From La Spezia the atmosphere changes with the altering landscape, the plain of the River Magra opening out as an introduction to Toscana.

Riomaggiore lies in a narrow valley carved out of the rugged coastline.

Following page: Vines on terraced slopes surround a village in the Cinque Terre region, home of many of Liguria's wines.

THE REALM OF SPAGHETTI

Paolo Battista Agnesi of Pontedassio bought himself, in 1824, a water mill which had been endowed by the king with the privilege of using the water of the river five days a week. It was the best mill in the area, and its acquisition marked the beginning of the production of the famous Pasta Agnesi. Today the pasta is produced in the modern plant of Imperia and shipped all over the world.

In Pontedassio the ancestral home of the Agnesi family has been transformed into a spaghetti museum, the Museo degli Spaghetti. Here the history of pasta is traced back to Etruscan times, and there are records of Papal bulls regarding quality control for spaghetti. The first grinding vat used in the mill is on display and technical information on the making of pasta is available. Humorous prints and drawings show the differences in traditions between the north of Italy and the south.

Originally the best grain was imported from Russia on Genovese ships and the Agnesi family had its own vessel called the *Paolo Battista* in honor of the dynasty's founder. Four times a year, in the port of Oneglia, children would gather to await the *Paolo Battista*, and the first who spotted the vessel on the horizon and brought the news to the family was rewarded with a fragrant *focaccia.*

In 1279 Ponzio Bastone of Genova left in his will a basket of *maccheroni*, clearly one of his most prized possessions. The Genovese have the same attitude to pasta today. Only the best grains and water are used now, as they were then, to make this wonderful product.

A visit to the Spaghetti Museum can be arranged by calling the Agnesi plant in Imperia—an experience well worth the effort.

MARY EVANS PICTURE LIBRARY

An illustration from Harper's Monthly Magazine *of 1885 showing* maccheroni *hanging on racks to dry. In those days it was common in Italy to see a* maccheronaro *selling pasta from his stall set up on the street corner.*

PETER JOHNSON

RECIPES OF LIGURIA

Antonio Carluccio

PETER JOHNSON

Marinated Fresh Anchovies

Trenette al Pesto

Pasta with Pesto Sauce

This sauce unites garlic, basil, grated cheese and olive oil, all Italian ingredients *par excellence*.

30 to 40 fresh basil leaves
1 tablespoon coarse salt
1 large garlic clove
1 tablespoon pine nuts
2 tablespoon grated pecorino or Parmesan cheese
5 tablespoons virgin olive oil
14 oz (440 g) trenette *(thin lasagne)*

Grind the basil and salt in a mortar. Add the garlic and pine nuts and grind until you obtain a smooth paste. Add the cheese and the olive oil and mix well.

Cook the *trenette* in plenty of lightly salted boiling water for 7 or 8 minutes. Drain and mix a small amount with a little of the sauce. Distribute on heated plates, placing a teaspoon of sauce in the middle of each serving.

SERVES: 4

Pasta with Pesto Sauce

Acciughe Marinate

Marinated Fresh Anchovies

This dish should be prepared with the freshest of anchovies. If you can buy them when they have just been caught, all the better, as they will marinate quickly, leaving the meat firm and tasty.

12 oz (375 g) fresh anchovies
Marinade:
3 tablespoons olive oil
juice of $1\frac{1}{2}$ lemons
1 garlic clove, finely chopped
1 tablespoon finely chopped parsley
1 small dried crushed hot red chili pepper
salt and freshly ground black pepper

Clean and fillet the anchovies well, taking good care to shave off all the bristles and fins. Wash and dry the separated fillets and arrange them in a shallow dish.

Mix the marinade ingredients together and pour over the fish. Leave to marinate for at least 4 hours before serving. The anchovies can be kept refrigerated for a couple of days.

SERVES: 4 to 6

Burrida

Ligurian Fish Stew

The *burrida* from Genova contains a greater variety of fish than the one made in Sardegna. A uniquely Ligurian flavor is given by the pine nuts.

1 small onion, finely sliced
6 tablespoons virgin olive oil
1 garlic clove, finely chopped
1 tablespoon finely chopped parsley
$1\frac{1}{4}$ lb (625 g) canned peeled tomatoes, finely chopped
6 anchovy fillets, preferably the salty type
2 tablespoons pine nuts
1 oz (30 g) dried porcini *(boletus) mushrooms, soaked*
4 tablespoons dry white wine
1 teaspoon aniseed
3 lb (1.5 kg) mixed fish, such as turbot, monkfish, and swordfish, or large shrimp (king prawns)
salt and freshly ground pepper

In a large skillet sauté the onion gently in the oil until glassy. Add the garlic and parsley and continue to sauté for 1 minute. Add the tomatoes.

In a mortar grind the anchovies, pine nuts and drained *porcini* to a pulp. Dilute with the wine and add to the sauce, together with the aniseed. Mix well.

Place the pieces of fish one next to the other in the sauce, covering them with a little of it. Add the salt and pepper and cook, stirring occasionally, for 15 minutes, or until the fish is tender.

Serve hot with garlic bread, spread with mayonnaise flavored with chili paste.

SERVES: 6

Nocciole d'Agnello con Carciofi

Lamb Noisettes with Artichokes

The tenderloin is the most tender cut of lamb and, in this recipe, it should be accompanied by equally tender artichokes. During the spring you will be able to find the tenderest artichokes; in Pinzimonio they can even be eaten raw. Canned artichoke hearts may be substituted, if necessary.

4 small artichokes
1 slice lemon
1 tablespoon capers, preferably salted
4 tablespoons olive oil
1 lb (500 g) lamb tenderloin (fillet) cut in 1-in (2.5-cm) thick slices
1 bunch green onions (scallions or spring onions), chopped
2 oz (60 g) prosciutto, with fat, cut into strips
4 tablespoons meat broth (stock)
2 tablespoons chopped parsley
salt and freshly ground black pepper

Wash the artichokes, pull off the tough outside leaves, trim off the tops and cut into quarters. If they have "chokes", remove them with a sharp knife. Put aside in a bowl of cold water with the slice of lemon.

Put the capers to soak in cold water to wash off surplus salt or vinegar. Heat the olive oil in a medium-sized saucepan and sauté the noisettes, turning them so that they brown on each side. Remove from the pan and keep warm.

Add the scallions and prosciutto to the pan, sauté briefly over high heat and then add the artichoke pieces. Stir-fry for 5 or 6 minutes.

Add the broth and the capers, reduce the heat and cook gently for a further 10 to 15 minutes, or until the artichokes are cooked.

Return the noisettes to the pan, add the parsley, black pepper and salt (if necessary), mix the meat together with the artichokes and serve straight away.

SERVES: 4

Ligurian Fish Stew, Lamb Noisettes with Artichokes

PETER JOHNSON

PETER JOHNSON

Artichokes and Onions, Sautéed Eggplant

Carciofini con Cipolline

Artichokes and Onions

This simple recipe makes an ideal vegetarian meal.

1 lb (500 g) small artichokes or 4 large artichokes, cut into quarters
1 lemon
6 tablespoons olive oil
6 oz (185 g) pearl onions, peeled
4 garlic cloves, coarsely chopped
2 tablespoons capers, drained
1½ cups (12 fl oz/375 ml) meat broth (stock)—a bouillon cube can be used
salt and freshly ground pepper
1 bunch fresh parsley, coarsely chopped

Clean the artichokes, pull off the tough outer leaves. Cut off the tops and the stalks about 1 in (2 cm) from the base. Eliminate the "choke" in the middle. Wash and cover with lemon juice, to avoid discoloration.

Pour the oil in a lidded pan, add the onions and sauté over moderate heat for 5 minutes. Add the garlic, capers and artichokes. Add the broth and the salt and pepper, cover and cook gently for 20 minutes over low heat. Add the parsley and serve hot or cold.

SERVES: 4

Melanzane al Funghetto

Sautéed Eggplant

Funghetto suggests a cooking method similar to that for preparing mushrooms, and eggplant cooked in this way does indeed taste like mushrooms.

8 tablespoons olive oil
1 lb (500 g) eggplant (aubergine) peeled and diced
2 garlic cloves, sliced
1 teaspoon salt
2 tablespoons chopped parsley
1 teaspoon chopped basil
freshly ground black pepper

Heat the olive oil in a large skillet and when hot add the cubed eggplant and slices of garlic, with salt to encourage the exuding of water. Cook over moderate heat, stirring frequently, until the eggplant is cooked—this will take about 25 to 30 minutes.

Drain off any excess oil and mix in the parsley and basil. Season with more salt, if necessary, and pepper, and serve.

SERVES: 4

PETER JOHNSON

Sweet Ravioli

Ravioli Dolci

Sweet Ravioli

Ligurians are credited with having invented the raviolo. Made with a sweet filling, ravioli are a delightful way to complete a meal.

Dough:
4 eggs
¾ cup (6 oz/185 g) sugar
2⅔ cups (1 lb 3 oz/600 g) all purpose (plain) flour
1 teaspoon baking powder
4 oz (125 g) butter
grated rind of ½ lemon
grated rind of ½ orange
Filling:
12 oz (375 g) ricotta
⅓ cup (3 oz/90 g) sugar
3 oz (90 g) semisweet (dark) chocolate, finely grated
2 oz (60 g) candied lemon or orange peel, finely chopped
2 tablespoons pine nuts
½ teaspoon ground cinnamon
1 tablespoon orange liqueur (Cointreau or Grand Marnier)
powdered (icing) sugar

For the dough: Beat the eggs with the sugar and then add the other ingredients. Work well, then set to rest in a cool place for at least for 30 minutes.

For the filling: Mix the ricotta with the sugar and beat well. Add all the other ingredients and mix until smooth.

To make the ravioli: Preheat the oven to 350°F (180°C). Roll out 2 sheets of pasta ¼ in (5 mm) thick. On one, place teaspoonfuls of filling in a row 2 in (5 cm) apart. Cover with the second sheet of pasta and press with your fingers all around each little mound of mixture to stick the two pasta sheets together. Using a wheel cutter, cut a square around each mound of mixture to form a "raviolo" 3 in x 3 in (8 cm x 8 cm).

Place the ravioli on a well-buttered tray and bake for 20 minutes. Cool, then dust generously with powdered sugar. Serve cold, with whipped cream.

SERVES: 8 (makes 16 ravioli)

Pesche Ripiene al Forno

Baked Stuffed Peaches

For this recipe you need those lovely big peaches with the yellow flesh, typical of Liguria. This dish can be made well in advance as baked peaches are excellent cold, but they should not be served straight from the fridge.

4 ripe peaches
2 tablespoons unsweetened cocoa powder
4 amaretti *cookies (macaroons), crumbled*
2 egg yolks
2 tablespoons sugar plus 2 or 3 drops vanilla, or 2 tablespoons vanilla sugar
1 tablespoon pine nuts

Preheat the oven to 400°F (200°C). Cut the peaches in two and remove the stones. Scoop out some of the flesh from the middle of the peaches to make room for the filling.

Mix the cocoa with the crumbled *amaretti*, egg yolks, sugar, vanilla and pine nuts, blending well. Fill the cavities of the peaches with this mixture.

Butter an ovenproof dish and place the peach halves in it, side by side. Bake for 15 to 20 minutes. Serve either hot or cold.

SERVES: 4

Baked Stuffed Peaches

PETER JOHNSON

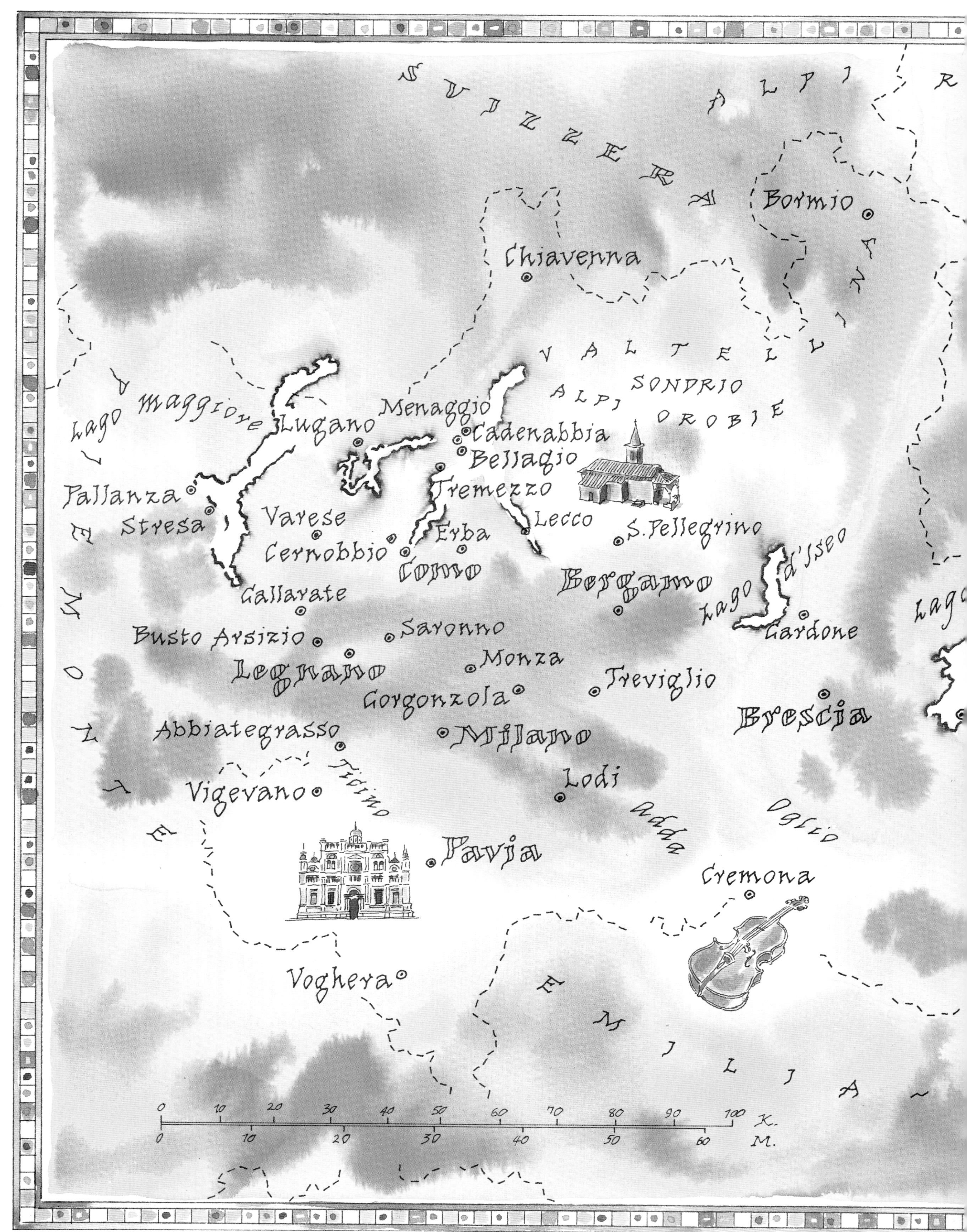

SVIZZERA
ALPI
R
Bormio
Chiavenna
VALTELLINA
SONDRIO
ALPI OROBIE
Lago Maggiore
Lugano
Menaggio
Cadenabbia
Bellagio
Tremezzo
Pallanza
Stresa
Varese
Cernobbio
Erba
Lecco
S. Pellegrino
Como
Bergamo
Lago d'Iseo
Gallarate
Busto Arsizio
Saronno
Gardone
Legnano
Monza
Treviglio
Gorgonzola
Brescia
Abbiategrasso
Milano
Ticino
Vigevano
Lodi
Adda
Oglio
Pavia
Cremona
Voghera
EMILIA
PIEMONTE
Lago
K.
M.

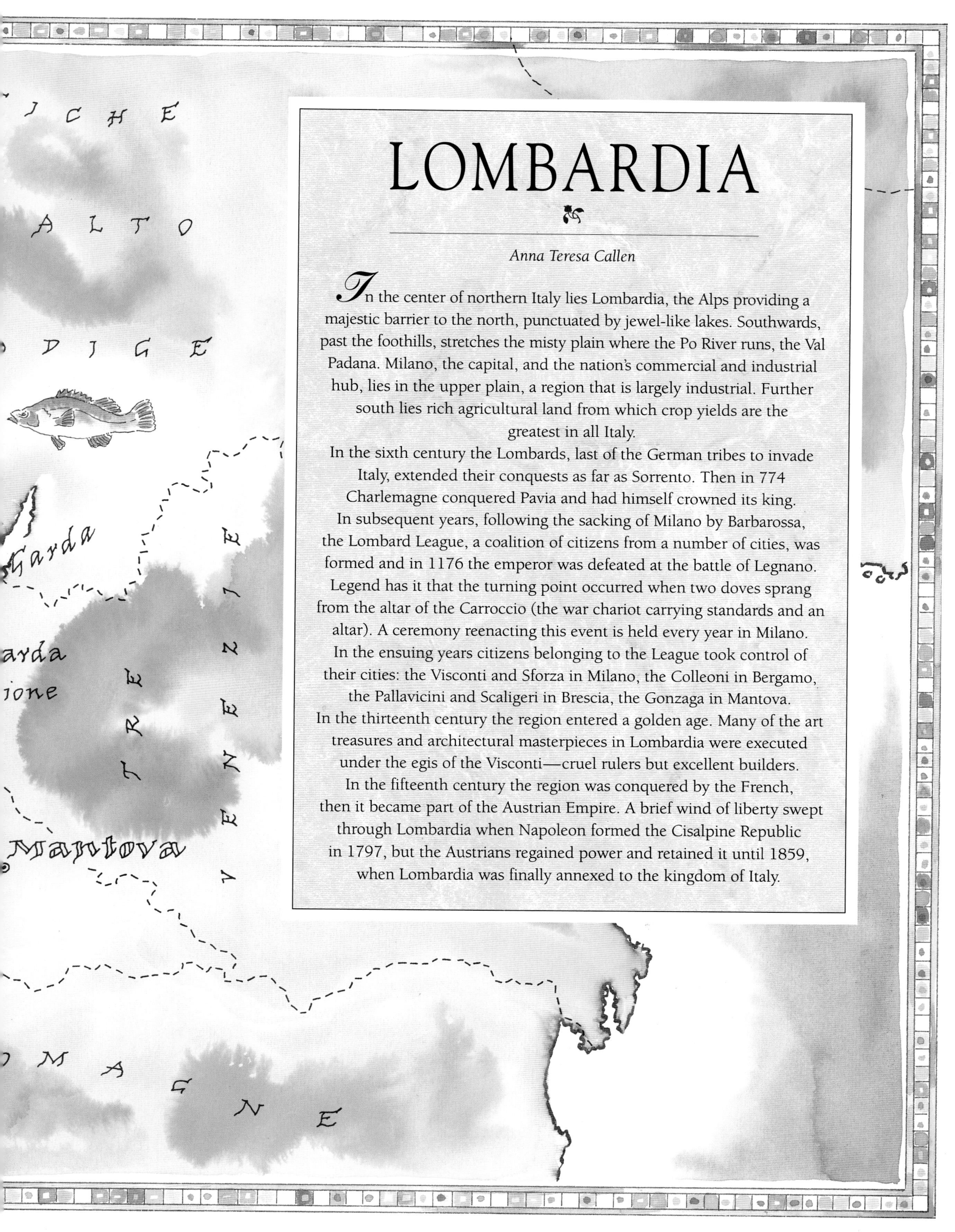

LOMBARDIA

Anna Teresa Callen

In the center of northern Italy lies Lombardia, the Alps providing a majestic barrier to the north, punctuated by jewel-like lakes. Southwards, past the foothills, stretches the misty plain where the Po River runs, the Val Padana. Milano, the capital, and the nation's commercial and industrial hub, lies in the upper plain, a region that is largely industrial. Further south lies rich agricultural land from which crop yields are the greatest in all Italy.

In the sixth century the Lombards, last of the German tribes to invade Italy, extended their conquests as far as Sorrento. Then in 774 Charlemagne conquered Pavia and had himself crowned its king.

In subsequent years, following the sacking of Milano by Barbarossa, the Lombard League, a coalition of citizens from a number of cities, was formed and in 1176 the emperor was defeated at the battle of Legnano. Legend has it that the turning point occurred when two doves sprang from the altar of the Carroccio (the war chariot carrying standards and an altar). A ceremony reenacting this event is held every year in Milano.

In the ensuing years citizens belonging to the League took control of their cities: the Visconti and Sforza in Milano, the Colleoni in Bergamo, the Pallavicini and Scaligeri in Brescia, the Gonzaga in Mantova.

In the thirteenth century the region entered a golden age. Many of the art treasures and architectural masterpieces in Lombardia were executed under the egis of the Visconti—cruel rulers but excellent builders.

In the fifteenth century the region was conquered by the French, then it became part of the Austrian Empire. A brief wind of liberty swept through Lombardia when Napoleon formed the Cisalpine Republic in 1797, but the Austrians regained power and retained it until 1859, when Lombardia was finally annexed to the kingdom of Italy.

LEO MEIER

Harvesting figs on the shores of Lake Como. There are usually two crops a year, the first ripening in July and the second being picked from late August to October.

Culinary Characteristics

In this region when it comes to food one thinks primarily of Milano's specialties—minestrone, risotto, *ossobuco,* and *costolette alla milanese.* Then there is *panettone,* a buttery yeast cake containing seedless raisins and candied peel, symbol of the city, and the sugary *colomba*, made in the shape of a dove to commemorate the doves of the battle of Legnano. But apart from these cakes, which are traditional at Christmas, the above dishes are eaten more elsewhere in Italy than in Milano itself.

Culinary independence is found in every province of the region. The yellow Milanese risotto is practically ignored in Mantova, which has its own version. The famous polenta with birds *alla bergamasca* remains a specialty of Bergamo, and Pavia's popular frog stew is seldom eaten elsewhere.

The cultivation of rice is widespread in the low-lying regions of Lombardia. An extensive system of waterways, draining swampland and providing irrigation in dry areas, was initiated in the twelfth century and took nearly 300 years to complete, Leonardo da Vinci's genius playing a considerable part in its design. Galeazzo Maria Sforza started rice cultivation in the fifteenth century, and he then made a gift of twelve sacks of grain to the Duke of Ferrara in order that he could start his own seedlings.

Rice, eaten much more than pasta, is one ingredient that is used widely throughout the region. Others are polenta, butter, cream, and the aperitif Campari, a Milanese invention.

The cooking of the Lombards, some say, is for people in a hurry. Why waste time eating? So the Milanesi invented one-dish meals. Rice, like pasta, is a first course everywhere in Italy but in Milano. Here *ossobuco* comes with risotto. In Mantova a pork chop rests on a bed of white risotto. *Cassoela*, stewed pork, is a dish in which meat and vegetables are cooked together. And polenta with other foods or solely with condiments also becomes a meal in itself.

Sugar beet, maize, wheat, vegetables, and fruit are also extensively produced. Agriculture is concentrated in the province of Sondrio along the Adda River and in the hills of Valtellina, where Lombardia's best wines are produced.

Fish is abundant throughout the region in rivers and lakes. Highly prized are tench, carp, pike, perch, and especially eels and sturgeon from the Po.

Without a doubt the people of Lombardia are carnivores. More farm animals are raised here than anywhere else in Italy. Pork is eaten in large quantities and rabbit is celebrated in Erba with a special annual fair. Beef, unlike the rest of Italy where it is often of poor quality, is tender, juicy, and full of flavor. Cows give superb milk and butter is used for cooking rather than oil. The ready availability of milk makes this very much a cheese-producing region. Some of the finest cheeses in all Italy are made here—gutsy Gorgonzola, soft and mild Bel Paese, creamy *robiola*, runny *taleggio*, and *mascarpone*, a fresh cream cheese that is also eaten as a dessert.

The Capital of the North

Milano is a sophisticated and cosmopolitan city, the second largest in the country, following Roma. There are records of the most sumptuous banquets being held in Milano in the past, with gilded food served and a bewildering number of dishes. One can still eat well here. There are restaurants that serve classic dishes like *ossobuco, costolette*, flattened and breaded veal chops, or *bollito misto* with all its components—veal, beef, capon, tongue, and sometimes a chewy *zampone* (stuffed pig's trotter)—and its obligatory accompaniments, *salsa verde*, green sauce, or *mostarda,* a fruit concoction from Cremona. The "poor parts" of animals, too, such as offal, trotters, and heads, continue to be turned into gastronomic delights, people going out of their way to find a restaurant or *gastronomia* that sells *busecca*, tripe with vegetables, or *nervetti*, veal trotter turned into a savory salad.

The leisurely side of life in Milano is much in evidence in the cafés and restaurants under the glass roof of the majestic nineteenth-century Galleria, where people meet to gossip or for a meal. Nearby is the opera house of La Scala, built in 1778, at which composers such as Rossini, Bellini, and Verdi made their debuts, and where some of the greatest conductors have worked. Singers of the caliber of Tebaldi, Callas, Gigli, and Pavarotti have been lionized and sometimes castigated by the demanding Milanese public.

Signorile, genteel, describes Milano perfectly. If you stroll in the city on a Sunday morning when there are no shops open to distract you from the quiet elegance of the via Manzoni, it is like returning to the past. At 10 via Moroni is one of the nicest small museums, the former residence of Poldi-Pezzoli, a discriminating art collector, who bequeathed his palace and superb collection to the city. Window shopping on the ultrafashionable via Monte Napoleone is another pleasant way to spend an afternoon.

REGINA MARIA ANZENBERGER

Balloon seller in the piazza Duomo, Milano.

Milano's vast, shop-filled Galleria, where there are some delightful cafés.

VISUM/MICHAEL WOLF

LEO MEIER

Herding goats in the foothills of the Alps near Brescia. Lombardia is justly famous for its cheeses and among these is caprino, *a goat cheese only available from the farms.*

The Duomo, northern Italy's largest cathederal, was commissioned in 1386 by one of the Visconti. Its pink marble façade is now pink once more, thanks to a thorough cleaning. Don't miss the adventure of climbing up to the roof, in amongst the pinnacles, statues, flying buttresses, and walkways. The city lies below and on a clear day you can see the Alps in the distance.

Not far from the Duomo is Castello Sforzesco, the immense stronghold of the powerful Sforzas. In the nineteenth century it was the scene of the struggle between the Milanese and Austrians which culminated in Milanese victory in the famous battle of the Cinque Giornate, five days. Practically no town in Lombardia is without a street called Cinque Giornate. Enriched with numerous major artworks, the Castello is now a peaceful museum.

Outings from Milano

Milano is a perfect point from which to take excursions to explore the surrounding region. Once past the city's industrial sprawl, there are many delightful places in which to have lunch or spend a night or two.

Bergamo lies in the foothills of the pre-Alps. The lower town is modern, with well-designed avenues and piazze; the upper town, perched on its bastions, is almost bucolic. Hanging gardens and pergolas decorate cobblestoned streets, squares, and ancient monuments. There is a Donizetti museum here, Donizetti being a native son, and you can visit his humble home. At the Galleria of the Accademia Carrara, one of Italy's finest museums, there are masterpieces by Botticelli, Bellini, Pisanello, Tiziano, Tiepolo, and Guardi.

Bergamo is at the edge of the district of Brianza, where high quality cheeses and meat are found. Its food is best described as vigorous, rich, and tasty. Polenta is often a main dish, like the famous *polenta e uccelli*, polenta and birds, which, incidentally, also appears as a dessert, with the polenta made of sponge cake and the birds of chocolate. *Polenta taragna*, made with a mixture of buckwheat and corn, is stirred for a long time with a *tarello* (cane), hence its name, until it is quite thick. Once it has hardened it is sliced and dressed with liberal amounts of sweet butter and grated *bitto*, a cheese from Valtellina.

Don't skip Brescia because of its commercial and industrial aspect. Beyond the suburban belt, the city is replete with surprises: Medieval churches, twinkling fountains, Roman ruins, gardens, solitary squares, and an old castle. Brescia is also the gateway to emerald-green Garda, the largest lake in Italy, with thick vegetation and lush gardens sloping down to the shore.

Sirmione, perched on the tip of a narrow peninsula that juts into the lake, is a fishing village entered through a crenellated castle. Sunny squares with umbrella-dotted cafés, cool streets with elegant boutiques, and charming *trattorie* make Sirmione the most popular spot on Lake Garda. In the hills are the Grotte di Catullo, Caves of Catullus, the ruins of the Roman poet's villa.

On the western shore of the lake, at Gardone, is Il Vittoriale, the villa where Gabriele D'Annunzio, Italy's poet-warrior, lived the last decades of his life. The estate is a high-terraced enclave and has a war memorial and a theater.

In this district the cuisine is linked to that of Venezia, especially in the south and on the Riviera Bresciana. Stop at a *trattoria* for a dish of fresh fried fish, accompanied by *polenta taragna* and a glass of Lugana, a graceful white wine from the area just south of the lake.

Dusk at Limone sul Garda on the north-western shore of placid Lake Garda.

INTERNATIONAL PHOTOGRAPHIC LIBRARY

Gorgonzola

Not far from Milano lies the town of Gorgonzola. Its claim to fame is, of course, the cheese that is made there. Records show that it was already being made in the eleventh century.

There are two stories that relate how the cheese first came to be made. When the cows were brought down from the mountain pastures in the fall the herds would pass through Gorgonzola. The milch cows would be tired and in need of milking, giving the people large amounts of milk, which they would then turn into cheese. The cold curds from the evening would be mixed with the warm curds of the morning's milking and they would not completely bind together, fissures forming in the cheese, along which would grow mold. Initially the cheese, creamy white with greenish blue veins, was called *stracchino di Gorgonzola*, from *stracco*, tired, as it was made from the milk of tired cows.

The other story tells of a Gorgonzola innkeeper who had a large stock of *stracchino* cheese. On checking his supplies he discovered that some had grown mold. He served this moldy cheese to his customers with some anxiety, but they thought it was delicious, and asked for more. As a result local producers began to concentrate on making moldy cheese.

Mantova, Cremona, and Pavia

If you can, spend a night on the lake and return to Milano through Mantova, Cremona and Pavia. In Medieval times Mantova was one of the most stable political entities in Europe, thanks to the wise rule of the Gonzagas. Francesco Gonzaga and his brilliant wife, Isabella d'Este, surrounded themselves with many significant Renaissance figures, among them the architect Leon Battista Alberti, the painter Mantegna, and the musician and composer Claudio Monteverdi. The fortress-like Gonzaga Palace, second only to the Vatican in size, is reason enough itself to stop in Mantova. It is filled with curiosities, courts, quarters, apartments, and pavilions filled with priceless masterpieces. An inventory of Gonzaga possessions in 1627 disclosed more than 2000 paintings alone.

Mantova is an agricultural center, sugar beet and wheat being its main crops. Mulberry trees are cultivated for silkworms. When it comes to food, Mantova takes its lead from Oltrepò, beyond the Po, which is in Emilia-Romagna. Some of the local specialties are *riso e trigoli*, rice and water chestnuts; *agnoli ripieni*, ravioli stuffed with capon, marrow, cinnamon, cloves, cheese, and egg; *mariconde*, little balls of cheese, breadcrumbs, and egg, cooked in broth; and fish and eels from the Mincio River, which embraces the city, and the Po. Dishes that might once have pleased the Gonzagas—chicken with black grapes, liver with orange sauce and the imposing dessert, *torta di tagliatelle*—can be found at a number of the city's best restaurants.

Cremona is one of the most striking cities in Lombardia. There are beautiful palaces and squares, the Duomo has a magnificent Romanesque façade and there is a bell tower, the tallest in Italy, built in the thirteenth century. Cremona's gastronomy is also influenced by Emilia-Romagna. Do not miss *antipasti* with local prosciutto, unusual salami, and *cotechini*, sausages. *Marubini*, served with butter and Parmesan, or in broth, are ravioli filled with grated toasted bread, marrow, *grana* cheese, and eggs. *Mostarda*, a spicy, chunky mixture of candied fruits and mustard, similar to chutney, usually served with *bollito misto*, roasts, and even fish, is the city's best known delicacy.

Many visitors skirt Pavia to rush to the famous Certosa nearby, the Carthusian monastery that was founded by the Visconti in 1396, but the city, especially the old town, delightfully cut off from the traffic, is charming, with its green courtyards, Medieval towers, and churches. The university, which has prestigious law and medical schools, dates back to 1361, and was attended by Petrarch, Columbus, and Goldoni.

Pavia's culinary gift to Italy is *zuppa alla pavese*, eaten in both the humblest of homes and palaces. A meal fit to revive even the moribund, it is a bowl of delicate broth in which a slice of fried bread rests, topped with an egg and a good deal of grated Parmesan.

Towards the Alps

The excursion one always takes from Milano is to its extraordinarily picturesque lakes, undoubtedly the most romantic feature of northern Italy. The best way to see Lake Maggiore is by boat. Its splendid villas open on to the lake but are enclosed by forbidding walls on the landward side. Stresa, the main town on the lake, sits at the entrance of the bay of Pallanza, another charming village. Isola

Bella, not far from Stresa, is an enchanting place to visit, with its terraced gardens, exotic plants, grottoes, and white peacocks.

Lake Como and its towns—Cadenabbia, Bellagio, and Menaggio—have been a source of inspiration to scores of writers and musicians. Verdi composed most of *La Traviata* here. Stendhal vividly describes the lake in his novel *The Charterhouse of Parma*. Magnificent villas grace its slopes—Villa Carlotta at Tremezzo; Villa Serbelloni, now a hotel, at Bellagio; Villa Melzi, nearby, and the exclusive Villa d'Este at Cernobbio, which has been a luxurious hotel since 1873.

The cuisine of the lake district is mostly based on the fish from its waters—trout, perch, tinca (similar to white fish), and *agoni* (a type of shad), the favorite of the Milanese when they come here. Local ravioli are filled with fish, and eels from the River Adda appear in risotto. The ubiquitous polenta is mostly baked or pan fried. Meat and local game are eaten widely.

In the Sondrio region, close by the Alps, *mortadella di fegato*, a liver-like bologna, rich sausages, and *bondiola*, a kind of salame, are local specialties. In the beautiful Valtellina Valley, with its terraces of stone, small amounts of red wine of excellent quality are made. The best known are Sassella, Inferno, Grumello, Sfursat, and Valgella. Valtellina's most famous dish is *pizzocheri*, buckwheat noodles layered with potatoes and leeks and cooked with grated cheese and butter. Buckwheat is also used in *chiscioo*, a savory pastry filled with cheese and eaten hot, and in *sciatt*, fritters shaped like tails. All the dishes here stem from a rich peasant gastronomy, closely related to that of Switzerland, which lies only a few miles to the north.

LEO MEIER

A mild day in Nesso on the shores of Lake Como brings an old woman outside her door to sort wool for spinning and enjoy the sunshine.

LOMBARDIA

DOC Wines

1. *Botticino*
2. *Capriano del Colle*
3. *Cellatica*
4. *Colli Morenici Mantovani del Garda*
5. *Franciacorta*
4. *Lambrusco Mantovano*
6. *Lugana*
7. *Oltrepò Pavese*
8. *Riviera del Garda Bresciano*
9. *San Colombano al Lambro*
10. *Tocai di San Martino della Battaglia*
11. *Valcalepio*
12. *Valtellina (Grumello, Inferno, Sassella, Sfursat, Valgella)*

Other Wines

Groppello della Valtenesi

RECIPES OF LOMBARDIA

Antonio Carluccio

PETER JOHNSON

Bresaola della Valtellina

Bresaola from Valtellina

Valtellina is a region to the north-east of Milano which is famous for its beef. Bresaola is marinated beef that is salted then air-dried. Sliced thinly, it is a wonderful deep ruby color, and is sweet and aromatic.

8 oz (250 g) bresaola, very thinly sliced
2 tablespoons virgin olive oil
juice of ½ lemon
plenty of freshly ground black pepper

Spread the slices of bresaola on a large plate, overlapping them only slightly. Sprinkle with oil, lemon juice and pepper and serve with *grissini,* bread sticks.

SERVES: 4

Risotto con Luganighe

Risotto with Sausage

Risotto is synonymous with Milano. This version is quite rich and could well be served as a main course, followed simply by a salad.

3 oz (90 g) butter
1 small onion, very finely chopped
10 oz (315 g) luganiga *sausage (pure pork), chopped in small pieces*
4 tablespoons dry white wine
2 cups (10 oz/315 g) Arborio rice
8 cups (2 qt/2 l) meat broth (stock), boiling
¼ teaspoon powdered saffron
½ cup (2 oz/60 g) freshly grated Parmesan cheese

Put 2 oz (60 g) butter in a pan, add the onion and the *luganiga.* Sauté until brown, then add the wine. Pour in the rice and cook for a few moments to enable the juices to penetrate the grains. Whilst continuing to stir, add the hot broth little by little. After 10 minutes add the saffron, diluted in some hot broth.

After 20 minutes, remove the pan from the heat. The consistency of the risotto should be not too runny but also not too stiff. Add the Parmesan and the rest of the butter. Stir well and serve immediately.

SERVES: 4

Bresaola from Valtellina

Minestrone alla Milanese

Vegetable Soup Milanese Style

The Milanese claim to have created minestrone, made throughout Italy.

2 oz (60 g) bacon, cut into strips
2 oz (60 g) butter
2 garlic cloves, coarsely chopped
3 tablespoons coarsely chopped parsley
2 zucchini (courgettes), cubed
2 carrots, cubed
2 celery stalks, cubed
2 ripe tomatoes, finely chopped
2 large potatoes, cubed
6 oz (185 g) fresh borlotti *beans or 1 medium can* borlotti *beans*
12 oz (375 g) Savoy cabbage, cut into strips
1 fresh rosemary sprig
several sage leaves
10 oz (315 g) pork rind, without the fat
nutmeg
salt and freshly ground pepper
8 cups (4 pt/2 l) broth (stock)
1 cup (6 oz/185 g) Arborio rice
¾ cup (3 oz/90 g) freshly grated Parmesan cheese

Put the bacon strips in a large, heavy saucepan with the butter and sauté over moderate heat for 5 minutes. Add the garlic and sauté for another 2 minutes. Add the parsley, zucchini, carrot, celery, tomatoes, potatoes, *borlotti* beans, cabbage, rosemary and sage.

Sprinkle the pork rind generously with nutmeg, salt and pepper and then roll and bind it with kitchen string. Add it to the saucepan, along with enough broth to thoroughly cover all the vegetables.

Bring to a boil and simmer for at least 1 hour, adding more broth if necessary. Add salt and pepper to taste, and the rice. (If you are using tinned *borlotti* beans, it is at this point that they are added.)

Cook for another 20 minutes or so, stirring frequently. Mash some of the potato cubes to give the soup a thicker consistency. Serve with a slice of the pork rind roll in each bowl, sprinkled with Parmesan cheese.

SERVES: 6 to 8

Risotto with Sausage, Vegetable Soup Milanese Style

PETER JOHNSON

PETER JOHNSON

Veal in Tuna Sauce

Vitello Tonnato

Veal in Tuna Sauce

This unusual combination of meat and fish results in a very tasty dish. It is popular throughout Italy, but perhaps this version from Lombardia is the easiest to make. The cut of veal generally used is the *girello* or eye of silverside, which provides very fine, close-textured slices when cut across the grain.

2 lb (1 kg) boned leg of veal or eye of silverside
1 carrot, chopped
2 celery stalks, cut into pieces
1 onion
6 oz (185 g) tuna fish in oil
2 tablespoons drained capers, plus a few extra for decoration
6 anchovy fillets
¾ cup (6 fl oz/180 ml) fresh mayonnaise
gherkin pickles for decoration
salt and freshly ground black pepper

Boil the meat with the carrot, celery and onion and a pinch of salt for 1 hour. Cool, then slice thinly and arrange on a dish.

Put the vegetables, together with the tuna, capers and anchovies, through a food processor to produce a smooth paste, the consistency of thick cream, and mix with the mayonnaise. Add salt and pepper to taste, spread the sauce over the veal and decorate with gherkins and capers.

SERVES: 12

Ossobuco alla Milanese

Braised Veal Shanks

This method of preparing *ossobuco* is typical of Lombardia, and more precisely of Milano.

4 cross-cut veal shanks, 1½ in (3 to 4 cm) thick, cut from the middle of the shin where the bone is rounded on both sides and the meat is dense
salt
all purpose (plain) flour for dusting
4 tablespoons olive oil
1 small onion, sliced
1 lb (500 g) canned peeled tomatoes, strained of ½ their juice
juice and ½ the grated rind of 1 large orange
1 cup (8 fl oz/250 ml) dry red wine
salt and freshly ground black pepper

Dust the veal shanks with salt and flour. Heat the olive oil in a cast-iron casserole and sauté the veal shanks 2 at a time on both sides, taking great care not to damage the marrow in the center or to allow it to fall out. Remove the shanks from the casserole and put to one side.

In the same oil, sauté the onion until transparent then add the tomatoes, breaking them up in the casserole with a wooden spoon while cooking. Cook over high heat so that the tomatoes reduce. After 5 minutes add the orange juice,

PETER JOHNSON

Braised Veal Shanks

orange rind and wine. Return the shanks to the sauce, still over high heat.

Season with salt and pepper and then reduce the heat, cover the casserole and simmer for 1 to $1\frac{1}{2}$ hours or until the meat begins to come away from the bone. Serve with rice.

SERVES: 4

Costolette alla Milanese

Veal Chops Milanese

It is important for this very simple but extremely tasty dish, to remove all the fat from the chops and to beat them slightly, so that they are not more than about ½ in (1.5 cm) thick. An incision with the tip of the knife into the edge of the meat, opposite the bone, will stop the meat from shrinking.

4 veal chops (cutlets) with the bone, without fat, about 6 or 7 oz (200 g) each
2 eggs, beaten
plenty of fresh breadcrumbs
3 oz (90 g) butter
salt and freshly ground pepper
1 lemon, quartered
4 parsley sprigs

Dip the chops in the eggs, then press them down into the breadcrumbs, patting them on each side to shake off the superfluous crumbs.

Heat the butter in a large skillet and seal the chops on each side for 2 to 3 minutes. Lower the heat and cook for another 8 minutes each side until crispy. (Fry only 2 at a time.)

Salt and pepper just before serving and decorate with the parsley and lemon.

SERVES: 4

Veal Chops Milanese

PETER JOHNSON

Sweetbreads Fricassee, Milanese Stewed Pork

and some more broth. Simmer for a further 30 minutes. The dish should be neither too dry nor too soupy. Serve hot with polenta.

SERVES: 8

Fricassea di Animelle

Sweetbreads Fricassee

Simple ingredients prepared with great care are the key to this recipe.

1 lb (500 g) blanched sweetbreads, cleaned of all membrane, sliced ½ in (1 cm) thick
all purpose (plain) flour for dusting
2 oz (60 g) butter
1 small onion, very finely sliced
1 small carrot, very finely cubed
6 oz (180 g) fresh porcini *(boletus) mushrooms or 20 dried ones, soaked*
salt and freshly ground pepper
¾ cup (6 fl oz/180 ml) dry white wine
4 tablespoons milk
1 tablespoon chopped parsley

Roll the sweetbreads in flour, sauté in butter until golden and set aside. Add the onion and sauté until glassy. Add the carrots and mushrooms. (If using the dried ones, also add a little of the soaking water.) Salt and pepper to taste.

Return the sweetbreads to the skillet, add the wine and cook for another 5 minutes. Add the milk and stir gently. Sprinkle with parsley and serve hot.

SERVES: 4

Cassoela

Milanese Stewed Pork

This dish is cooked in Lombardia to celebrate the killing of the pig. It is supposed to be cooked with all the bits and pieces that remain after the pig has been processed into various specialties.

3 tablespoons olive oil
1 large onion, finely sliced
13 oz (410 g) pork skin, without fat, sprinkled with nutmeg, salt and pepper, rolled and tied up with kitchen string, and cut into chunks
2 fresh pig's feet (trotters), quartered
1½ lb (750 g) meaty pork belly
1 lb (500 g) meaty pork spare ribs
12 cups (3 qt/3 l) broth (stock)—bouillon cubes can be used
2 celery stalks, cut into small chunks
2 large carrots, coarsely chopped
1 lb (500 g) Savoy cabbage, coarsely shredded
10 oz (315 g) luganiga *sausage (pure pork), cut into chunks*
salt and freshly ground pepper

Put the oil in a large heavy saucepan and gently sauté the onion until glassy. Add the rolled pork skin, the feet, the pork belly and the spare ribs, and cover with broth. Simmer for 1 hour.

Add the celery, carrots, cabbage and the sausage, with salt and pepper to taste,

Bollito Misto

Boiled Mixed Meats

In Lombardia, there are many different ingredients available for the *bollito*, such as calf's head and feet which, when boiled, will become quite gelatinous. Make sure to include the famous *zampone*, stuffed pig's foot, available from any good Italian delicatessen.

1 beef tongue, about 3 lb (1.5 kg), preferably one that has been soaked in brine
1 boiling chicken, about 4 lb (2 kg)
1 lb (500 g) beef brisket
4 carrots
5 celery stalks
2 onions

1 large fresh rosemary sprig
8 potatoes
salt and freshly ground black pepper
1 zampone *(stuffed pig's foot/trotter)*
Green Sauce:
10 anchovy fillets
50 drained capers
⅓ cup (1½ oz/45 g) breadcrumbs
1 large bunch flat-leafed parsley
1 garlic clove
2 tablespoons wine vinegar
1½ cups (12 fl oz/375 ml) olive oil

Clean the tongue of fat and gristle. Clean and wash the chicken.

Put the tongue into a very large, heavy saucepan (large enough to take the chicken, tongue and beef), cover with cold water and bring to a boil. Skim away the froth that comes to the surface every now and again. Boil for 1 hour, then add the beef, chicken, carrots, celery, onions, rosemary and a little salt and pepper. Continue to boil the meats together for a further 2 hours. The boiling chicken and the beef should be tested to see if they are cooked after 1½ hours. They should be tender but not falling apart. During the final ½ hour of boiling add the potatoes.

In a separate saucepan boil the *zampone*. The cooking time is usually specified on the package: most *zampone* are precooked so that 20 minutes will be sufficient.

When the tongue, chicken and beef are cooked, remove them from the saucepan. Allow the tongue to cool a little before peeling off the skin. Allow all the meats to stand for 10 minutes before carving. Arrange slices of all the meats on a large, heated serving plate. You may ladle a little of the stock onto the slices to keep them moist. Arrange the potatoes and other vegetables with the meats and serve with green sauce.

For the sauce: Put all the ingredients except the olive oil into the blender and process until you get a thick paste. Then slowly add the olive oil, intermittently blending, until you obtain a smooth, thick sauce. The amount of oil that will be needed will depend upon the size of the bunch of parsley.

You may wish to add salt and pepper, but usually the capers and anchovies are seasoning enough.

SERVES: 8

Boiled Mixed Meats

PETER JOHNSON

Funghi Fritti

Deep Fried Mushrooms

All the edible mushrooms you can lay your hands on are good for this dish.

2 lb (1 kg) mixed wild mushrooms, cleaned weight
4 eggs
salt and freshly ground pepper
oil for deep frying
breadcrumbs for coating
3 lemons, quartered (optional)

Cut the larger mushrooms into mouthful-sized chunks; leave the small ones whole. Beat the eggs, adding salt and pepper to taste. Pour some oil into a large skillet to a depth of at least ¾ in (2 cm) and heat.

Dip the mushrooms in the eggs, allow the surplus to run off, then roll in the breadcrumbs. Place gently in the hot oil and sauté, in batches, until they are light gold and crispy all over. Serve garnished with lemon, if desired.

SERVES: 6

Bietole al Burro

Swiss Chard with Butter

Cooking vegetables this way conserves the vitamin content and enhances their flavor.

1 lb (500 g) Swiss chard, with stalks
1½ oz (45 g) butter
¾ cup (6 fl oz/180 ml) water or broth (stock)
salt and freshly ground black pepper

Wash and cut the chard into 1-in (2-cm) slices. Heat the butter in a large saucepan, and when melted add the chard. Increase the heat, mix well, then add the water and salt and pepper. Cover the pan and cook for about 7 minutes. Serve hot.

SERVES: 4

Fave Fresche alla Pancetta

Broad Beans and Bacon

The smaller tender broad beans are best for this recipe but they are difficult to find, as the growers prefer to sell the larger ones. Broad beans cooked in this way make a good accompaniment to game and other strongly flavored dishes.

3 tablespoons olive oil
1 small onion, chopped
2 oz (60 g) smoked bacon, in match-stick slices
1 lb (500 g) broad beans, podded weight
salt

Heat the olive oil in a saucepan and sauté the onion until glassy. Add the bacon and stir-fry together until golden. Add the broad beans and the water and cook, covered, until tender: about 5 to 7 minutes. Season with salt, if necessary, and serve hot.

SERVES: 4

Topinambur con Cipolle

Jerusalem Artichokes with Onions

Resembling a ginger root rather than a globe artichoke, Jerusalem artichokes are best when they are small. Cooked in this way they are delicious with delicate meats such as veal or chicken.

1 lb 6 oz (680 g) Jerusalem artichokes, peeled weight
juice of ½ lemon
1½ oz (45 g) butter
5 oz (150 g) onion, thinly sliced
¾ cup (6 fl oz/180 ml) water or broth (stock)
salt and freshly ground black pepper
2 tablespoons chopped parsley

Peel the artichokes, roughly chop them and put in water with the lemon juice to prevent discoloring.

Heat the butter and sauté the onion. When it is glassy, add the artichokes, together with the water or broth and some salt and pepper. Simmer gently for 30 minutes.

The liquid should be of a syrupy consistency once the artichokes are cooked. Serve sprinkled with parsley.

SERVES: 4

Deep Fried Mushrooms, Jerusalem Artichokes with Onions, Swiss Chard with Butter, Broad Beans and Bacon

PETER JOHNSON

PETER JOHNSON

Trifle

Tiramisù

Trifle

There are many recipes for *Tiramsù*, which means "pick me up" or "lift me up", perhaps referring to the large number of calories in it!

2 egg yolks
2 tablespoons sugar
1 packet (2 teaspoons) vanilla sugar
1 lb (500 g) mascarpone *cheese*
¾ cup (6 fl oz/180 ml) strong black coffee
1 tablespoon Kahlua, or other coffee liqueur
24 small savoiardi *sponge fingers*
1 to 2 tablespoons unsweetened cocoa powder

Put the egg yolks, sugar and vanilla in a bowl and mix gently to a creamy consistency. Fold in the *mascarpone* to obtain a cream.

Mix the coffee with the coffee liqueur. Dip the *savoiardi* for a second or two in the coffee mixture, making sure they do not become too soggy.

Starting with the *savoiardi*, arrange on individual plates, alternating layers of sponge fingers and *mascarpone*, ending with *mascarpone*.

Dust the servings generously with cocoa powder and put into the fridge for an hour to two to set and chill.

SERVES: 4 to 6

Crostata di Mirtilli

Blueberry Tart

This tart is wonderful when made with freshly gathered wild blueberries, but in many places this is simply not possible. Strawberries, raspberries and blackberries make fine alternatives.

Pastry:
2¼ cups (9 oz/280 g) all purpose (plain) flour
¼ cup (2 oz/60 g) sugar
pinch of salt
4 oz (125 g) unsalted butter
4 tablespoons dry sherry
Filling:
1½ lb (750 g) fresh blueberries
½ cup (4 fl oz/125 ml) water
juice of ½ lemon
⅔ cup (5 oz/155 g) sugar
1 envelope or 1 tablespoon (¼ oz/8 g) powdered gelatin

For the pastry: Sieve together the flour, sugar and salt, add the butter cut into small pieces and mix together with your fingertips until the butter has completely crumbled. Add the sherry and mix lightly to make a dough. Cover and put aside in a cool place for at least 1 hour. Preheat the oven to 350°F (180°C).

Roll out the pastry and line a 10-in (25-cm) pie pan. Prick the surface and bake blind for 15 to 20 minutes, or until the pastry is cooked.

For the filling: Wash the berries and choose 6 oz (185 g) of the least good-looking ones. Put them in small saucepan with the water, the lemon juice and the sugar. Boil until the juice takes on some color and becomes slightly syrupy. Remove from the heat, stir in the gelatin and leave to cool a little.

When the pastry and the syrup have cooled, spread the jellied syrup evenly over the flan base. Arrange the remaining berries in a decorative way on the top, making concentric circles. Leave for a little while to set before serving.

SERVES: 6 to 8

Blueberry Tart

PETER JOHNSON

A U S T R
SVIZZERA
Bressanone
Merano
TRENTINO ~
ALTO ADIGE
Cortina d'Ampezzo
ALPI
FRI
Tolmezzo
Tagliamento
Bolzano
DOLOMITI
Belluno
VENE
Spilimbergo
Trento
Vittorio Veneto
Pordenone
GIU
Rovereto
Valdobbiadene
VENETO
Conegliano
Lago di Garda
Bassano del Grappa
Piave
COLLI LESSINI
Bacchiglione
San Dona
Castelfranco Veneto
Treviso
Garda
Vicenza
Burano
Torcello
Murano
Brenta
Verona
Padova
Venezia
COLLI EUGANEI
Chioggia
Legnago
Adige
Cavarzere
LOMBARDIA
Po
Rovigo
Delta del Po
MARE
EMILIA~ROMAGNA
0 10 20 30 40 50 M.
0 10 20 30 40 50 60 70 80 Km.

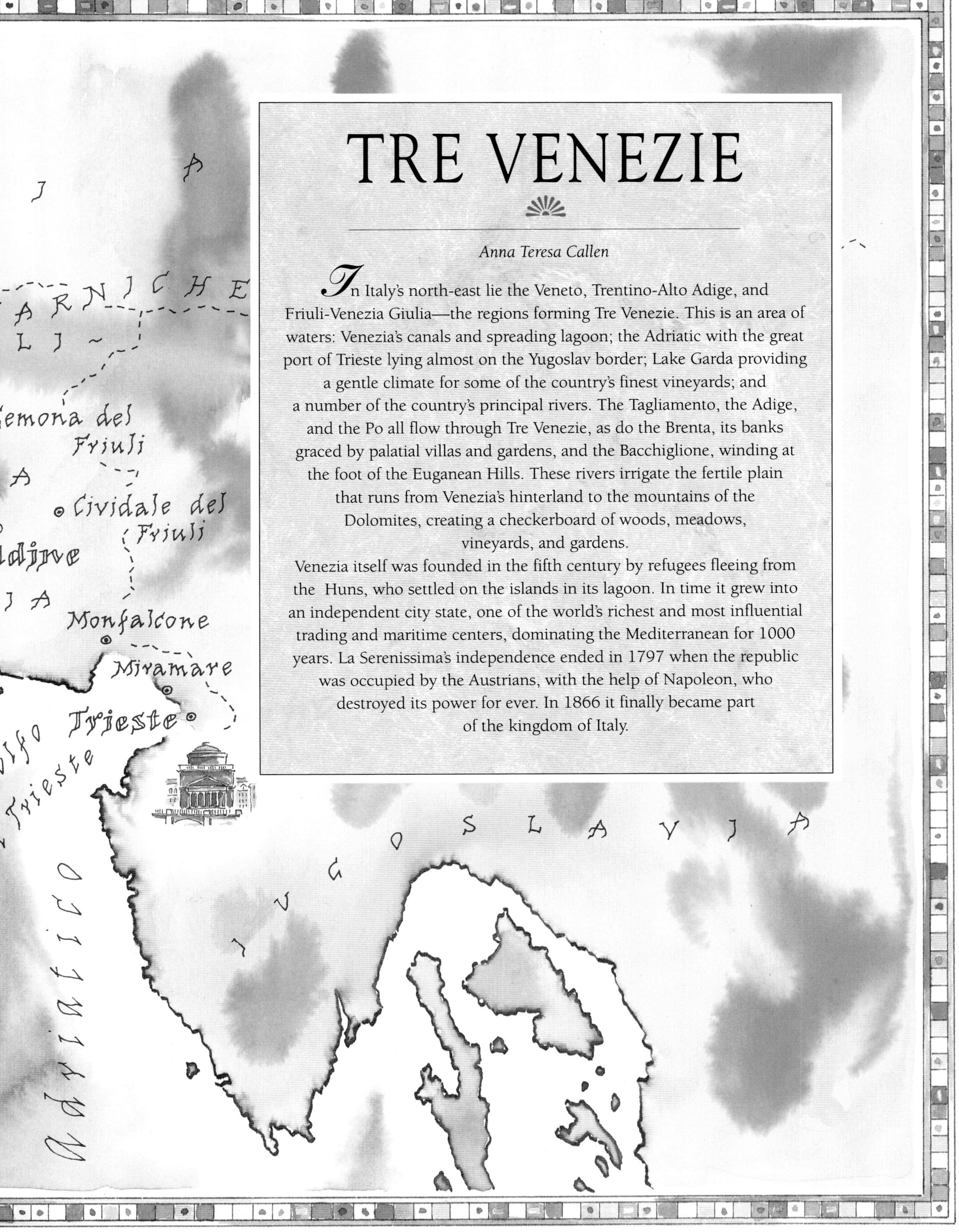

TRE VENEZIE

Anna Teresa Callen

In Italy's north-east lie the Veneto, Trentino-Alto Adige, and Friuli-Venezia Giulia—the regions forming Tre Venezie. This is an area of waters: Venezia's canals and spreading lagoon; the Adriatic with the great port of Trieste lying almost on the Yugoslav border; Lake Garda providing a gentle climate for some of the country's finest vineyards; and a number of the country's principal rivers. The Tagliamento, the Adige, and the Po all flow through Tre Venezie, as do the Brenta, its banks graced by palatial villas and gardens, and the Bacchiglione, winding at the foot of the Euganean Hills. These rivers irrigate the fertile plain that runs from Venezia's hinterland to the mountains of the Dolomites, creating a checkerboard of woods, meadows, vineyards, and gardens.

Venezia itself was founded in the fifth century by refugees fleeing from the Huns, who settled on the islands in its lagoon. In time it grew into an independent city state, one of the world's richest and most influential trading and maritime centers, dominating the Mediterranean for 1000 years. La Serenissima's independence ended in 1797 when the republic was occupied by the Austrians, with the help of Napoleon, who destroyed its power for ever. In 1866 it finally became part of the kingdom of Italy.

RAY JOYCE

A pair of carved horses, painted in silver, prance on the prow of a Venetian boat.

SOME VENETIAN SCENES

If you can, approach Venezia from the sea. Watching this fairytale city emerge from the waters of the lagoon is an unforgettable sight. Built on 118 tiny islands and linked by 400 bridges and about 3000 *calli*, as the narrow streets are called, Venezia is blessedly without cars. Her people go about by water transport—gondolas, *vaporetti*, water buses, *motoscafi*—or on foot.

Napoleon called Venezia's main piazza, the piazza San Marco, "the living- room of Italy". With its classical arcaded buildings on three sides, and the magical Basilica di San Marco with its Byzantine cupolas and Romanesque façade dominating the eastern end, it is one of the most beautiful squares in the world. Begun in 828 and completed in the eleventh century, the Basilica, with its blending of architectural styles, illustrates Venezia's position at the crossroads between east and west. The Palazzo Ducale or Doge's Palace, from which affairs of the Venetian Republic were conducted, is built alongside the Basilica, its southern façade looking out over the lagoon.

The fashionable Caffè Florian and its rival, Quadri, across the piazza, are perfect places to stop for a *cappuccino* or a Campari. If you are in a shopping mood, the shops of the Marzaria display some of the best of Italian *alta moda*. Signs on the walls will guide you to the Rialto Bridge, leading to the bustling produce and fish markets. As in the past, this is still the city's commercial center.

Why not return to piazza San Marco by gondola? Just before the color leaves the sky and the busy Grand Canal has quietened, such a trip is pure magic. Before you board, settle on a price for your ride and buy a bottle of bubbly Prosecco di Conegliano wine from a nearby shop.

A boatman makes his way down the main canal on the island of Murano, just north of Venezia. Since the thirteenth century Murano has been renowned for its glass.

HANS WOLF/THE IMAGE BANK

BOUNTY FROM THE LAGOON

The cuisine of Venezia had rustic beginnings. When the people from terra firma took refuge from the barbarians on the lagoon's islands they hunted birds and wild animals and, of course, they fished. Salt and pepper were later brought to these shores by the gilded galleons of the Republic. Saffron arrived with returning Crusaders, as did tarragon. Ginger, which had disappeared with the ancient Romans, was brought back by Marco Polo from China. All this initiated trade on a scale that provided La Serenissima with untold riches.

Venezia's cuisine today reflects the levels of sophistication that it reached during the city's golden age. Earthy and marine flavors exude from moist risotti, often married to vegetables, fish, and meat. Fish, of course, is the pillar of Venetian cuisine. *Granseola*, a typical *antipasto*, is poached crab dressed with olive oil, salt, a touch of pepper, and lemon juice, and presented in its rosy shell. Fragrant *broeti*, fish stews, and shellfish combinations are what make Venezia and the ports on its lagoon a paradise for fish lovers. Expert grilling and frying produces food that is both juicy and crunchy. As for non-fish dishes, try the *fegato alla veneziana*, liver Venetian style, cooked with onion and vinegar, and the extraordinary *masoro alla valesana,* a traditional dish of wild duck.

For a change of scenery take a trip to some of the islands in the lagoon. In Murano you can watch the glass blowers; in Burano, women create exquisite laces as they sit in front of their vividly painted houses. Torcello, perhaps the most enchanting of all the islands, is where Venezia began more than 1500 years ago. Lunch in a *locanda* where the food tends to be homey—gnocchi, *tagliarini verdi gratinati*, green noodles au gratin, grilled meat, fresh fish.

THE MARCA TREVIGIANA

In summer wealthy Venetians headed for their country villas, many of them in the Marca Trevigiana, the Treviso district. During the Middle Ages villa dwellers created such an atmosphere of gaiety that the Marca became known as the Marca *gioiosa e amorosa*—a district of joy and love.

When it comes to food, Treviso maintains the Venetian tradition of high living, evident from the variety of produce in its colorful markets. *Radicchio*, the pride of Treviso, explodes in shades of red, even having its own market. And behind the Palazzo dei Trecento, where the city council used to meet, there is a market selling nothing but mushrooms.

As in most of the Veneto, poultry is widely eaten. Goose is flavored with celery, and the ubiquitous *faraona*, guinea hen, is served with *peverada,* a sauce made with vinegar, lemon juice, garlic, anchovies, chicken livers, *grana* (a cheese similar to Parmesan), breadcrumbs, peppercorns, lemon peel, and ginger. *Trippa alla trevigiana,* tripe, is a local specialty eaten on market days because it can be counted on to be fresh. *Lievero in tecia*, a specialty from Vittorio Veneto, is hare cooked in *peverada* containing the hare's liver and sausages.

This is wine territory. The most famous, Prosecco, is a golden wine with a fruity taste and a sparkle. The best is made in Valdobbiadene and in Conegliano, site of one of the first wine schools in Italy. Also produced in this area is Tocai, which differs from the syrupy sweet, more famous Hungarian wine of the same name. The local Tocai grape is turned into a dry, crisp wine which is excellent with fish and *antipasti*, as is the Verdiso, so-called because of its greenish hue.

RADICCHIO ROSSO

For most of the year the vegetable markets of the Veneto, and particularly in Treviso, bloom ruby-red and pink with this crisp, leafy vegetable that has a pleasantly bitter flavour, similar to endive.

The people of Treviso believe that their *radicchio*, which grows in tight bunches of smooth elongated red leaves with white stalks, is superior to the more common rounded variety that comes from Castelfranco Veneto.

The round *radicchio* is flower-like in appearance, somewhat resembling an old-fashioned rose. Its coloring and flavor are less pronounced, and it is not as tender as the Treviso *radicchio*, but it is easier to find.

When mixed with slices of fennel, *radicchio* makes a wonderful winter salad. It is quite frequently cooked—brushed with oil and grilled, or deep-fried, *alla giudia.* There is also a traditional risotto made with the Treviso *radicchio.*

RAY JOYCE

The rounded radicchio from Castelfranco Veneto.

LA SERENISSIMA'S FESTIVALS

Venezia is famous for its many festivals. For 700 years the Regata Storica, a gondola race, has been passing under the same bridges and beside the same weather-stained palazzi. The Regata, on the first Sunday of September, starts with a procession of gondolas and *bissoni,* eight-oared boats, rowed by sailors wearing historic garb in the colors of their *sestrieri,* districts. People crowd along the canal, on the bridges, and on balconies to cheer the competing sailors.

The Festa del Redentore, Feast of the Redeemer, is held on the third Sunday of July. All Venezia takes part in this feast, called "famous night" because it lasts till dawn. Boats and gondolas, festooned with flowers and Chinese lanterns, crowd the Giudecca Canal, loaded with enthusiastic spectators watching the fireworks display.

Perhaps the most impressive ceremony of all is Lo Sposalizio del Mare, the Marriage of the Sea, on Ascension Day. A solemn procession of boats, led by the gilded state galleon, *Bucintoro,* sail on the lagoon which flows to the sea. Here the person representing the Doge tosses a blessed ring into the water, renewing with this gesture the marriage of La Serenissima with the sea, dating from 1311.

The gayest of the festivals by far is Carnevale, which takes place during the dreary month of February. Out of the mists appear damsels and cavaliers in eighteenth-century costume, harlequins and colombines, ladies and gentlemen in dominos, crowding into the piazza San Marco and the converging *calli.*

When snow falls the city becomes a fantasy land, sparkling with ice crystal decorations, but the unavoidable stairs and bridges can be treacherous. If trestles are lined up on the riva degli Schiavoni or in piazza San Marco, don't think they are preparing for a market. You will have to walk on them if the dreaded *acqua alta,* high water, comes. But no matter how cold it is or how high the water rises, at Carnevale the air seems to warm up and blow the mist away. Food is very much a part of Carnevale. There are mountains of gnocchi and lasagne oozing rich sauces; yards and yards of piquant sausages; succulent roasts and *pastizade,* stews; *fritole,* fried pastries similar to donuts; and *galani,* ribbons of crunchy pastry sprinkled with powdered sugar.

The international Biennale d'Arte Contemporanea, the Contemporary Art Biennale, one of the world's most important art shows, is held during the summer months in even years. The bulk of the art works are exhibited in permanent pavilions on the Lido; the rest are placed at random throughout the city. It is intriguing to see an ultramodern sculpture set in an ancient courtyard or *campiello.*

ARTHUS BERTRAND/EXPLORER

The color and movement of dancing during Carnevale brightens up a winter's day in the piazza San Marco.

Left: A barge loaded with produce from the markets. Below: In summer, the crowds gather all along the Grand Canal for the spectacle of the Regata Storica, the participants' costumes and boats much as they were 700 years ago.

SILVIO FIORE/FIOREPRESS

GUIDO ALBERTO ROSSI/THE IMAGE BANK

MILAN HORACEK/BILDERBERG

Small red and yellow plums are dried in the sun for a day or so and then sorted for preserving in alcohol.

Along the Brenta

A delightful way to travel from Venezia to Padova is by boat along the Brenta River. A replica of the *Burchiello*, an eighteenth-century boat, immortalized by Tiepolo in several of his paintings, navigates the Brenta from 24 March to 26 October. It is an enchanting all-day journey, traveling past a polychromy of old houses and villas, with their gardens and spreading trees. The boat visits several villas, including Palladio's Villa Foscari, called La Malcontenta, the unhappy one, built for a member of the Foscari family who banished his wife there. Lunch is served in Oriago at a riverside restaurant where the cooking is typically regional, with inventive seasonal specialties, served with the ubiquitous polenta.

Padova is the agricultural hub of the Veneto region. Its people are fond of pointing out that their city has "un santo senza nome, un prato senza erba ed un caffè senza porte" ("a saint without a name, a meadow without grass and a coffeehouse without doors"). Padova's nameless saint is its protector, San Antonio, always referred to as "the saint". The meadow is Prato della Valle, which is not a meadow but a square. In its center is a garden surrounded by a canal adorned with statuary. The café is the Pedrocchi, given to the city by a benefactor who stipulated that it must stay open day and night, a tradition only interrupted during the last war.

The Basilica di Sant'Antonio, a monumental composite of styles—Romanesque, Gothic, Moorish, and Byzantine—houses many works of art by Sansovino, Lombardi, and Mantegna, and an altar group by Donatello. Among a multitude of other artworks worthy of mention are the frescoes by Giotto in the Cappella degli Scrovegni and those by Mantegna at the Chiesa degli Eremitani.

Padova's university was founded in 1222. It is one of the most important universities in Italy, Galileo being one of its more controversial members of staff. It is here that the Teatro Anatomico, theater of anatomy, was built in 1594, the first of its kind in Europe. Close by is the piazza delle Erbe, where the daily market takes place. It is well worth a visit.

Padova's cuisine is based mostly on vegetables, rice, and legumes. Many recipes begin with the world-famous *gallina padovana,* a local large-breasted hen. Fowl, like ducks, geese, and guinea hens, are prepared with great care. There is an ancient proverb that praises "Vincentine wines, Trevigian tripe, and Venetian women", to which Padovani modestly add their *pan padovan*, the local bread. It is indeed praiseworthy, especially the crusty *ciopete*, rolls, and the *pan biscotto* that crumbles in your mouth.

If *risi e bisi* is a bone of contention between "Venezia bella e Padova sa sorella" ("beautiful Venezia and Padova her sister"), both claiming to have invented it, *risotto alla padovana*, made with chopped veal and chicken livers, is exclusive to Padova. In summer fresh peas are used; in winter, sliced mushrooms.

While cultivated mostly in Piemonte and Lombardia, rice has become the favorite food of the Veneti. The countryside is rich in vegetables—zucchini, cabbage, asparagus, peas, cauliflower, and mushrooms—which are liberally used in simple risotti. More substantial, and reserved for special occasions, are those made with chicken liver, duck, eel, and *tinca,* a sweet fish from the Bacchiglione River and Lake Garda.

In the Padova area pasta is mostly *bigoli*—dark, home-made, thick, round noodles, dressed with sauce. One of the most popular sauces is made with onion sautéed slowly in olive oil until creamy, after which sardines and anchovies are

Preceding pages: An aerial view of La Serenissima reveals the city in all her richness, the Grand Canal winding past decaying, beautiful palaces and out into the lagoon.

JOHN CALLANAN/THE IMAGE BANK

Palladio, arguably the finest architect of the Renaissance, was much influenced by the Roman architect Vitruvius. Many fine Palladian buildings can be seen around the city of Vicenza in the Veneto.

added. On Good Friday the sauce is enriched with tuna fish. Poultry, especially duck, a favorite of the Veneti, is also used to flavor *bigoli*. *Bigoli coi rovinazzi* is made with a mixture which must include cocks' combs, a local penchant.

The pig provides many delicacies. Nothing is wasted, the Veneti excelling with their salami, sausages, prosciutti, and other preserved meats. *Museti* are made with the pig's skin; *bondole*, with pork, beef, and cured tongue; *luganiga* is a thin fresh sausage. And there are the *osi de porco*, the pig's bones that add flavor to many heart-warming *minestre*.

Palladio's Legacy

Vicenza, north-west of Padova, has one of the richest architectural heritages in all Italy, thanks to Palladio, whose work so greatly influenced the development of Western architecture. The majority of his masterpieces are in Vicenza, where he spent most of his life—the Basilica, symbol of the city; La Loggia del Capitano; and the Palazzo Chiericati, now the civic museum. All three buildings exemplify Palladio's obsession with Roman antiquity. His last work, the enchanting Teatro Olimpico, should not be missed. There are ninety-five statues ranged around this intimate, semi-circular theater, giving an air of classical grandeur, and the fanciful stage set provides an extraordinary, three-dimensional perspective. Among Palladio's villas, the best known and the most frequently copied is La Rotonda, just outside Vicenza.

The most popular bird for the table in Vicenza and its province is the turkey. *Paeta al malgaragna* is a young female turkey wrapped in pork fat, cooked on a spit, and basted with pomegranate juice. The dish is served with *peverada* sauce made with turkey innards flavored with onion, rosemary, and pepper.

INTERNATIONAL PHOTOGRAPHIC LIBRARY

Loads of fodder being transported by horse and cart, the peaks of the Dolomites providing a dramatic backdrop.

The Home of Romeo and Juliet

At the foot of the Lessini Hills lies the ancient city of Verona, filled with architectural marvels that range from a Roman arena to a Renaissance marketplace. It is the setting for the story of Romeo and Juliet, first recounted by Matteo Maria Boiardo, a fifteenth-century writer, and later immortalized by Shakespeare. You can see the hapless Juliet's house, complete with balcony, at 17 via Cappello. Castelvecchio, the most impressive Medieval structure in the city, is a sprawling castle on the banks of the Adige that was once a stronghold of the powerful Scaglieri. It is now a fascinating museum.

Perhaps the most enchanting square in Italy is here—the piazza delle Erbe, vegetable square, bordered by Baroque and Renaissance buildings. During the day the piazza is the site of a colorful, noisy vegetable market where all the produce of the area is artfully displayed.

The people of Verona are the most dedicated gnocchi eaters. Another traditional dish is *risotto alla veronese*, made with chopped ham and mushrooms. The pride of the city, however, is *pandoro*, golden bread, a dome-shaped, spongy vanilla cake, often served with *zabaione*.

Going north, Lake Garda narrows between towering cliffs and offers a glorious approach to the Dolomites. Wild fowl abound, and fish are plentiful. The climate, mild in winter and breezy in summer, is Mediterranean. There are groves of orange, lemon, and olive trees, and vineyards flourish. Mellow Soave, refreshing Bardolino, and Valpolicella, light and dry, all come from here.

When you dine in one of the pleasant *trattorie* along the lake shore ask for local wine. You may be served an unlabeled full-bodied Verduzzo or a simple house wine. The intense Recioto, that takes its name from *orecchie*, ears, is a dessert wine that is made with only the outer "ears" of a bunch of grapes. Being more exposed to the sun these grapes are the sweetest and, after being picked, they are dried in the sun to bring out the sweetness even more.

Austria's Culinary Legacy

Trento, capital of Trentino-Alto Adige, surrounded by magnificent mountains, sits serenely around its castle, the Castello del Buon Consiglio, the Castle of Good Advice. The Austrians occupied the city up to 1918, and their culinary legacy is evident. The famous *Knödel* of the Alto Adige, where German is spoken as much as Italian, have become *canederli*. *Nockerln* are *gnocchetti,* and sauerkraut is *crauti.*

There are many *Gulasches* and *sguazet*, made with different meats and eaten with a polenta in which the cornmeal is mixed with other flours and even potatoes and onions. *Lepre alla trentina*, hare marinated in butter, lard, onion, pine nuts, raisins, cinnamon, lemon rind, and sugar, is found nowhere else in Italy. *Probusti* are salami made with pork and veal with a touch of garlic. They are smoked over white birch and eaten boiled with *crauti*—a truly delicious dish.

This region makes wonderful salami and prosciutti, including speck. Trout and eel abound and are prominent in the local cuisine. In *trotelle alla trentina* the trout is sautéed and dressed with a lemon-mint sauce containing raisins. Eel is usually simply roasted or cooked in wine. In coffee houses, pastries and cakes are elaborate and Austrian in style, while in the home they tend to be rustic. Many contain dried fruit, and cornmeal is sometimes used instead of flour. *Zelten* is a

Umbrellas cover the stalls of the vegetable market in the piazza delle Erbe, Verona. Now lined with old palaces and houses, the square was once a Roman forum, where chariot races were held.

WALTER LEONARDI/SPERANZA

Vines in the afternoon sunlight alongside a farmhouse in Alto Adige. Hemmed in by the Alps, space for grape growing is limited, but many of the wines produced in the region are of exceptional quality.

rich Christmas cake similar to, but lighter than, fruitcake. Strudel, filled with either savory or sweet ingredients, is eaten everywhere.

A dozen DOC wines are produced in this region: Merlot and Cabernet are the best known reds and the whites are Pinot, Riesling, Traminer, and Chardonnay.

On its course toward the Adriatic the Adige flows through valleys where rye, maize, wheat, oats, and barley grow. Rye, little seen in the rest of Italy, is widely used here. On the lower hills vines are grown extensively. Since the vineyards are at an altitude of 4000 feet (1220 meters) they are tended with extra care. Some prized Italian sparkling wines are produced here from the Pinot Blanc grape.

The food in this region is markedly Teutonic, with echoes of Austro-Hungarian finesse. Dishes like the ever-present *canederli* and gnocchi are listed on menus as *tirolesi*, for this was once the Austrian South Tyrol. Polenta is layered with meat or wurst, and topped with bechamel. Pasta for ravioli is made with rye flour and fillings often contain cabbage or sauerkraut and caraway seeds. Dishes of Italian origin, like *spezzatino di vitello*, veal stew, and *arrosto stufato*, braised roast, become *Kalbsragout* and *Schmorbraten*.

Breads are highly regarded in this region. One, *Schüttelbrot*, shaken-up bread, is so called because of the violence used to knead it. When baked it is so hard it must be broken with a hammer. Understandably it is mostly used for dunking in wine or soup. *Schlagbrot* is soft and is delicious with butter and speck.

Bolzano, capital of Alto Adige, has, through the centuries, been a major crossroads between Italy and Germany. The architecture is typically Tyrolean with painted roofs and gaily decorated façades and the people's dress and speech show that this is a truly northern city. The frescoes in the fifteenth-century Castel Roncolo depict Tyrolean court scenes of the era and many restaurants have a turn-of-the-century Viennese ambience.

Set in a sun-drenched basin, looking out on some of the most famous peaks of the Dolomites, Cortina, for all its fame, has remained an unspoiled village. Playground of the rich and famous, it has splendid hotels and superb summer and winter sports. Treat yourself to an afternoon tea or a drink at one of the luxury hotels, but go to one of the family-run restaurants for lunch or dinner.

Tre Venezie's Easternmost Region

Friuli-Venezia Giulia is the easternmost part of Tre Venezie. The population is greatest on the Friuli plain, where the soil is most fertile. Roughly half the district is mountainous: the Carso massif bordering Yugoslavia is a bastion of bare rocks. The mountainous regions do provide some sustenance, however. Game abounds, there are trout in the streams, and sheep and goats are raised on small farms. Fruit from sparse orchards is much sought-after, and kiwi fruit is now being grown. Superb pork products are made using the small, dark native pigs.

The Friuliani have a way with vegetables and herbs. Soups are varied and light. *Brovada* is a sourish soup made with turnips and vinegar. *Cialson*, the local ravioli, are also served in soup. Spices, especially cumin, are often used: in a classic *jota*, a vegetable soup made with sauerkraut, it is essential.

Desserts, elaborately worked, are made with simple ingredients. The *gubana*, a specialty of Cividale, is shaped like a giant donut. *Millefeuille* pastry is filled with nuts, spices, and a dash of liqueur. *Castagnole*, chestnut-shaped sweet gnocchi, are everywhere in Friuli, as is *pinza*, a bread sweetened with sugar and dried figs.

Udine, the ancient Utina of the Romans, is the capital and historic center of Friuli. Fortunately the 1976 earthquake that severely damaged this region left this handsome city and its monuments practically unscathed.

In Friuli the focal point around which families gather or restaurant tables are set is the *fogolar*, hearth. For local fare go to a *trattoria*. Sit near a *fogolar* and relax with a glass of local wine, and then have a dish of stuffed vegetables, flaky pastries filled with cheese, or crepes with rabbit and walnuts.

On the Adriatic

Trieste, set on a gulf with rolling hills as a backdrop, is the most important seaport on the northern Adriatic. Because of its geographic position and its history, the cooking of Trieste is eclectic. *Gnocchetti di fegato,* liver dumplings, are a reminder of Austrian ties. Venezia's influence is apparent in its many risotti, including its own version of *risi e bisi*. It also has its own variation of *brodetto,* the fish stew so popular along the entire Italian coastline. Made with local fish, the sauce contains vinegar, wine, and sometimes tomatoes, and is always served with grilled polenta. There are many rich desserts. Typical are *strucoli*, similar to strudel, which like *presniz*, an Easter specialty, are made with a variety of ingredients.

Trieste has many restaurants, some modestly called *osterie,* which should not be missed. Tender kid from the island of Cherso, delicate custard-filled *bignes,* dipped in chocolate, and refreshing *gelati* are specialties. The wines, often served in rustic pitchers, are excellent.

For travelers making the round trip, the road back to Venezia takes them through coastal towns, past small coves and sandy beaches. At the end of this journey what could be more pleasant than a final night sitting on the terrace of the Hotel Danieli or at a simple *trattoria* sipping an aperitif and watching the last of the light fading from the waters of the lagoon.

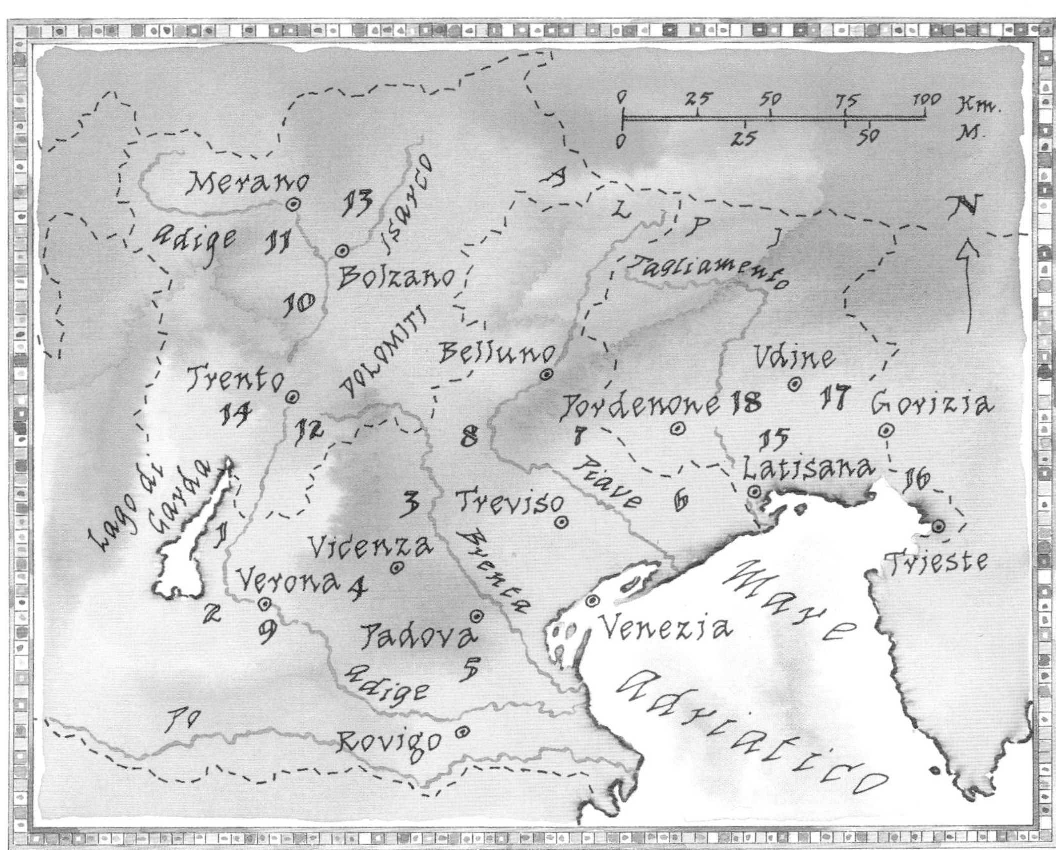

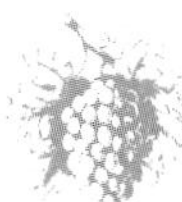

VENETO

DOC Wines

1. Bardolino
2. Bianco di Custoza
3. Breganze
4. Colli Berici
5. Colli Eugani
4. Gambellara
4. Lessini Durello
6. Lison-Pramaggiore
7. Montello e Colli Asolani
6. Piave
8. Prosecco di Conegliano-Valdobbiadene
9. Soave
10. Valdadige
1. Valpolicella

TRENTINO-ALTO ADIGE

DOC Wines

11. Alto Adige/Südtiroler
11. Caldaro
12. Casteller
10. Colli di Bolzano
11. Meranese di Collina
13. Santa Maddalena
12. Sorni
11. Terlano
14. Teroldego Rotaliano
14. Trentino
13. Valle Isarco

FRIULI-VENEZIA GIULIA

DOC Wines

15. Aquilea
16. Carso
17. Collio Goriziano
17. Colli Orientali del Friuli
18. Grave del Friuli
16. Isonzo
15. Latisana

RECIPES OF TRE VENEZIE

Antonio Carluccio

PETER JOHNSON

Peverasse in Cassopipa

Mussel Chowder

Chioggia, the fishing port on the southern arm of Venezia's lagoon, is known for its fine mussels.

4 tablespoons olive oil
1 small onion, sliced
4 lb (2 kg) black fleshy mussels, scrubbed (buy only closed ones)
6 tablespoons dry white wine
2 tablespoons chopped parsley
salt and freshly ground pepper

Place the oil in a large, heavy pan and sauté the onion gently. Add the mussels and put the lid on the pan. After about 10 minutes shake the contents vigorously, as if you are trying to make the mussels at the top of the pan go to the bottom.

When all the mussels are open (discard those that are still closed), add the wine and parsley. Salt to taste and add lots of freshly ground pepper. Serve hot with crusty bread.

SERVES: 4

Bigoli in Salsa

Bigoli with Special Sauce

Bigoli are huge spaghetti freshly made with wholemeal flour in the Veneto.

2 large onions, finely sliced
2 oz (60 g) butter
4 tablespoons olive oil
8 anchovy fillets
12 oz (375 g) freshly made bigoli *or* bucatini *pasta*
salt and freshly ground pepper
1 tablespoon finely chopped parsley

In a large pan, sauté the onion in the butter and oil over moderate heat. When glassy, add the anchovy fillets and stir a few times until they dissolve.

Cook the *bigoli* in plenty of boiling salted water until *al dente*. Mix with the sauce, adding 1 or 2 tablespoons of the cooking water. Be sparing with the salt, over-generous with the pepper, and sprinkle with parsley. Serve immediately.

SERVES: 4 to 6

Mussel Chowder, Black Rissotto, Bigoli with Special Sauce, Seafood Salad, Carpaccio, Marinated Sardines

Carpaccio

Raw Beef Carpaccio

Mr Cipriani of the Cipriani Hotel in Venezia invented the original version of this dish to honor the painter Carpaccio, contrasting the red of the meat and the white/off-white of the sauce. There are hundreds of versions of this dish throughout the world, because Mr Cipriani would not give away the recipe.

12 oz (375g) fillet of beef, sliced and beaten very thinly
2 anchovy fillets
2 tablespoons freshly made mayonnaise
juice of ½ lemon
½ teaspoon Tabasco
2 tablespoons English mustard
salt and freshly ground pepper

Beat the meat between 2 sheets of transparent plastic until very thin. Mix all the other ingredients in a blender to make the sauce. Salt and pepper to taste.

Place the meat, the slices overlapping, on 4 separate plates and decorate with the sauce by making a grid pattern using a small syringe.

SERVES: 4

Risotto Nero

Black Risotto

This typically Venetian dish has a slightly funereal appearance, but it tastes exceptional. It can be found on the menus of all the finest restaurants in Venezia.

1 lb (500 g) small cuttlefish, to make 10 oz (300 g) when cleaned
2 tablespoons olive oil
1 oz (30 g) butter
1 small onion, chopped
½ cup (4 fl oz/125 ml) white wine
2 cups (12 oz/375 g) Arborio rice
6 cups (3 pt/1.5 l) fish broth (stock)
generous nut of butter
salt and freshly ground black pepper

Clean the cuttlefish, discarding the eyes, the mouth (in the middle of the tentacles), the little backbone and the interior, but you must retain the little silvery-blue bag, the ink container. Set this aside and wash the rest well. Slice the body and tentacles into ½-in (1-cm) pieces.

Heat the oil and butter in a large, heavy pan. Add the onion and sauté over moderate heat until it becomes glassy. Add the cuttlefish and continue to cook for at least another 10 minutes. Add the wine and, without increasing the heat, cook for another 5 minutes. Pour in the rice and allow it to absorb the flavor for a couple of minutes, stirring gently with a wooden spoon.

Bring the fish broth to a boil and gradually add it to the rice, a ladle at a time, stirring as the grains absorb the liquid as they cook. Make sure you use only as much broth as is needed—do not drown the rice. Continue to stir and add the broth until the rice appears cooked (about 20 to 25 minutes).

When the rice is nearly ready, add the cuttlefish ink to the last ladle of broth and stir into the rice.

Remove from heat, add the nut of butter and salt and pepper to taste. Transfer to a serving dish and serve hot.

SERVES: 4

Sardine in Saor

Marinated Sardines

"*In saor*" means that the fish is sautéed and then put in a cooked marinade of water, oil, vinegar and herbs. This is a typical summer dish, and many varieties of fish are prepared in this way.

2 lb (1 kg) sardines, cleaned, scaled and thoroughly dried
all purpose (plain) flour for dusting
corn oil for frying
Marinade:
8 tablespoons olive oil
2 onions, sliced
3 garlic cloves, sliced
1 tablespoon white sugar
1 cup (8 fl oz/250 ml) wine vinegar
1 cup (8 fl oz/250 ml) white wine
4 bay leaves
1 fresh rosemary sprig
salt
1 tablespoon whole peppercorns

Dust the fish thoroughly in flour. Heat oil, which should be about ½ in (1 cm) deep, in a large skillet. Sauté the fish over moderate heat until crisp and golden on each side. Place on paper towels to drain.

For the marinade: Heat the olive oil in a pan and sauté the onions. When they become glassy, add the garlic and cook together, stirring to prevent the garlic from browning, for 3 or 4 minutes. Then add the sugar, vinegar, wine, bay leaves, rosemary, salt and peppercorns. Bring to a boil and remove from the stove.

Lay the fish side by side in a shallow earthenware dish. Pour the hot marinade over them and leave for at least 24 hours before serving.

SERVES: 4

Insalata di Mare

Seafood Salad

A variety of fish can be used in this salad, preferably shellfish of some kind, and some shrimp. Squid, cuttlefish or octopus are essential for both appearance and texture.

1 lb (500 g) mussels, scrubbed (buy only closed ones)
12 oz (375 g) squid, cleaned weight
6 oz (185 g) large shrimp (king prawns), cleaned weight
4 shelled scallops, about 5 oz (155 g)
juice of 1 lemon
3 tablespoons olive oil
salt and freshly ground black pepper
1 tablespoon chopped parsley
1 small bunch chives chopped

Put a cup of water in a large saucepan with a lid, add the mussels and steam them over high heat, shaking the pan from time to time, for 7 or 8 minutes. Cool, then shell the mussels.

Clean the squid, remove the transparent bone and the head. Keep the tentacles whole in bunches and do not cut the body at this point.

Bring a saucepan of water to a boil and add some salt, the squid, shrimp and scallops. The cooking time for these depends on their size, but they should not take more than 10 to 15 minutes. Remove the shrimp after 5 minutes. The squid, too (if they are small ones), will be cooked in 5 minutes. Test for tenderness and drain when cooked.

Cut the scallops and shrimp in half and large squid into ¾-in (2-cm) slices. Mix the mussels with the other seafood and leave to cool.

Dress with the lemon juice and olive oil, season with salt, pepper and parsley and scatter the chives over the top.

SERVES: 4

PETER JOHNSON

Bean Soup

Sopa de Fasoi

Bean Soup

This simple but sophisticated soup is often eaten cold in the summer.

1 cup (6 oz/200 g) dry borlotti *beans, or 2 medium cans* borlotti *beans*
4 tablespoons virgin olive oil
1 small onion, finely chopped
2 oz (50 g) prosciutto cubes (on the fatty side)
1 small fresh rosemary sprig, or 1 teaspoon dried rosemary
2 cups (16 fl oz/500 ml) broth (stock), or less if you like the soup thicker
5 oz (150 g) pasta for soup, such as anellini *or* conchigliette
salt and freshly ground pepper

Soak the dry *borlotti* beans for at least 24 hours. Use fresh water for cooking, which will take about 1½ hours. (If you are using tinned beans, sieve half of them and reduce them to a purée.)

Put the olive oil in a large, heavy pan, add the onion, prosciutto and rosemary, and sauté gently.

Add the beans and the broth and bring to a boil. Add salt and pasta, cook for 10 minutes and serve warm with a little stream of virgin olive oil in each bowl, and lots of freshly ground pepper.

SERVES: 4

Crauti e Salsiccie

Sausages and Sauerkraut

This recipe, influenced by Austria, is common to the whole of the Veneto.

2 oz (60 g) prosciutto fat, cut in small cubes
3 tablespoons olive oil
1½ lb (750 g) luganiga *sausages (pure pork)*
2 lb (1 kg) canned sauerkraut
2 large Granny Smith apples, grated
½ teaspoon cloves
plenty of broth (stock)
salt and freshly ground pepper

In a large skillet, sauté the prosciutto fat in the oil. Add the *luganiga*, brown each side and set aside.

In the same fat place the sauerkraut, apples and cloves, with sufficient broth to cover them, and cook for approximately 1 hour, adding more broth if required. Put the sausages back in the skillet for the last 30 minutes.

Season with salt and pepper and serve with boiled potatoes.

SERVES: 4

Lepre in Salmì

Jugged Hare

Hare is sought-after game and its preparation is careful and long. This marinade is sweetened with raisins.

1 large hare, about 4 lb (2 kg), in pieces
all purpose (plain) flour for dusting
8 tablespoons olive oil
Marinade:
2 cups (16 fl oz/500 ml) red wine
⅓ cup (2 oz/60 g) raisins
5 cloves
grated rind and juice of 1 orange
10 bay leaves
1 large fresh thyme sprig
1 fresh rosemary sprig
2 garlic cloves
1 tablespoon honey
1 bunch celery leaves
1 large carrot, finely chopped
1 teaspoon mustard
Sauce:
1 oz (30 g) dried porcini *(boletus) mushrooms*
1 small onion, finely chopped
1 oz (30 g) butter
2 oz (60 g) prosciutto, cut into strips

PETER JOHNSON

Jugged Hare, Goulash Friuli Style, Sausages and Sauerkraut

Prepare the marinade by mixing all the ingredients together in a large bowl. Leave the hare to marinate for 24 hours, turning from time to time.

Take the hare pieces from the marinade and dry with a cloth. Dust with flour, brown thoroughly in hot oil on all sides, then remove and put to one side. Heat up marinade. Deglaze the skillet with a ladle of the hot marinade.

Place the hare pieces in a cast-iron casserole and pour in the deglazed juices and enough marinade to cover. Bring to a boil, turn down the heat and simmer gently for 2 hours, until the hare is tender. After 1 hour of cooking add the dried *porcini,* crumbled.

Meanwhile, to finish the sauce, sauté the onion in butter in a skillet until it becomes glassy, then add the prosciutto. Take the hare pieces from the casserole and place on a warmed serving dish. Strain the liquid and add it to the onion and prosciutto; stir well and simmer for a few minutes longer, seasoning to taste.

Pour the sauce over the hare and serve, if possible, with polenta crusts as an accompaniment.

SERVES: 8

Gulasch Friulano

Goulash Friuli Style

Each of the three regions of Tre Venezie believes it makes the real *gulasch*, which came originally from Hungary, via the Austro-Hungarian Empire. This Friulian version is perhaps the most appealing.

3 oz (90 g) prosciutto fat, cut in small cubes
1 oz (30 g) butter
2 large onions, finely chopped
1 hot red chili pepper, chopped
2 lb (1 kg) lean beef, cut in large cubes
1 lb (500 g) canned peeled tomatoes, chopped
2 tablespoons tomato paste
1 tablespoon dried rosemary
1 tablespoon dried sage
2 bay leaves
¾ cup (6 fl oz/180 ml) broth (stock)
1 tablespoon sweet paprika
salt to taste

Sweat the fat in a large skillet with the butter. When it starts becoming crispy, add the onions and chili. Sauté the onions until they turn glassy, then add the meat, tomatoes, tomato paste, rosemary, sage and bay leaves.

Bring everything to a simmer, add some broth, the paprika and salt and cook over moderate heat for 1½ hours or until the meat is tender. (Add some more broth if it starts to dry out.)

Serve with boiled potatoes or freshly cooked macaroni.

SERVES: 4

Fegato alla Veneziana

Calf's Liver Venetian Style

This world famous dish exists in a number of versions.

1 large onion, finely sliced
6 tablespoons olive oil
1 lb (4 oz (625 g) calf's (veal) liver, thinly sliced
all purpose (plain) flour for dusting
2 tablespoons balsamic vinegar
salt and freshly ground pepper
1 tablespoon chopped parsley

In a large skillet, sauté the onion in the oil until glassy. Toss the liver in the flour.

Push the onion to one side of the skillet and fry the liver quickly, stirring often. When it is cooked, pour in the vinegar and stir-fry for 30 seconds. Salt and pepper to taste, sprinkle with parsley and serve hot.

SERVES: 4

Calf's Liver Venetian Style

PETER JOHNSON

Polenta con Funghi

Polenta with Mushrooms

Polenta with mushrooms is very much a dish of the mountains.

Sauce:
12 oz (375 g) fresh porcini *(boletus) mushrooms, plus 1 oz (30 g) dried* porcini
1 small onion, chopped
3 tablespoons olive oil
1 oz (30 g) butter
1 lb (500 g) canned peeled plum tomatoes, liquidized
salt and freshly ground black pepper
6 fresh basil leaves
Polenta:
6 cups (3 pt/1.5 l) salted water
2 cups (10 oz/315 g) cornmeal, or 1 packet (12 oz/375 g) Valsugana polenta
1 oz (30 g) butter
½ cup (2 oz/60 g) freshly grated Parmesan cheese

For the sauce: Clean and slice the mushrooms and soak the dried ones for 10 minutes in lukewarm water. In a skillet, sauté the chopped onion in the oil and butter over moderate heat, then add all the mushrooms. Cook together over high heat for 10 minutes. Add the tomatoes and continue cooking for another 20 minutes so that the water evaporates. When everything is fully cooked, add the salt and pepper and basil.

For the polenta: Bring the water to a boil in a large saucepan. Add the cornmeal, pouring in a thin, consistent stream, stirring constantly with a wooden spoon so that no lumps appear. Continue to stir the polenta until it starts to come away from the side of the saucepan. (This will take only 5 minutes if you are using Valsugana polenta, 30 minutes if you are using cornmeal.) When it is ready, add the butter and half the Parmesan.

Serve in shallow bowls, pouring some sauce into the middle of each and sprinkling the remaining Parmesan over the top.

SERVES: 4

Sour Pork,
Polenta with Mushrooms
PETER JOHNSON

Maiale in Saor

Sour Pork

The word "*saor*" used in the border region with Austria and in Venezia means sour, from the German "*sauer*"

2 oz (60 g) lard
2 lb (1 kg) lean pork, in one piece
1 fresh rosemary sprig
4 bay leaves
4 or 5 cloves
1 large onion, finely sliced
1 garlic clove, finely chopped
1 cup (8 fl oz/250 ml) dry white wine
1 cup (8 fl oz/250 ml) white wine vinegar
salt and freshly ground pepper
4 cups (2 pt/1 l) broth (stock)

Put the lard in a large, deep skillet and brown the meat for a few minutes. Add the rosemary, bay leaves, cloves, onion and garlic and stir-fry for a few minutes.

When the onion begins to turn glassy, add the wine and the vinegar, salt and pepper to taste and cook over low heat, turning occasionally, for 1½ hours. Check from time to time and add some broth, if necessary. Slice and serve with a spoon of the sauce on each serving.

SERVES: 4

PETER JOHNSON

Deep Fried Cauliflower Florets, Broccoli with Ginger

Fioretti di Cavolfiore Fritti

Deep Fried Cauliflower Florets

Even the everyday cauliflower assumes an air of sophistication when cooked in this way.

10 oz (315 g) cauliflower florets
2 eggs
salt and freshly ground black pepper
all purpose (plain) flour for dusting
½ cup (2 oz/60 g) dry breadcrumbs
olive oil for deep frying
1 lemon, sliced

Cook the cauliflower in boiling salted water until *al dente* (4 to 6 minutes). Drain and cool. Beat the eggs and season with salt and pepper. Dip the florets in the flour, then in the beaten eggs and finally roll in the breadcrumbs.

Heat the oil in a deep fryer and cook the florets 3 or 4 at a time. Serve with slices of lemon.

SERVES: 4

Broccoli allo Zenzero

Broccoli with Ginger

Ginger was known to the Romans, who imported it from Egypt.

1 lb (500 g) broccoli florets
4 tablespoons olive oil
2 garlic cloves, sliced
a walnut-sized piece of ginger, peeled and cut into thin strips
salt and freshly ground black pepper

Cook the broccoli in boiling salted water until *al dente* (4 to 6 minutes), then drain and keep warm.

Heat the oil and sauté the garlic and ginger together for a few minutes, taking care not to let the garlic brown.

Place broccoli on a warmed serving dish, pour the garlic and ginger over it, season and serve.

SERVES: 4

Fagiolini al Burro e Pangrattato

Grean Beans and Fried Breadcrumbs

The crunchiness of the breadcrumbs combined with the tender beans is both unusual and delicious.

2 cups (4 oz/125 g) fresh breadcrumbs, coarsely crumbled
10 oz (315 g) green beans, trimmed
4 oz (125 g) butter
salt and freshly ground black pepper

Preheat the oven 450°F (230°C). Lay the crumbs on an oven tray and roast for 5 or 6 minutes, until golden.

Cook the beans in boiling salted water until *al dente* (4 to 6 minutes). Meanwhile, melt the butter in a small skillet. Stirring, add the breadcrumbs and continue to stir until they have soaked up the butter and turned brown. Season with salt and pepper. Cover the freshly boiled beans with the breadcrumb mixture.

This is an excellent accompaniment for chicken or fish.

SERVES: 4

Finocchi Gratinati

Fennel au Gratin

It is a pity that this delicious dish, well known and appreciated in Italy, is seldom eaten abroad.

2 lb (1 kg) fennel bulbs, round, fat and firm
1½ oz (45 g) butter
salt and freshly ground black pepper
¼ cup (1 oz/30 g) dry breadcrumbs

Wash and clean the fennel. Cut off the stalks and the hard base, and cut each bulb in half lengthwise.

Preheat the oven to 400°F (200°C). Boil the fennel in salted water for 15 minutes, drain and cool a little.

Butter an ovenproof dish, cut the fennel into ½-in (1-cm) slices and lay in the dish, slightly overlapping. Dot with butter, season with salt and pepper, and sprinkle with breadcrumbs. Bake for 15 to 20 minutes, until brown and crispy.

SERVES: 4

Fennel au Gratin,
Green Beans and Fried Breadcrumbs

PETER JOHNSON

Rumpot

Frutta Secca al Rum

Rumpot

Dried fruit was a staple of the seafarer, so the addition of rum was not surprising.

juice and rind of 4 oranges
1¼ cups (10 oz/315 g) sugar
10 cloves
1 cinnamon stick
4 cups (2 pt/1 l) water
2½ cups (10 oz/315 g) dried apricots
2½ cups (10 oz/315 g) dried pears
2½ cups (10 oz/315 g) dried peaches
1½ cups (10 oz/315 g) dried prunes
2 cups (10 oz/315 g) dried golden raisins (sultanas)
2½ cups (10 oz/315 g) dried apple rings
2½ cups (16 fl oz/500 ml) dark rum

Put the orange juice, rind, sugar and spices with the water in a saucepan over high heat and boil for several minutes to reduce a little. Discard the rind and the spices and filter the liquid through muslin or cheesecloth. Add the fruit, mixed together.

Bring to a boil, cook for 8 to 10 minutes and set aside to cool. When the mixture is completely cold, pour over the rum, mix well and preserve in airtight jars.

Store the rumpot for a couple of months so that the flavors can develop fully, and then serve as an accompaniment to vanilla ice cream, with whipped double cream, or simply by itself.

SERVES: 10

Pesche al Limone

Peaches and Lemon

This light summer dish is simplicity itself. It should be prepared a couple of hours before serving so that the flavors are fully developed.

2 lb (1 kg) ripe white peaches
$\frac{2}{3}$ cup (5 oz/150 g) superfine (caster) sugar (increase or reduce to taste)
juice of 2 lemons
1 teaspoon ground cinnamon

Slice the peaches quite thinly and put them in a bowl with the sugar. Sprinkle with the lemon juice and the cinnamon and then place in the fridge, stirring from time to time.

While the peaches can be served with whipped cream, they are delicious simply eaten by themselves.

SERVES: 6

Mele Cotogne Sciroppate

Quinces in Syrup

Quinces have a most distinctive flavor, but they cannot be eaten raw. Cooked in this way they are delicious, without the syrup, as a tart filling.

4 large quinces or 2 lb (1 kg) smaller ones
1 cup (8 oz/250 g) sugar
rind and juice of 1 lemon
1 cinnamon stick, 4 in (10 cm) long
10 cloves
water to cover

Peel, core and slice the quinces thinly. Put them in a saucepan with the sugar, lemon and spices. Cover with water and simmer until the quinces can be pricked easily with a knife—this will take about 1 hour.

Remove the quinces from the pan and boil the liquid rapidly in order to reduce it to a syrup. Strain, pour over the quinces and serve cold.

SERVES: 6

Quinces in Syrup, Peaches and Lemon

PETER JOHNSON

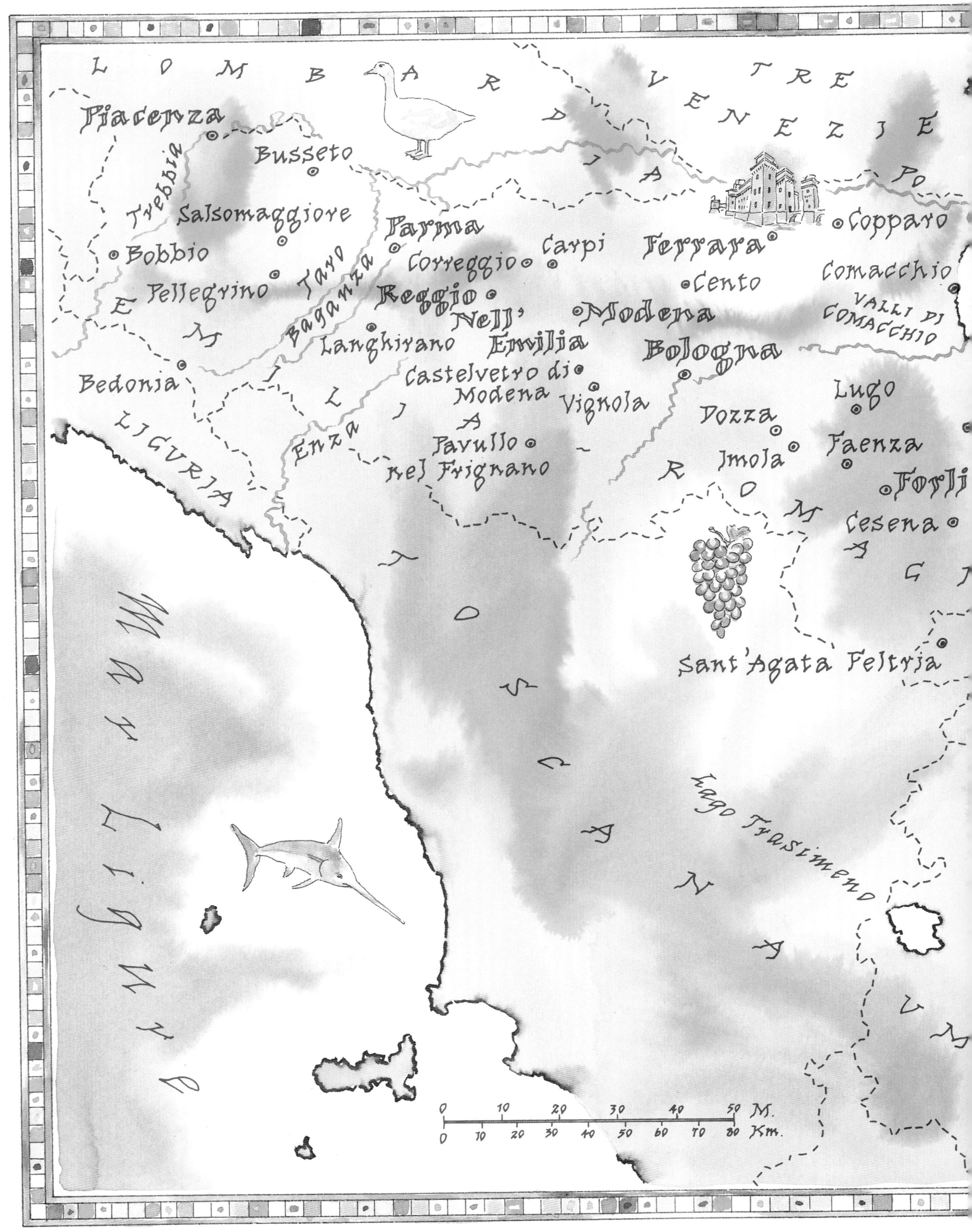

LOMBARDIA
VENEZIE
TRE
Po
Piacenza
Busseto
Trebbia
Salsomaggiore
Bobbio
Parma
Carpi
Ferrara
Coppari
Taro
Baganza
Correggio
Cento
Comacchio
Pellegrino
Reggio Nell' Emilia
Modena
Valli di Comacchio
Langhirano
Bologna
Bedonia
Castelvetro di Modena
Vignola
Lugo
Dozza
Liguria
Enza
Pavullo nel Frignano
Imola
Faenza
Forlì
Cesena
Emilia Romagna
Toscana
Sant'Agata Feltria
Lago Trasimeno
Umbria
0 10 20 30 40 50 M.
0 10 20 30 40 50 60 70 80 Km.

EMILIA-ROMAGNA AND MARCHE

Mary Beth Clark

Vermillion poppies blanketing the fields...Trees laden with ripe peaches, apples, and pears...Sweet milk aged into golden wheels of Parmesan...Faience bowls brimming with handmade *pappardelle,* lasagne, and tortellini...Paper-thin slices of finely-cured prosciutto, *culatello,* and *mortadella*...Delicate, briny aromas wafting from tureens of fresh Adriatic stews. This is but part of what awaits you in Emilia-Romagna and Marche.

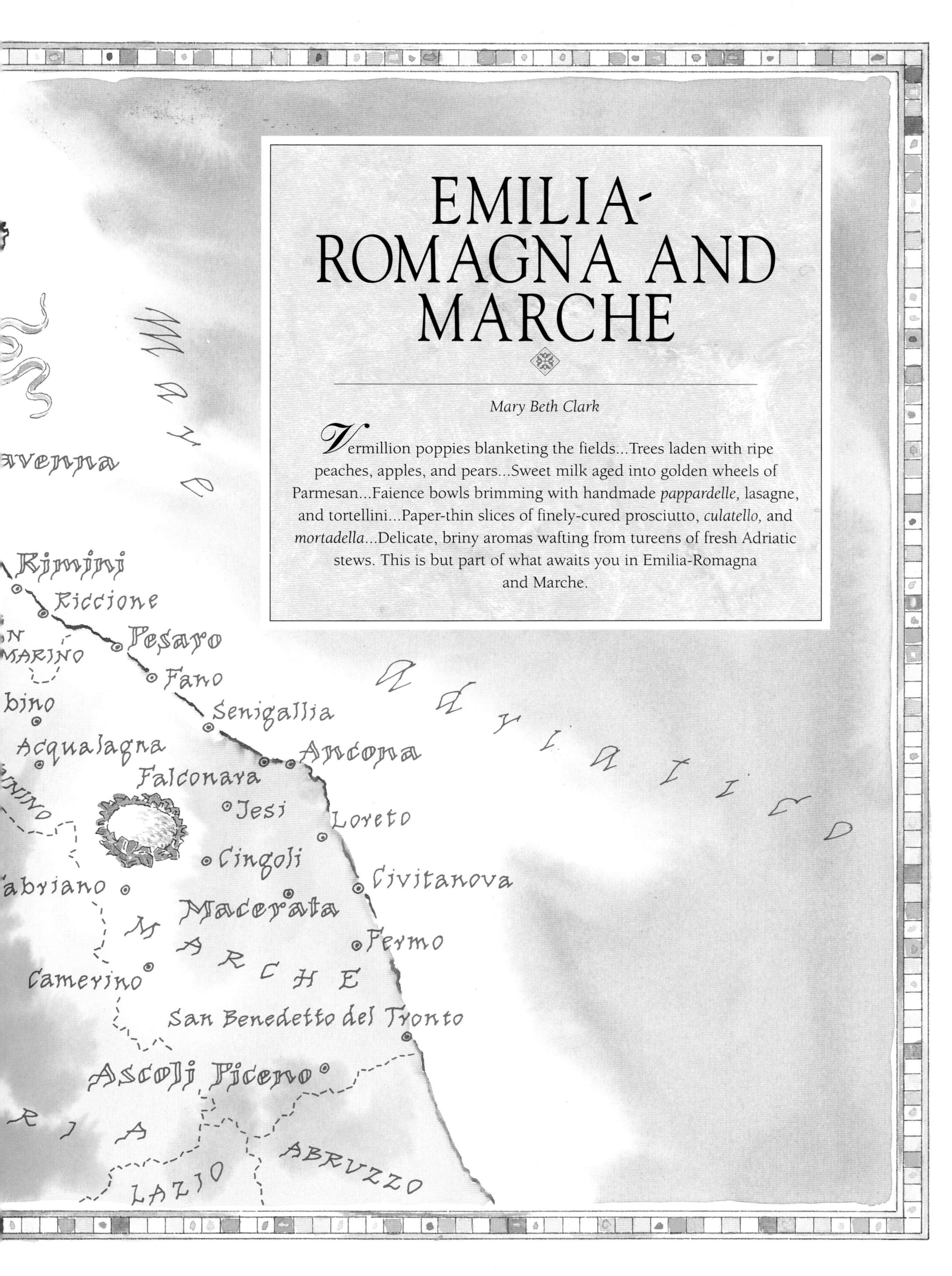

GIULIANO COLLIVA/THE IMAGE BANK

Fruit and vegetables in profusion, as stallkeepers set up their displays for another busy day at the markets.

Rich Soils and a Bountiful Sea

A rich alluvial plain extends the length of Emilia-Romagna, providing one of the prime agricultural areas in all Italy. The region produces one-fifth of the country's wheat, half its sugar beet, and a major proportion of its fruit. Supplementing these are grapes grown for the table, for wine-making and equally important, for *aceto balsamico*, balsamic vinegar, the regional gustatory treasure. Strawberries, asparagus, potatoes, zucchini, and wild and cultivated mushrooms are also exported. Pig farms provide one-fourth of total Italian production of cured pork products, such as prosciutto from Langhirano, *mortadella* from Bologna and *zampone*, stuffed pig's trotter, from Modena. Often, milk for drinking is imported, reserving the highly-prized local milk for making *stracchino, squacquerone*, mozzarella, ricotta, Grana Padano, and most importantly, the king of cheeses, the majestic Parmigiano-Reggiano—Parmesan.

The Po River flows eastwards along Emilia-Romagna's northern border. Although dwindling, the river's sturgeon population yields a coarse-grained caviar that is a specialty of central Italy. Along the coast from the border with Venezia down to San Benedetto del Tronto, the southernmost part of Marche, the bountiful sea offers an immense range of produce, including *calamari* (squid), *polpo* (octopus), *seppia* (cuttlefish), *triglia* (red mullet), *cefalo* (grey mullet), *sogliola* (sole), *pesce spada* (swordfish), *aragosta* (spiny lobster), and *cannocchie* (similar to saltwater crayfish).

The life and culture of Emilia-Romagna are rooted firmly in the land and sea. Even the temperature, the winds, and the humidity are acknowledged as major influences on the proper production of prosciutto, *aceto balsamico*, and Parmigiano-Reggiano. Intimacy with land and sea is quietly reflected in the people themselves. Strong-willed, pragmatic and yet religiously respectful of nature, they are among the friendliest of Italians.

Although occupying only a small amount of land, Marche is of strategic significance, and as a consequence was a province of Augustus, a former frontier of the Franks, and part of Charlemagne's empire, who later gave the region to the Church. The Pope fought several powerful local families to maintain supremacy and as a legacy of these warlike times many cities still staunchly retain their individual character. Accompanying this today is an intermingling of religious and good-humored pagan rituals—a pragmatic approach that enables people to honor the Church and nature simultaneously.

Marche borders Emilia-Romagna in the north and the Umbrian Apennines in the west, Abruzzo in the south and the Adriatic Sea in the east. Deep, narrow valleys have been cut by its rivers and a narrow coastal plain runs the length of the region. Breezes from the sea combined with cool mountain air give the region an equable climate. The bucolic terrain is reflected in the calm, diligent, good-natured Marchean temperament. Industry depends largely on agriculture, zootechnics, tourism, and fishing.

Poppies bloom in the meadows of Emilia-Romagna. This is prosperous farming country, and the area is well known for the richness of its dishes.

The Cuisine of Emilia-Romagna

Emilia-Romagna's cooking is a mixture of agrarian, coastal, and court cuisines. Emphasized are wheat and rice, and vegetables such as carrots, celery, potatoes, onions, zucchini, spinach, artichokes, asparagus, green beans, and tomatoes. Pork

RENNIE ELLIS/SCOOPIX

CHARLES C. PLACE/THE IMAGE BANK

Murals of biblical scenes and events from the lives of the saints can be seen in churches and on façades throughout Italy.

forms the basis for many dishes whether fresh, when served as pork loin with *porcini* sauce, braised in milk to a creamy tenderness, or used as flavoring in the form of *pancetta*. Veal also dominates main dishes, usually as *scaloppine, costoletta*, or *nodino*. Often ground chicken and turkey are used as stuffing for pasta or *galantina*, producing light, delicate dishes. Game is abundant and every fall brings wild boar, pheasant, guinea hen, and hare to the table. Snails and frogs' legs add further variety. To bring out natural flavorings diced onion, carrot, celery, and minced parsley are favored, with virtually no garlic or pepper being used. Bologna's specialties often include a twist of nutmeg, whereas the people of Parma favor a pinch of mace. Parmigiano-Reggiano finds its way into most dishes as flavoring or as a golden-brown topping, when not served as is next to thinly sliced *mortadella*, prosciutto, or salame.

Emilia-Romagna is mainly butter-and-lard and pork-and-pasta country. While olive groves used to flourish here, they were uprooted to make way for faster-ripening, larger-yielding crops. Consequently, olive oil never gained a stronghold here as it did in southern Italy, but is used rather as a mild accent. The climate has also inevitably influenced the cuisine. Extremes of temperature are typical, except along the Adriatic coast. Fat in the form of butter, cream, cheese, and lard is needed during the winter to fuel the body and keep it warm, while during the summer the emphasis tends to be on simple grilled and roasted meats, poultry, fish, and shellfish.

Typical daily fare usually includes at least one serving of home-made pasta, which is consumed in vast quantities. Nowhere is this more apparent than in Emilia. Every day local *sfogliatrice* (women who make hand-rolled and -shaped pasta) cut this tender dough into *linguine, fettuccine,* lasagna, and *tagliatelle*, pinch or roll it into *farfalle* and *garganelli* or shape and stuff it to make *tortellini, anolini,* and ravioli. Stuffed pasta is exemplary throughout the region: squares, crescents, and rounds are stuffed with cheese, meat, poultry, fish, shellfish, and vegetables. Each city has its own pasta shape and filling with its own particular name.

Piacenza is known for *anolini* made with finely-ground pork and vegetables and the delicate *tortelli alla piacentina,* stuffed with creamy ricotta and *mascarpone.* Pork-curing country begins here, with *pancetta* used to flavor pasta sauces and braised dishes such as *trippa piacentina*, tripe simmered with white beans, carrots, celery, garlic, sage, tomato, and white wine. *Batu,* preserved goose, is an ancient recipe similar to the French *confit d'oie*, served with pasta or polenta, and should not be missed.

To the east near the Lombardia border is Busseto, the birthplace of the composer Guiseppe Verdi. A specialty of this tiny town and of Parma is *culatello* made from the top round of the pig's leg, cured and aged in a similar fashion to prosciutto. Its texture is silky satin, its color translucent ruby. Begin your meal with paper thin slices—it is "*meraviglioso*!"

PARMA THE GRACIOUS

Known as "The Gracious", Parma is one of the major food centers of Italy. During the nineteenth century the Duchess Maria-Luigia, second wife of Napoleon Bonaparte, introduced Austrian and French court-style cooking to the town and some of the favorite dishes of this much-loved benefactress, such as stuffed pasta flavored with wild green herbs, and lasagna made with chicken liver and cream sauce, are very much part of the local cuisine. Candied violets, spinach, and angelica are essential to make *torta di Maria-Luigia.*

Birthplace of Arturo Toscanini, music has always flourished in Parma. The exquisitely gilded Teatro Regio is considered one of the most important and difficult testing grounds for opera singers.

Parma is world famous for Parmigiano-Reggiano cheese, the production of which it shares with Reggio-Emilia and three other designated areas of the Enza Valley. It is famous also for prosciutto, which flavors all sorts of dishes, from sauces to desserts. The *alla parmigiana* style of cooking means that grated or shaved Parmesan tops the dish, accented by a simple butter or broth sauce. To capture the essence of Parma, order *anolini* accented with cinnamon, nutmeg, clove, and tomato paste and served with a prosciutto sauce topped with a golden mound of grated Parmesan. To sample Parma's excellent foods for a picnic, slip on your walking shoes and set out with confidence. Every block will tantalize you with food shops offering salads, cold meat and seafood dishes, fresh pastas, and miniature pastries that are Parma's wonderful marriage of Italian, French, and Austrian techniques. Try *spongata*, a specialty dating from the Middle Ages, made with pine nuts, walnuts, spices, and herbs—"*superba!*"

PROSCIUTTO

Prosciutto di Parma, Parma ham, is made from pigs fed on the whey from Parmesan cheese-making, grain, and chestnuts, with production controlled by the Consorzio del Prosciutto di Parma. Production is between the Taro and Baganza Rivers, a region coinciding with most of the area assigned to the making of Parmesan.

Thought to have been first produced in Salsomaggiore near Parma, because of its free salt deposits, today this prosciutto is still cured with only sea salt, lard, and black pepper. Twenty to thirty miles (about forty kilometers) south of Parma, the Langhirano area is considered the best for curing because of its dry microclimate.

The pigs are prized for the fat surrounding the leg, since a little fat must be eaten with the meat to truly appreciate its flavor. *Prosciutto di Parma* differs from the Friulian San Daniele prosciutto and the Tuscan prosciutto in being milder and softer. If you eat this Emilia-Romagnan specialty with bread and chunks of Parmesan sprinkled with a little *aceto balsamico*, you will capture the essence of the region in one delicious mouthful.

ROUSTAN/CAMERA PRESS/AUSTRAL

Curing the hams

Parmigiano-Reggiano

Recorded descriptions of this cheese date back to 1200-1300. In the fourteenth-century book of a hundred tales, the *Decameron*, Boccaccio writes "...and there was a whole mountain of Parmesan cheese, all finely grated, on top of which stood people who were doing nothing but making macaroni and ravioli". These were to be "rolled in cheese after cooking, the better to season them".

The Consorzio del Formaggio Parmigiano-Reggiano, a cooperative of around 950 cheesemakers, controls production and sales. Using over 1.4 million tons of milk, 2500 000 cheeses are produced annually. The *zona tipica* includes the entire provinces of Parma, Reggio Emilia and Modena, Mantua on the right bank of the Po River and Bologna on the left bank of the Reno River. Milk from other areas cannot be used.

Making Parmesan, an art handed down from father to son, begins daily before dawn. The previous evening's milk, allowed to rest overnight, and the following morning's milk are poured into huge v-shaped copper cauldrons. Fermenting whey is added, the milk is heated to 90° F (33° C) while being stirred slowly. When the heat is turned off, rennet is added, causing coagulation. The solids are turned over, then heated further. At this point the cheesemaster scoops up the curd in a shallow disc, smelling the aroma and checking the color. At just the right moment, the heat is turned off, the solids settle to the bottom and are shaped into huge loaves to be hung in cheesecloth to drain. Some of the remaining milky liquid, the whey, is siphoned off to be used as a fermenting starter for the next day's batch of cheese, while the rest feeds the pigs of the area, for making prosciutto. The curd is then placed inside a circular wooden mold and pressed for a few hours to release more whey. Later a matrix imprinted with the Parmigiano-Reggiano name is inserted, the cheese is turned at frequent intervals, and left to set for a few days. After soaking in brine for twenty to twenty-five days, each wheel is then dried in the sun. The cheesemaster and his relatives usually produce fourteen to twenty wheels each day, so it is indeed a family affair. Once the wheels are dried they are shipped to the *cascina*, storehouse, for maturing. In aging rooms holding from 100 000 to 200 000 cheeses each, these wheels weighing from 72 to 80 pounds (32 to 36 kilograms) are placed on huge wooden shelves.

With many impostors in the market, you must select wedges with a dark golden rind showing the words Parmigiano-Reggiano. Aged under eighteen months, *fresco*, young, goes well in salads and *antipasti*. Aged eighteen to twenty-four months, *vecchio*, old, is delicious eaten as is. Aged twenty-four to thirty-six months, *Stravecchio*, extra-mature, is ideal for grating. It has a delicate, buttery flavor and is often used as a seasoning, like salt and pepper. Do what the Italians do—save the rind and soften it in soup or stew. Then scoop the runny cheese onto toasted bread, *e mangia bene*!

OUDDEKEN/CAMERA PRESS/AUSTRAL

Cheeses spend a period of up to three years maturing in the aging rooms of the storehouse.

As the cheese begins to solidify, the cheesemaker stirs it with an enormous metal brush called a spino.

OUDDEKEN/CAMERA PRESS/AUSTRAL

Prosperous Modena

Ruled by the house of Este for centuries, today Modena has the highest per capita income in the region. It is the home town of Luciano Pavarotti, Ferrari sports cars (made in nearby Maranello), Maserati sports cars, and *zampone*, stuffed pig's trotter. Boiled and served with *lenticchie,* lentils, *zampone* is a must for Christmas dinner because the lentils denote coins, bringing a prosperous New Year. Most restaurants serve delicious *bollito misto* which includes *zampone*, beef, veal, turkey, or chicken, and sometimes a cured pork sausage, *cotechino*, that has been gently boiled to a melt-in-the-mouth tenderness. Serve this with *salsa verde*, a piquant cold green sauce made from pickled cornichons, parsley, onions, and herbs, and you have a truly outstanding meal. Flat griddle breads such as *ciacci montanari*, ricotta fritters, are a specialty of Modena. *Tijelli*, made with lard and wheat flour and baked between two tiles, themselves resemble tiles.

Modena is dominated by one product exported worldwide, *aceto balsamico*, the family treasure more valued than wine. It's in *aperitivi*, *antipasti*, and *dolci*. Recommended for alleviating the pain of childbirth, this vinegar was served as a cordial, elixir, and food flavoring by the Dukes of Este during the Renaissance. Near Modena in Castelvetro there is a shop that not only sells this vinegar but also supplies marinated fruits and vegetables, along with the outstanding liqueurs Laurino, flavored with bay leaves, and Nocino, made from green walnuts.

South, between Modena and Bologna, is Vignola, a picture of cherry blossom during May and June. Vignola cherries, the best in Italy, are used to make the famous *amarene*, preserved cherries, served with *torta* and *gelato*.

"La Grassa"

The regional capital, Bologna's recorded history goes back to Etruscan times. Its university, founded in the tenth century, is arguably the oldest in Europe, hence the city's epithet "*La Dotta*", "The Learned". Dante Alighieri studied here, as did Copernicus. Mozart frequented the historic Bologna Conservatory, which numbers Donizetti and Rossini among its students.

Bologna is also known as "*La Grassa*", "The Fat", for the rich table it sets. Its restaurants are among the best in all Italy. Almost all serve the gastronomic symbol of Bologna, *tortellini*, stuffed with another symbol, *mortadella*, a large sausage made from finely ground pork, and flavored with yet another symbol, nutmeg. Savor *tortellini alla bolognese*, *tortellini* with *ragù bolognese*, and *tortellini in brodo*, *tortellini* in chicken consommé, the traditional first course for holidays.

Bologna has a museum devoted exclusively to pasta, located in the town hall. Recorded are the exact dimensions for traditional pasta shapes, as well as the official recipe for the true *tortellini alla bolognese* and *ragù bolognese*. Next to the Basilica di San Petronio, with its astronomical calendar and twenty-two chapels, there are food stalls galore under the porticos, piled high with enticing fruit and vegetables. In the fall this market overflows with wild mushrooms and game.

The ancient city of Ferrara produces marvellous breads, pastries, and pasta. *Cappellacci*, the city's round-shaped, stuffed pasta is made with *zucca*, the yellow squash so favored in Lombardia. *Pasticcio* is a pasta pie made with *ragù*, *porcini*, and *balsamella*. *Lasagna di magro* is a traditional lasagna made with fish and shrimp instead of pork, showing the coastal influence. Typical pastries of Ferrara

Aceto Balsamico

In 1986, *aceto balsamico* became the first Italian vinegar to be granted DOC status. When buying, look for the initials MO, meaning made in Modena, and the DOC seal which guarantees a minimum of twelve years aging.

Located in *l'acetaia*, an attic or large space open to extremes of temperature, storage of *aceto balsamico* is in *la batteria*, a collection of old and new wooden barrels. These are used to age cooked grapes musts for up to 300 years or more.

A range of particular woods are used for making the barrels, to give this vinegar its sophisticated flavor and sweet aroma. The vinegar is "racked"—transferred from larger to smaller barrels—usually in winter, after the sediment settles. With this transference, new cooked grape must is added to the aged vinegar in a process called "*rincalzo*" or "tucking up". Over the years, evaporation and leakage reduce and concentrate the vinegar to a mahogany-colored, slightly viscous liquid redolent of fruit, wood, spices, and herbs.

Do with your *aceto balsamico* as the Modenese do. Try a few drops mixed with sparkling water as a *digestivo*, sprinkle it on strawberries or Parmesan, or flavor a sauce with it.

ROY/EXPLORER

Baling hay close to Corbola, on the lower reaches of the Po River. Spreading vines mark the border of the field.

are *ciambella*, a traditional ring-shaped Easter cake similar to the yellow sponge cake that is often served for breakfast, and *panpepato*, a chocolate Christmas cake flavored with honey, spices, and almonds.

East, towards the coastal town of Comacchio, is the Valli di Comacchio, Italy's largest lagoon and basin of the Po River. This region is famous for eel-farming: *valli* does not mean valley but loosely refers to the eel farming reservoirs. A miniature Venezia, Comacchio extends over thirteen islands complete with canals and bridges and has been famous from antiquity for its salt flats. The eels are considered to be the best in Italy. Served as *anguilla in gratella* they are skewered between bay leaves and grilled; *anguilla marinata* are bathed in wine vinegar with sage, garlic, raisins, and pine nuts, and there is *zuppa di anguille di Comacchio*, a tomato-based soup ladled over crisp-toasted bread called *bruschetta*.

Ravenna was originally built by Augustus and in the fifth century became a Byzantine capital. There remain several Byzantine basilicas filled with exquisite mosaics well worth seeing, such as San Vitale with its stone-pine groves yielding *pignola*, pine nuts, and white and black truffles. This charming city has restaurants specializing in hearty fare as well as light fish dishes. Try *passatelli in brodo*, a breadcrumb and egg pasta in chicken consommé, and the Romagnan *garganelli con salsiccie*, elongated, ribbed pasta tossed with pieces of sausage and tomato. *Risotto d'anitra selvatica*, Arborio rice with wild duck sauce, is a particular specialty. Small, delicious fish croquettes are made here, called *polpettone di mare*.

An aerial view of Bologna, capital of Emilia-Romagna. The city still retains much of the character of a Medieval town, with arcades lining many of its main streets, and a wonderful array of towers, turrets, and campaniles.

Near the border with Marche is Rimini, the air of which is said to be essential for making the famous *brodetto di Rimini*, a fish soup without eels, unlike Comacchio's version, and flavored with onion, tomato, wine vinegar, and olive oil.

Other dishes specific to the coast that should be sampled are *canocchie*, crayfish-like crustaceans that are fried or grilled and served with lemon wedges, and *seppie in umido con piselli*, stuffed cuttlefish braised with green peas.

JAKE RAJS/THE IMAGE BANK

F. ROITER/THE IMAGE BANK

Even when on land, there is still a good deal of work for a fisherman to do.

The Cuisine Of Marche

Dominated by *la campagna* and *il mare*, the cuisine of Marche features dishes similar to those of Romagna and Umbria, with the marked presence of mushrooms and precious black and white truffles. Pork is stuffed and roasted into meltingly tender *porchetta* and cured in such products as *soppressata*, salame, *coppa*, and *prosciutto del Montefeltro*.

There is prized Chianina beef and there are chickens, snails, and lamb. Game such as rabbit, quail, guinea hen, and pigeon is plentiful in the hills, and is often flavored with marjoram or rosemary when roasted or grilled. The Adriatic yields fish and seafood in abundance, and while methods of preparation and cooking are uncomplicated, there are endless variations. *Brodetto*, fish and shellfish stew, can be found everywhere along the coast, each restaurant having its own secret recipe. A distinctive style of cooking fish, game, or poultry is *in potaccio*, braised with tomato, rosemary, garlic, onion, and white wine.

Home-made pasta is similar to that of Emilia-Romagna, however in Marche pasta is also served with fish; *passatelli* float in a fragrant fish broth and *ravioli ai filetti di sogliola* is a dish of ricotta-stuffed ravioli layered with filet of sole in a tomato sauce. During the colder months, polenta is often substituted for pasta and served with braised game. Vegetable dishes usually include tomatoes, fennel, the celebrated cauliflower of Jesi, bell peppers, cabbage, broad beans, and green peas. From spring through fall, peaches, apples, figs, and cherries are the perfect finish to a meal. Sheep's-milk cheeses, fresh or aged and aromatic with *serpillo*, a wild herb, or walnut leaves, marry well with fruit, sausage, and fresh breads.

In Pesaro, the birthplace of Rossini, try the famous *tournedos alla Rossini*. Here it is braised beef with ham, mushrooms, parsley, lemon, and pepper; in France it is grilled beef topped with *foie gras*. Going inland southwards amidst green hills with tall stands of cypress and vineyards is Urbino, a center of the arts where you can visit the beautifully restored birthplace of Raphael. At one of the town's *trattorie*, sample *la braciola*, rolls of stuffed, braised beef in a white wine sauce, or tiny snails cooked with garlic and herbs. Continuing south is Acqualagna, the center of the truffle market, and then Fabriano, an immensely wealthy and powerful city in the Middle Ages. This city and the surrounding area of Montefeltro are famous for their cured pork products, especially their version of proscuitto which differs from others in being salted, washed with vinegar, massaged with black pepper, and then smoked. *Cotechino* and *coppa marchigiana*, made with pork, almonds, pine nuts, and orange rind are distinctively delicious, too. In Macerata a sausage exemplifying Greek influence is *ciausculu*, finely ground lean pork mixed with several spices and cooked wine. *Vincisgrassi*, lasagne layered with butter and truffles, is a particular specialty that musn't be missed.

The Medieval town of Ascoli Piceno is renowned for its luscious gigantic green olives which are stuffed with ground meat, egg, and pecorino, dipped in batter and breadcrumbs, then fried and served piping hot, filling the air with their aroma. Grilled lamb or goat delicately flavored with wild herbs is excellent here.

For dessert there are local specialties such as *caciuni*, ravioli filled with pecorino, sugar, egg yolk, and lemon peel or *pestringolo*, a rich fruit cake made from dried figs, its surface studded with pine nuts and walnuts.

The Giostra della Quintana, Tournament of the Quintana, is held in Ascoli Piceno in early August, a colorful and noisy tribute to life in the region during the

The Palazzo Ducale in Urbino, completed in 1482. By the nineteenth century the palace was in a state of disrepair and was being used as a prison. Today it is fully restored, and part of it houses the Marche National Gallery.

SOLOMON/WHEELER/FOCUS

Middle Ages. Fifteenth-century costumes are worn by the townspeople in torchlight parades, at pageants and jousts, and there's much feasting.

The air of the ancient Greek port of Ancona is filled with the perfume of *brodetto*, made with an incredible variety of fish. Try other seafood dishes—whether ground and fried as croquettes, stuffed, or braised in a casserole, all embody the essence of the sea. South from Ancona, through laurel forests, is Loreto, shrine of the Virgin Mary that has drawn millions of pilgrims for over six centuries. At the southernmost tip along the coast of Marche is the port of San Benedetto del Tronto offering outstanding vegetables and *stoccafisso*, dried cod, and *code di rospo*, angler fish, prepared *in potaccio*.

Fairs in Marche tend to center around truffles...white truffles and black truffles everywhere! When planning your travels, make sure you contact a tourist office to find out what is going on. South of Urbino in Acqualagna fieras are held in mid-February and mid-August, and from the last week of October through the second week of November. South-west of San Marino, in Sant'Agata Feltria, a regional cheese fair is held in June and there is a fair for truffles and other produce from the region in October.

GERT WAGNER/BILDERBERG

Made from finely ground spiced pork, the huge mortadella from Bologna is related to the sausage known as boloney in the United States.

Regional Wines

In the Apennine foothills of Emilia-Romagna there are vineyards for mile after mile. The vines grow in the Colli Piacentini, south of Piacenza and in the Colli Bolognesi, extending from the central south almost to the coast. East of Bologna is Dozza, a tiny town of narrow cobbled streets, and in the Medieval Sforza fortress is the Enoteca Regionale Emilia-Romagna. Local wines are displayed here, and can be sampled. Next to the enoteca is the wine museum with its display of old winemaking equipment. On the first Sunday in June the town holds the Albana Wine Festival and there is a competition for the best balcony floral arrangement.

Among the most important regional wines to savor is Albana di Romagna, young and light with a hint of almond bitterness, produced dry, sweet, and sparkling. Along with Trebbiano di Romagna, a youthful white, usually made still and dry, this wine goes well with local fish dishes. Sangiovese di Romagna is a medium-bodied red with a flowery bouquet; Barbarossa di Bertinoro is a light robust red and Pagadebit is a medium-bodied white with spice and floral overtones. Lambrusco, a sparkling red produced dry and sweet, is probably the most popular wine. It is heavily consumed in the region as well as being exported.

Among the various wines of Marche, Verdicchio is prevalent and goes well with seafood. Verdicchio dei Castelli di Jesi and di Montanello are good table wines, with Verdicchio di Matelica being considered the best of this variety. Sparkling Verdicchio Pian delle Mura, a well-made *méthode champenoise* wine, is particularly good with pasta dishes and *vincisgrassi*. Rosso Piceno, a fruity and full red made from Sangiovese and Montepulciano grapes, and Rosso Conero, a robust dry red, are also good drinking.

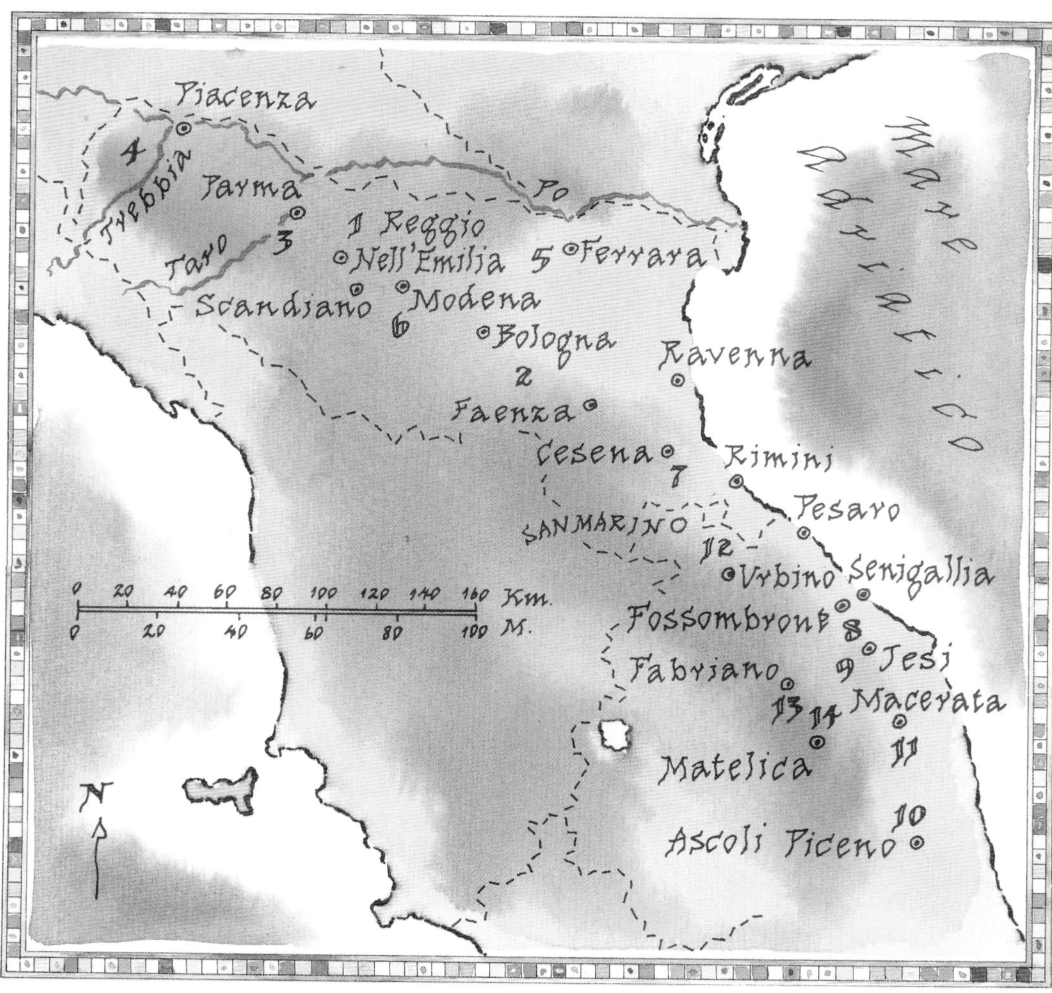

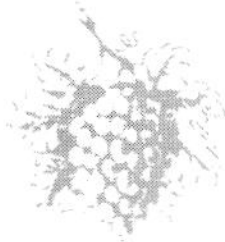

EMILIA-ROMAGNA

DOC Wines

1. *Bianco di Scandiano*
2. *Colli Bolognesi-Monte San Pietro-Castelli Medioevali*
3. *Colli di Parma*
4. *Colli Piacentini*
5. *Lambrusco di Sorbara*
6. *Lambrusco Grasparossa di Castelvetro*

1. *Lambrusco Reggiano*

5. *Lambrusco Salamino di Santa Croce*

7. *Sangiovese di Romagna*
7. *Trebbiano di Romagna*

DOCG Wines

7. *Albana di Romagna*

MARCHE

DOC Wines

8. *Bianchello del Metauro*
9. *Bianco dei Colli Maceratesi*
10. *Falerio dei Colli Ascolani*

8. *Lacrima di Morro*

9. *Rosso Conero*

11. *Rosso Piceno*
12. *Sangiovese dei Colli Pesaresi*

8. *Verdicchio dei Castelli di Jesi*

13. *Verdicchio di Matelica*
14. *Vernaccia di Serrapetrona*

Other Wines

Montepulciano delle Marche

Rutilus

RECIPES OF EMILIA-ROMAGNA AND MARCHE

Antonio Carluccio

Tortellini alla Bolognese

Filled Pasta Bologna Style

This is the best known of all the pastas made in the Emilia-Romagna region. Spinach, ricotta and even fish also make good fillings.

Filling:
2 oz (60 g) lean pork
2 oz (60 g) chicken breast
3 oz (90 g) roast beef
1 oz (30 g) butter
2 oz (60 g) mortadella
2 oz (60 g) prosciutto
nutmeg to taste
2 eggs
salt and freshly ground pepper
¾ cup (3 oz/90 g) freshly grated Parmesan cheese
Pasta:
See Tagliatelle al Prosciutto *recipe, p. 116*
7 cups (3½ pt/1.75 l) veal or chicken broth (stock)

For the filling: In a pan, gently sauté the pork, chicken and beef pieces on each side in the butter until most of the water has been exuded. Put them, together with the *mortadella* and the prosciutto, in a blender and grind finely. Add the nutmeg, eggs, salt and pepper and Parmesan and mix well.

For the *tortellini*: Roll the pasta out thinly into longish sheets. Cut into small squares 2 in x 2 in (5 cm x 5 cm) and place in the middle of each a teaspoon of filling. Brush the edges of the square with water to enable them to stick together. Fold each *tortellino* into a triangle first, pressing the edges to seal the filling in, then roll it around your finger and press together the two extremities to form a little ring. (Make the pasta in a fresh and non-ventilated room to avoid it drying out too quickly. When it dries it becomes brittle and unworkable.)

Boil the *tortellini* in the broth for 5 to 6 minutes. Serve in the broth with a little Parmesan sprinkled on top.

SERVES: 6 (makes 60 *tortellini*)

Ragù Bolognese con Tagliatelle

Bolognese Sauce on Tagliatelle

Variations of this most famous of all pasta sauces include chicken offal or dried *porcini*.

Sauce:
3 oz (90 g) butter
1 tablespoon olive oil
1 small onion, finely chopped
1 celery stalk, finely chopped
1 carrot, finely chopped
2 oz (60 g) lean bacon, finely chopped
5 oz (155 g) ground (minced) beef
7 oz (220 g) lean pork, coarsely chopped
½ cup (4 fl oz/125 ml) dry white wine
pinch of nutmeg
salt and freshly ground pepper
2 tablespoons tomato paste
2 cups (16 fl oz/500 ml) meat broth (stock)
¾ cup (6 fl oz/180 ml) milk
½ cup (2 oz/60 g) freshly grated Parmesan cheese
Pasta:
See Tagliatelle al Prosciutto *recipe, p. 116*

Put in a pan 2 oz (60 g) butter, olive oil, onion, celery, carrot and bacon and sauté gently for 10 minutes.

Add the ground beef and the pork. Stir-fry for a few minutes over a gentle heat and let cook for an additional 10 minutes. Add the wine and allow it to evaporate. Add nutmeg, salt and pepper and tomato paste, diluted with broth, and cook for at least 1 hour, adding more stock if the mixture starts to dry out.

Add the milk, the rest of the butter, mix well and serve on freshly made and cooked *tagliatelle*. Sprinkle with the Parmesan.

SERVES: 4

Prosciutto e Melone

Prosciutto and Melon

This pleasant summer dish can also be made with ripe fresh figs.

12 slices cantaloupe (rockmelon)
12 slices prosciutto, freshly and thinly sliced
freshly ground black pepper

Display the cut melon on a plate and cover with the prosciutto slices. Grind a little black pepper over them.

Grissini, bread sticks, accompany this dish extremely well.

SERVES: 4

Prosciutto and Melon, Tagliatelle with Prosciutto

PETER JOHNSON

Filled Pasta Bologna Style, Bolognese Sauce on Tagliatelle

Tagliatelle al Prosciutto

Tagliatelle with Prosciutto

Making pasta is one of the simplest and most pleasurable things in life.

Pasta:
$2\frac{1}{2}$ cups (10 oz/315 g) all purpose (plain) flour
3 eggs
pinch of salt
Sauce:
1 onion, finely chopped
3 oz (90 g) butter
3 oz (90 g) prosciutto, cut into strips
salt and freshly ground pepper
$\frac{1}{2}$ cup (2 oz/60 g) freshly grated Parmesan cheese

For the pasta: Mix the flour with the eggs and a pinch of salt. When they are mixed well, work with the palms of your hands on a wooden surface. Knead the dough using the weight of your shoulder, working until it is smooth and elastic. Put to one side to rest for 30 minutes.

Taking a little of the pasta at a time, roll it with a rolling pin to obtain a thin strip. Using either a cutting machine or a knife, cut the pasta into small or large ribbons, and the *tagliatelle* are ready.

For the sauce: Sauté the onion in the butter. When it becomes glassy, add the prosciutto and sweat for a minute. Season with salt and pepper.

Cook the pasta in plenty of boiling salted water until *al dente*. It will only take 2 or 3 minutes, a little longer if cut thicker. Drain. Mix well with the sauce and Parmesan cheese and serve.

SERVES: 4

Agnello alla Brace

Grilled Lamb on Charcoal

This is one of the best ways of eating lamb in the Marche region. If you can, use a charcoal grill, as this will give the meat the most authentic flavor.

2 oz (60 g) prosciutto fat (ask an Italian delicatessen to save some for you)
1 tablespoon finely chopped rosemary
1 garlic clove, finely chopped
1 teaspoon sage leaves
salt and freshly ground pepper
12 spring lamb chops (cutlets), trimmed of all fat

Place the prosciutto fat, rosemary, garlic and sage in a blender or mortar, and reduce them to a sort of paste. Mix in a little salt and pepper. Spread the mixture on each side of the chops, keeping them packed tightly together for a couple of hours, allowing the flavor to penetrate the meat. Grill the chops without any oil—the fat will moisten them sufficiently. Serve at once.

SERVES: 4

Quaglie San Leo

San Leo Quails

Quails are the favorite game in Marche. Those that are wild have much more flavor than the ones bred domestically.

8 quails, cleaned
salt and freshly ground pepper
3 oz (90 g) prosciutto, finely chopped
8 sage leaves, finely chopped
1 oz (30 g) pistachio nuts, ground
3 oz (90 g) butter
8 slices smoked bacon
2 carrots, finely chopped
2 celery stalks, finely chopped
1 leek, sliced
2 tablespoons finely chopped parsley
1 cup (8 fl oz/250 ml) white wine
$\frac{3}{4}$ cup (6 fl oz/180 ml) meat broth (stock)

Singe the quails quickly over a flame to remove any small feathers after plucking. Salt and pepper the quails inside and out.

Mix the prosciutto, sage and pistachios together and stuff each bird with the mixture. Divide half the butter into 8 and place a knob inside each bird. Wrap a slice of bacon around each bird and bind together with kitchen string and cocktail sticks.

Melt the rest of the butter in a large pan, add the quails and brown them on each side for 5 minutes over moderate heat. Add the carrot, celery, leek and parsley and sweat for 10 minutes.

Pour in the wine and the broth and cook for a further 10 minutes, allowing the liquid to evaporate. If there is still too much liquid, reduce over high heat. Transfer to a heated dish and serve.

SERVES: 4

Grilled Lamb on Charcoal (below), San Leo Quails (right)

PETER JOHNSON

PETER JOHNSON

PETER JOHNSON

Calf's (Veal) Kidneys with Garlic and Parsley

Rognoni di Vitello Trifolati

Calf's (Veal) Kidneys with Garlic and Parsley

The word *trifolati* originally meant the addition of truffles, but as the truffle is now a rare commodity the word has assumed a secondary meaning, denoting something fried with butter, garlic and parsley.

Anyone who is fortunate enough to come by some truffles may add a few slices of these to the kidneys, thereby transforming the dish into an extremely sophisticated meal.

2 calf's (veal) kidneys, cleaned, fat, and gristle removed
all purpose (plain) flour for dusting
2 oz (60 g) butter
2 garlic cloves, sliced
$\frac{1}{2}$ cup (4 fl oz/125 ml) dry white wine
salt and freshly ground black pepper
2 tablespoons chopped parsley

Slice the kidneys, roll them in flour and sauté in butter over high heat for around 5 minutes, turning constantly.

Add the garlic, and sauté for a few moments more. Add the wine and the salt and pepper and cook over high heat for a minute or so to reduce. Sprinkle with parsley and serve.

Serves: 4

Zampone con Lenticchie

Stuffed Pig's Foot with Lentils

Precooked *zampone* can be found in many Italian delicatessens.

2 cups (14 oz/440 g) large brown lentils
3 tablespoons olive oil
2 garlic cloves, sliced
1 lb (500 g) canned peeled plum tomatoes
1 zampone weighing about $1\frac{1}{4}$ lb (625 g)
good pinch of oregano
salt and freshly ground black pepper

Put a saucepan of water large enough to take the *zampone* on to boil. In a separate saucepan, simmer the lentils in boiling salted water for 15 minutes.

In a large pan heat the olive oil and briefly sauté the garlic; the moment it begins to color, add the tomatoes. Roughly break up the tomatoes, cooking them over moderate heat for 10 minutes until they reduce to a sauce.

Put the *zampone* in the saucepan of boiling water and simmer for around 20 minutes, or as long as instructed on the packaging.

When the lentils are cooked, drain them well and add to the tomato sauce, seasoning with the oregano, salt and pepper. Stir well and continue to cook for a further 10 minutes, testing the lentils, which should not be reduced to a mush but retain a "bite".

Serve the *zampone*, cut into $\frac{1}{2}$-in (1-cm) slices, with the lentils and possibly some *mostarda di Cremona*.

Serves: 4

Anguille di Comacchio in Umido

Stewed Comacchio Eels

The eels of Comacchio are the sweetest in all Italy.

4 tablespoons olive oil
1 carrot, finely chopped
1 celery stalk, finely chopped
1 onion, finely chopped
1 garlic clove, finely chopped
1 lb (500 g) filleted eel, cut into 2-in (5-cm) pieces
4 tablespoons dry white wine
a little meat broth (stock)
juice of 1 lemon
2 tablespoons coarsely chopped parsley
salt and freshly ground pepper

Heat the oil in a pan over moderate heat. Add the carrot, celery, onion and garlic and sauté gently for 10 minutes. Add the eel, the wine, and the broth. Braise for 15 minutes.

Once the liquor is reduced, add the lemon juice and the parsley. Add salt and pepper to taste, turn out onto a warmed platter and serve.

Serves: 4

Stuffed Pig's Foot with Lentils

PETER JOHNSON

PETER JOHNSON

Rape al Burro

Turnips with Butter

This is a typical winter dish that is now having a revival outside Italy.

2 oz (60 g) butter
1 lb (500 g) tender young turnips, peeled and sliced
½ cup (4 fl oz/125 ml) meat broth (stock)
salt and freshly ground black pepper

In a saucepan with a fitting lid, melt the butter, add the turnips and sauté for a minute or two, then pour in the broth. Bring to a boil, reduce the heat and simmer for approximately 10 minutes, covered. Season with salt and pepper and serve.

SERVES: 4

Cardi Burro e Parmigiano

Cardoon with Butter and Parmesan

This recipe is also suitable for celery, fennel, and zucchini (courgettes).

1 lb (500 g) tender white cardoon, cleaned and cut into 4-in (10-cm) pieces
2 oz (60 g) butter
½ cup (2 oz/60 g) freshly grated Parmesan cheese
grated nutmeg

Boil the cardoon for 15 minutes, or until tender, in salted water. Drain and in a baking dish layer the pieces, alternating with butter and Parmesan. Sprinkle with nutmeg and top with remaining cheese and butter.

Place in a 425°F (220°C) oven for 30 minutes or until brown on top. Serve with roast beef, or as a first course.

SERVES: 4

Asparagi alla Parmigiana

Asparagus with Parmesan

By adding a few slices of prosciutto and freshly boiled new potatoes, this becomes a delicious main course.

2 lb (1 kg) tender green asparagus, the lower parts of the stalk peeled, if necessary
4 tablespoons hot clarified butter
4 tablespoons freshly grated Parmesan cheese

Tie the asparagus in bunches and place upright in a tall, narrow saucepan in boiling water, the tips protruding. Test after 15 minutes. The asparagus stalks are cooked when they just fail to bend when a little force is used.

Clarify the butter and keep warm. Drain the asparagus and display it on a longish plate. Pour the butter over and grate Parmesan cheese on top. Under no circumstances use already grated cheese—the difference is too great!

SERVES: 4

Preceding pages: Turnips with Butter, Cardoon with Butter and Parmesan, Fried Potatoes with Garlic and Rosemary, Asparagus with Parmesan, Mixed Sautéed Wild Mushrooms

Patate Fritte con Aglio e Rosmarino

Fried Potatoes with Garlic and Rosemary

This is another wonderful recipe containing simple but effective ingredients. The combination of rosemary and garlic give an unmistakably Romagnan flavor.

8 tablespoons olive oil
1 lb (500 g) potatoes, peeled, cut into ½-in (1.5-cm) cubes
8 large garlic cloves, unpeeled
1 fresh rosemary sprig, crumbled
salt and freshly ground black pepper

Heat the olive oil in a large skillet, and when hot add the potato cubes. Spread them well out over the pan, but do not stir-fry until they form a golden crust.

Turn the potatoes over and add the garlic. Fry together to brown on all sides. Just before the cooking is complete add the rosemary, salt and pepper.

SERVES: 4

Funghi Misti in Umido

Mixed Sautéed Wild Mushrooms

A mixture of wild mushrooms from a mushroom hunt provides an opportunity to have this colorful, flavorful dish. It makes an excellent accompaniment to game dishes.

5 tablespoons olive oil
1 small onion, sliced
1 large tomato, chopped
2 bay leaves
1 fresh rosemary sprig
1½ lb (750 g) mixed mushrooms (oyster, field, porcini, hedgehog), wiped rather than washed clean, if possible
salt and freshly ground black pepper

Heat the oil in a large pan, sauté the onion and when it becomes golden add the tomato, bay leaves and rosemary.

Cook for a minute or two and then add the mushrooms. Continue cooking for 20 minutes more over low heat, stirring occasionally. Season with salt and pepper and serve.

SERVES: 4 to 6

Crostata di Ricotta

Ricotta Tart

The abundance of dairy products in Emilia-Romagna and Marche has inspired the people to use them in many ways. In other parts of Italy the tart is simply filled with jelly.

Pastry:
4 oz (125 g) unsalted butter
¼ cup (2 oz/60 g) sugar
4 tablespoons dry sherry
pinch of salt
2 cups (8 oz/250 g) all purpose (plain) flour
Filling:
2 egg yolks
⅔ cup (5 oz/155 g) superfine (caster) sugar
rind of ½ lemon, chopped
2 lb (1 kg) very fresh ricotta
1½ oz (45 g) candied orange peel, chopped in ¼-in (5-mm) pieces
1½ oz (45 g) candied lemon peel, chopped in ¼-in (5-mm) pieces
1½ oz (45 g) angelica, chopped in ¼-in (5-mm) pieces
1½ oz (45 g) semisweet (plain) chocolate, chopped in ¼-in (5-mm) pieces

For the pastry: Work together the butter, sugar, sherry and salt to a smooth consistency. Add the flour and work to obtain a stiffish dough. Put aside, covered, in a cool place for about 1 hour.

PETER JOHNSON

Apricot Tart, Ricotta Tart

For the filling: Beat the egg yolks with the sugar until creamy, then add the chopped lemon rind. Beat the ricotta with a fork until light, then add it to the egg mixture. Finally, stir in the candied peel, angelica and chocolate pieces.

Preheat the oven to 370°F (190°C). Roll out ¾ of the pastry and use it to line the bottom and sides of a shallow pie pan 12 in x 8 in (30 cm x 20 cm). Pour in the ricotta mixture and spread it evenly. Roll out the rest of the pastry and cut into strips ¾ in (2 cm) wide. Arrange the strips in a lattice over the filling. Bake until the top starts to turn brown (40 minutes to 1 hour). Serve cold.

SERVES: 10

Crostata di Albicocche

Apricot Tart

A good Moscato naturale makes a fine accompaniment to this dessert, which can be made with dried apricots.

Pastry:
2½ cups (10 oz/315 g) all purpose (plain) flour
3 large egg yolks
⅔ cup (5 oz/155 g) superfine (caster) sugar
5 oz (155 g) unsalted butter
½ oz (15 g) butter to butter the pan

Filling:
1 cup (11 oz/345 g) apricot jelly (jam) diluted, if necessary, with a little water
2 lb (1 kg) freshly cooked apricot halves, or 3½ cups (1 lb/500 g) dried apricots cooked in water, lemon juice and sugar for 20 minutes

For the pastry: Combine flour, egg yolks, sugar and butter and mix into a dough. Put aside, covered, in a cool place, for 30 minutes.

Preheat the oven to 350°F (180°C). Butter a 12 in x 8 in (30 cm x 20 cm) pie pan, line it evenly with the dough, pressing it out with your fingers. Spread with the jelly and cover with the drained apricot halves. Bake for 30 to 45 minutes. Serve cold.

SERVES: 6 to 8

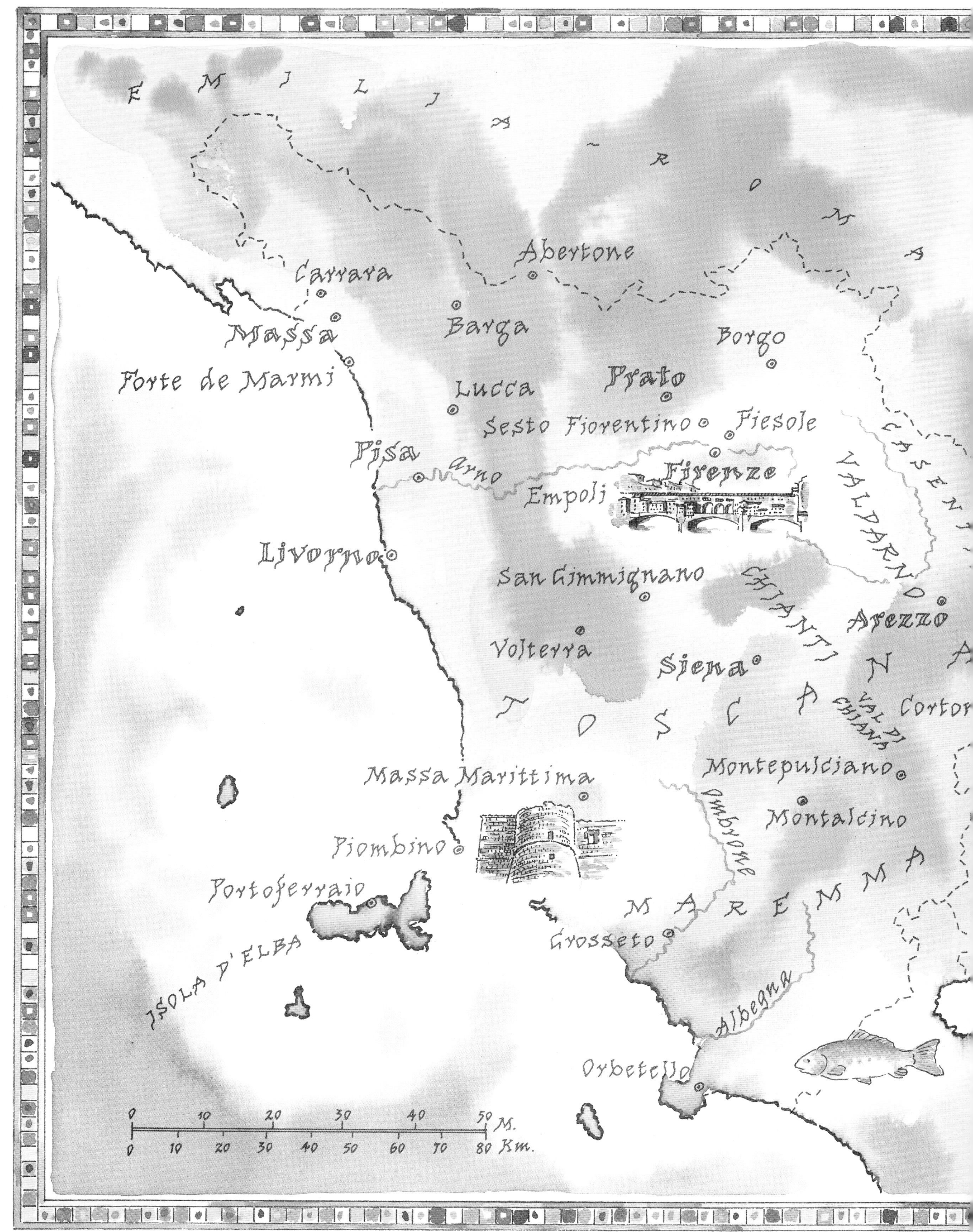
E M I L I A ~ R O M A
Abertone
Carrara
Massa
Barga
Borgo
Forte de Marmi
Lucca
Prato
Sesto Fiorentino
Fiesole
Pisa
Arno
Firenze
Empoli
VALDARNO
CASENT
Livorno
San Gimmignano
CHIANTI
Arezzo
Volterra
Siena
T O S C A N A
VAL DI CHIANA
Corton
Massa Marittima
Montepulciano
Montalcino
Ombrone
Piombino
Portoferraio
M A R E M M A
Grosseto
ISOLA D'ELBA
Albegna
Orbetello
0 10 20 30 40 50 M.
0 10 20 30 40 50 60 70 80 Km.

TOSCANA AND UMBRIA

Don Andrea Scirè Borghese and Donna Marisa Borghese

For many, Toscana and Umbria exemplify Italian culture. This was where the Etruscans settled, the people who brought civilization to Roma, and it is said that the purest Italian is spoken by the people of Siena. In Toscana and Umbria, despite the increasing spread of industry, there are still towns and cities largely unchanged since Medieval times, with their walls and towers of rosy and pale gold stone, havens of tranquility and beauty in an increasingly hectic world.

RAY JOYCE

A high relief marble by Luca della Robbia on one of the choir stalls in the Cathedral of Santa Maria del Fiore, Firenze.

The City of the Lily

Firenze, heart of Toscana and home of the Renaissance, lies in a green hollow surrounded by hills, silvery with olive groves and topped by villages like Bellosguardo, Belvedere, and Fiesole. It is uniquely endowed with monuments and historic buildings, many housing works created by Tuscan genius throughout the centuries, artists like Giotto, Botticelli, Fra Angelico, Paolo Uccello, Michelangelo, and Leonardo da Vinci. The Palazzo Vecchio, on the piazza della Signoria, forms the city's heart. Nearby is the Uffizi Gallery with its unparalleled collection of paintings, and across the Ponte Vecchio, which spans the River Arno, are the magnificent Pitti Palace and the Boboli Gardens, designed during the Renaissance. The city is not large, enabling the visitor to discover these wonders, and the many others, on foot.

The magnificent Cathedral of Santa Maria del Fiore was begun prior to 1300 and it waited nearly 600 years for its final façade to be completed, integrated in the best Tuscan-Gothic style by the warm polychromy of its marblework. This ability to harmonize the diverse parts of a project is a particularly Tuscan quality. Together with the gifts of inspiration and tenacity, it helps explain the greatness of so much Tuscan achievement.

A Simple Cuisine

Tuscan cusine is superb in its simplicity, a gastronomic art rather than a mere necessity for survival. Ingredients are treated in an uncomplicated but well defined way to enhance their flavors without burying them beneath elaborate sauces or garnishes. Fine Tuscan olive oil, plentiful herbs, and vegetables are the basic ingredients.

A famous Tuscan dish, *crostini*, consists of slices of toast covered with a variety of tasty ingredients, the most popular being *crostini ai fegatini di pollo*, with chicken livers. A highly prized variant includes the addition of ground *milza*, veal spleen, onions, capers, ham fat, olive oil, butter, sage, pepper, Vin Santo or Marsala, and Parmesan cheese. An ideal balance to such a rich *antipasto* would be the light tomato soup, *pappa al pomodoro*, a soup considered so healthy, mainly because of the quantities of garlic used, that the Sienese recommend it for babies.

Perhaps the best known Florentine dish is *bistecca alla fiorentina*. The basic recipe is no secret but cooking details are jealously guarded by those in the restaurant trade. To be perfect, the steak—a T-bone or sirloin—should come from a young steer and be the thickness of index and middle fingers joined together. It is grilled over charcoal without basting and kept four fingers high above the coals for no more than four to five minutes on each side. A proper *fiorentina* is never well done. When one side is cooked the meat is turned and sprinkled generously with sea salt. Then it is turned again to get rid of the excess salt, seasoned with freshly ground black pepper, and its surface covered with a fine stream of virgin olive oil. It is brought sizzling to the table, where it is served with lemon wedges.

For a more sophisticated main course it would be difficult to go past *anitra all'arancia*, orange duck. This delicacy, proudly claimed by the French as their own *caneton à l'orange,* originated in Toscana. The French learned of it in the sixteenth century when a team of chefs accompanied members of the Medici family to Paris. And another popular Florentine main course is *pollo alla diavola*, chicken split open, flattened, then fried under weights, with chili.

TONY STONE WORLDWIDE/THE PHOTO LIBRARY

Firenze's Cathedral of Santa Maria del Fiore is one of the world's largest cathedrals. Its walls are faced with multicolored marble in geometrical designs, and the magnificent dome was designed by Brunelleschi.

As for desserts, Florentine *zuccotto* is a semi-chilled whipped cream and chocolate sponge cake looking like half a pumpkin, moistened with liqueur, at its heart a mixture of strawberries and cream. From Pistoia come *brigidini*, wafer-like pastries flavored with aniseed. Perhaps Toscana's most famous cake of all is the *panforte*, from Siena, a cake containing almonds, hazelnuts, spices, and fruit. Also Sienese are the well known almond cookies called *ricciarelli*.

The Home of Chianti

Toscana is the home of Chianti, with its bulbous straw-covered bottle, a worldwide synonym for Italian wine. Even though it is by far the most popular of the region's wines, however, Chianti is only one of many Tuscan wines well worth tasting. Chianti can vary greatly in quality from one producer to another. A general guide to quality is the appellation, Chianti Classico, supported by a picture of a black rooster or, as a second choice, a scantily clad boy, on a label glued to the neck of the bottle. These are the registered marks adopted by wine producers from the officially designated Chianti region. Good quality Chiantis are also produced in the hills around Firenze (Colli Fiorentini), Pisa (Colline Pisane), and Arezzo (Colli Aretini).

Similar to Chianti but more prestigious is the Vino Nobile di Montepulciano, a dry red wine dating back to the eighth century. It is produced in the area of Montepulciano, at the southern end of the Val di Chiana, and is called noble probably because it was favored by the Tuscan nobility, who would have been able to afford to cellar it.

An enduring favorite among the whites is Vernaccia di San Gimignano, a medium bodied, strongly flavored, pale golden dry wine. While resting from his labors, Michelangelo relished a draught of Vernaccia, describing it as something that "kisses, licks, bites, tingles, and stings". Michelangelo's appreciation of a good wine is embodied in his statue of Bacchus, the god of wine, one of the treasures in the Bargello Museum in Firenze. Another highly recommended white is Galestro, a recently established wine from the hills of central Toscana.

One of Italy's finest wines, Brunello di Montalcino, produced from Sangiovese grapes, comes from the hills of Siena. It is smooth and robust, with a high alcohol content. Ideally suited for aging, a good vintage may have a life in excess of fifty years, if properly cellared.

A glass of sweet smelling, liqueur like Vin Santo, holy wine, makes a delightful conclusion to a meal, although it is also often served as an aperitif. The name is said to derive from the fact that the priest celebrating mass was accustomed to receive from the congregation their most prized wine.

It is said that in the nineteenth century Barone Ricasoli developed the original formula for Toscana's most famous export, Chianti, at his castle at Brolio. The grapes he used were from vineyards that had once been owned by Galileo.

ENRICO FERORELLI/DOT/COLORIFIC

Tuscan Staples

Bread is essential to Tuscan cuisine. With a hard crust and compact crumb, the traditional saltless Tuscan loaf originally substituted for pasta—such as *pappardelle*, *pici*, and *tortelli*—which was considered quite a luxury. Many old recipes call for slices of bread to provide the necessary carbohydrates, a need in part satisfied also by the widespread consumption of potatoes and chestnuts.

And beans must not be overlooked. The Tuscans have a multitude of ways of preparing their humble but delicious beans, introduced to the region around 1500 by the Medici Pope, Clemente VII. They make bean *antipasti*, bean soup, and serve beans with tuna. In Lucca they excel in the preparation of *fagioli al fiasco*, fresh haricot beans cooked over charcoals in a glass flask, generally a Chianti bottle, in order to minimize movement, preserve the texture of the beans, and keep in the flavor.

Olive oil is still the main source of fat, essential to give that distinctive earthy taste characteristic of so many Tuscan dishes. The best oils are produced in the hills of Lucca, a beautiful, small city famous for the natural beauty of its surroundings as well as for the works of art enclosed within its fortified walls. The prized local olives are used in the district's specialty *agnello con le olive*. Other Lucchese treats are fried eels and various game dishes, including *folaghe alla Puccini*, coot cooked in wine with a sauce of anchovy fillets, herring roe, smoked salmon, olive oil, and lemon juice. The dish is named after Giacomo Puccini, born in Lucca in 1858, composer of *Madama Butterfly*, *La Bohème,* and *Tosca*, among the most famous of all operas.

Arezzo, the easternmost of Toscana's cities, stands on a hilltop overlooking fertile farming land. Arezzo was the birthplace of the great fourteenth-century poet Petrarch justly considered, with his friend Boccaccio, the reviver of classical Italian literature. But whether visiting Arezzo to pay homage to Petrarch or to attend the centuries-old folkloristic event, the Giostra del Saracino, on the first Sunday of September, make a point of trying some of the local specialties such as *pollo al tegame,* chicken casserole with mushrooms or with green peas, or pheasant with truffles, those rare and precious tubers that grow in the countryside around Arezzo, Firenze, Grosseto, and Siena.

Other specialties to try here are the pork dishes, sometimes spit-roasted, and eels caught in the nearby Canale Maestro. Hare, too, is popular. A notable dish is *pappardelle con la lepre*, fettucine-like egg noodles with hare sauce. Sometimes hare is prepared *agrodolce*, sweet and sour, a method also used for cooking roe buck and wild boar. To accompany such dishes try a Chianti dei Colli Aretini.

Prosciutto and sausages made from wild boar are still produced in Pisa and Siena but come mainly from Grosseto, in the Maremma area in the south-west. Protection of the boars is increasing, however, because of their dwindling numbers, and such products are becoming less common.

Rather than have a restaurant meal you could have a *panino*, an Italian-style sandwich, prepared in a quality delicatessen. A few slices of locally dried and cured meats make a tasty filling. Although Toscana does not produce preserved meats on a large scale, sufficient is made to cater for the local market. Typical are *mortadella ai semi di finocchio*, mortadella flavored with aniseed, *salsicce allo zenzero*, pork sausages with chili, a specialty of Siena, the small *salamino* of the Valdarno area, south-east of Firenze, and the juniper-flavored smoked ham of the Casentina area north of Arezzo.

Cacciucco

Cacciucco, a rich fish stew and the prize of the province of Livorno, makes a heavenly main course. The use of tomatoes and hot chili peppers might hint at a southern origin for the dish but the Livornese are adamant that their version is the best in all Italy and far surpasses Marseilles' famous *bouillabaisse*.

A mixture of fish is used, depending on what is available from the catch, but rock fish must be included, and sometimes some octopus or even crab or lobster, is added. The wine specified is generally white, but sometimes a local red is favored.

A peculiarity of the preparation of *cacciucco* in Viareggio is the addition to the pot of a stone from the bottom of the sea. This is believed to enhance the flavor and to make the *cacciucco's* bouquet sufficiently impressive to convince Neptune to overlook the theft of the various ingredients from his kingdom.

It is thought that the many fish stews of the Mediterranean stem from an Athenian recipe, spread throughout the region by the Greeks.

LEO MEIER

At the fish market.

WOLFGANG STECHE/VISUM

JOHN G. ROSS/SUSAN GRIGGS AGENCY

Even today, in parts of Umbria, farming methods are largely traditional. On this farm a pair of oxen have yet to be replaced by a tractor.

You might wish for a second *panino* with cheese. Pecorino toscano, produced from sheep's milk, is a piquant alternative to the milder Parmesan. From the Chianti region in springtime comes another well known sheep's milk cheese called *marzolino*, named after the month of March. This can be enjoyed either fresh or after it has matured.

An affinity with the food of Liguria, largely based on vegetables, olive oil, and flavorsome herbs, is evident in the areas of Massa and Carrara, home of the famous white marble from which the major proportion of Italian sculptures over the years have been chiseled.

In the nearby mountainous Garfagnana area, covered with forests of fir, pine, maple, and beech, a preference for pork meat is dictated by the cold climate and the strong influence of neighboring Emilia. Typical of the Garfagnana is a dish offering a unique blend of flavors: a chestnut polenta served with pork meat, accompanied by a slightly bitter root vegetable called *scorzonera*.

Landlocked Umbria

East from Arezzo lies mountainous Umbria, with its ancient citadel towns keeping watch over the valleys. It is the only region in central and southern Italy not touched by the sea, but the abundance of water from its rivers, springs, and lakes, together with the natural shelter offered by mountain caves, attracted settlers to the area as early as Paleolithic times.

About 1000 BC people from the north, known later as the Umbrians, arrived, and were followed in turn by the Etruscans. The Etruscans, experienced in

Preceding pages: A crop of sunflowers ripens in the heat of summer. Though the consumption of oils other than olive oil is still small in Italy, it is increasing.

agriculture, architecture, and the arts, were also fine hunters, skilled with the bow and arrow and at fishing with the line and hook. They introduced many crops, including the chestnut. Chestnut flour over the years has been used to bake a nourishing pie, still popular today, known as *castagnaccio*.

From the Etruscans the Umbrians learned the art of roasting. There is barely any food they cannot prepare to perfection on the spit, in the oven, or over a red hot grill, be it a piece of the locally bred Perugino beef, a succulent suckling pig, a goat, lamb, poultry, game, or fish.

The Region's Capital

Perugia, the regional capital, with its great fortified walls, is primarily Medieval in appearance, but is rich in relics of older civilizations, as a visit to the National Archaeological Museum will attest. Reminders of the city's grandeur in the Middle Ages and the Renaissance are numerous, among them the Duomo, the imposing Palazzo del Priore, the Fontana Maggiore, and the papal fortress known as La Rocca Paolina. At the National Gallery there are works by such artists as Perugino, Pinturicchio, and Piero della Francesca.

The University of Perugia, founded at the beginning of the fourteenth century, is one of the oldest in the whole of Europe. Today it is complemented by the university for foreign students to which students from all over the world come in their thousands.

Ideally you should reach Perugia for the first time by walking from the surrounding plain with its factories, although this will require a little effort and a comfortable pair of shoes. (It is in one of these factories that the world-famous "Baci", "kisses", are produced—delicious morsels of chocolate and hazelnuts.) First you will reach the new city then finally the old one, making your way through little lanes, often stepped and bearing romantic names. There are many ancient arches, one of which dates from Etruscan times, and numerous churches, ranging from the fifth century church of Sant'Angelo to those in Gothic and Baroque style. Once you have reached the top of the hill you'll probably be ready to try some of the local specialties.

As a first course, try *ombricelli umbri*, hand-made spaghetti with a tasty tomato sauce. This could be followed by *torello perugino alla ghiotta*, meat from a young bull spit-roasted over the *ghiotta*, a copper tray in which the juices and fat are collected and then enriched with olive oil or butter, anchovies, capers, and wine. This mixture is used firstly to baste the cooking roast, then as a sauce.

Take a stroll on the corso Vannucci and visit Sandri, the oldest cake shop in the city, its decor unchanged since the turn of the century. There you can sample delicious *pignoccate*, pine nut fondants, *pizza dolce*, a sweet pizza flavored with wine and lemon rind, and the *serpentone delle monache Cappuccine*, snake of the Capuchin nuns, a kind of strudel rolled to look like a coiled snake, with candied cherry eyes and a blanched almond tongue.

Home of St Francis

Assisi, with its Roman remains and enchanting Medieval buildings, is one of Italy's jewels. From the city there are views of such beauty that the city's most illustrious son, St Francis, was once compelled to exclaim: "I have never seen a place more beautiful than this, my native valley ..."

Umbria's Black Magic

The black truffle is one of the backbones of Umbrian cuisine. Luxurious meat and fish dishes with black truffles are prepared all over the region but also more modest foods like pasta and eggs are glorified by the magic tuber. Black truffles are also excellent in fine slivers in salads, or cut in little cubes and sautéed in butter, then added to a plate of rice or *fettuccine*, topped with freshly grated Parmesan.

November to March is the time of the year in which truffles are dug out, sometimes with the help of pigs, but mainly using specially trained dogs.

As a result of excessive demand and lack of protection, the yearly crops have been gradually declining. To preserve this delicacy for the gourmets of the twenty-first century, a great number of oak trees have been planted and truffle spores artificially inseminated.

Apparently some of these plantings are giving promising results, although all details on production are a well-guarded secret. This is understandable, since in Italy, at present market prices, you can buy a modest new motor car for less than the retail value of eight or ten pounds (four or five kilograms) of truffles.

MILAN HORACEK/BILDERBERG

WENDELY HARVEY

Assisi, home of St Francis, Italy's patron saint, still retains a tranquil Medieval air, despite its new buildings. Built from pink stone, it has an enchanting blush to it at dawn and dusk.

The town of Bastia, close to Assisi, claims to be the center of the region where the best *porchetta* is prepared. Every year, in September, they have the Fete of the Spit-roasted Pig, La Sagra della Porchetta, which rivals the one held each May not far from the Tuscan border in the village of Monte Santa Maria Tiberina. A treat in summer is to have slices of freshly carved *porchetta* combined with the sweet freshness of cantaloupe.

The fish eaten in Umbria come mainly from its rivers and from Lake Trasimeno, west of Perugia. The local chefs proudly offer *regina in porchetta*, roasted queen carp, tincs or perches with sage and olive oil, eels *al tegamaccio,* and a simple but delicious dish of slightly bitter-tasting tiny fish called *arborelle* or *lasche* fried in virgin olive oil. In the *trattorie* on the lake shores fish are prepared in a variety of ways, one of the most pleasing being *tagliatelle col sugo di pesce*, tagliatelle with a fish sauce.

Norcia and Cascia produce excellent fresh and matured cheeses like ricotta and pecorino. The prosciutto, salame, and pork sausages produced in Norcia are so well known in Umbria and Lazio that *norcineria* (things made in Norcia) is the name given to a shop that sells pork meat, wherever it comes from. The prosciutto produced here has a more robust and salty flavor than the better known ones produced around Parma and in San Daniele.

Umbria's Wines

Orvieto's Duomo with its breathtaking façade is one of the country's most beautiful buildings, and it is from the Orvieto region that Umbria's best known wines come. There are two varieties, one dry, one slightly sweet. In the past it was so highly esteemed that the great artist Pinturicchio demanded "as much Orvieto wine as he could drink" as a conditional over-payment when he was requested to decorate the walls of the Cathedral of Perugia.

The wines of Torgiano, to the south of Perugia, are wines of considerable consistency and quality. There the Lungarotti family has created a fascinating wine museum, which is well worth a visit. The family produces some interesting wine, such as Cabernet Sauvignon of Miraldolo, Rubesco Riserva, Torre di Giano, Vin Santo, and a sherry-style Solleone.

Other regional wines deserving of mention are the robust, red Sagrantino di Montefalco, the white Greco from Todi and the whites of the Colli del Trasimeno and of the Altotiberina area, near Città di Castello.

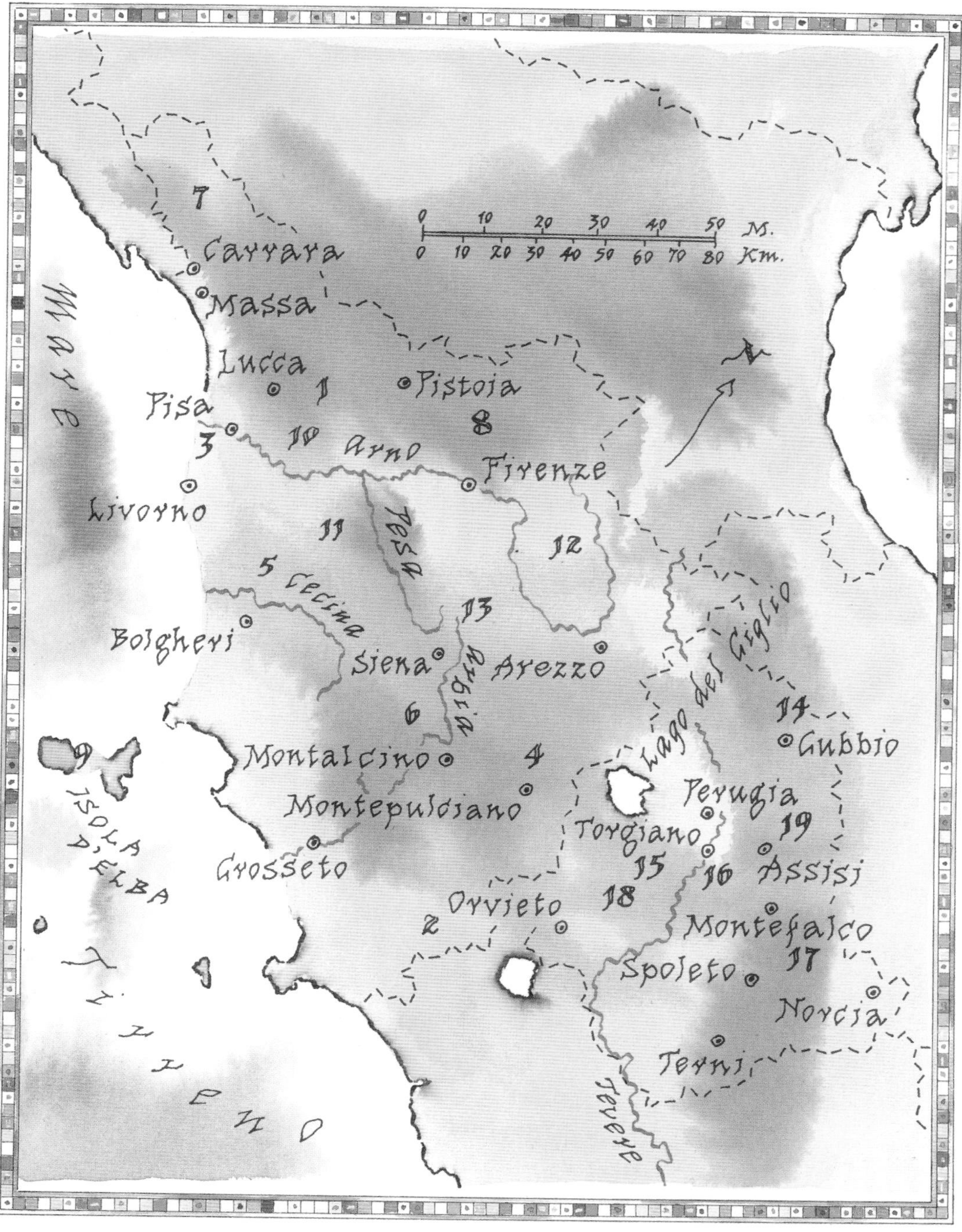

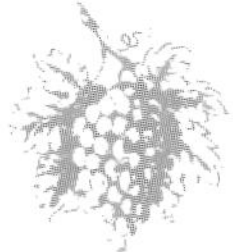

TOSCANA

DOC Wines

1. Bianco della Valdinievole
2. Bianco di Pitigliano
3. Bianco Pisano San Torpè
4. Bianco Vergine della Valdichiana
5. Bolgheri
7. Candia dei Colli Apuani
8. Carmignano
1. Colline Lucchesi
9. Elba
10. Montecarlo
11. Montescudaio
2. Morellino di Scansano
6. Moscadello di Montalcino
2. Parrina
12. Pomino
6. Rosso di Montalcino
13. Val d'Arbia
5. Vernaccia di San Gimignano

DOCG Wines

6. Brunello di Montalcino
11. Chianti
4. Vino Nobile di Montepulciano

UMBRIA

DOC Wines

14. Colli Altotiberini
15. Colli del Trasimeno
16. Colli Perugini
17. Montefalco
18. Orvieto
19. Torgiano

Other Wines

Solleone
Vin Santo

RECIPES OF TOSCANA & UMBRIA

Don Andrea Scirè Borghese and Donna Marisa Borghese

PETER JOHNSON

Panzanella

Salad of Raw Vegetables and Bread

This is a particularly handy dish, as it makes good use of leftover bread. It can be served as a summer snack, an appetizer or a salad.

1 lb (500 g) stale Italian country-style bread or French bread, sliced thickly
⅓ cup (3 fl oz/90 ml) extra virgin olive oil
2 tablespoons red wine vinegar
salt and freshly ground black pepper
1 cucumber, sliced
6 green onions (scallions or spring onions) or 2 onions, sliced
12 sweet basil leaves, cut in ¼-in (5-mm) strips
6 tomatoes, peeled and cut in wedges

Soak the bread in cold water. Squeeze gently in a clean cloth to remove excess moisture and store in the fridge for several hours.

In a jar, shake together the oil, vinegar and a pinch of salt and pepper. Place the cucumber, green onions, basil and tomatoes in a salad bowl. Lay the slices of bread on top, pour over the dressing, toss gently and serve.

SERVES: 6

Crostini di Fegatini

Chicken Liver Croutons

A famous Florentine *antipasto*, which makes an excellent snack for serving with drinks.

⅓ cup (3 fl oz/90 ml) virgin olive oil
8 oz (250 g) beef liver, well cleaned and cut in pieces
6 chicken livers
2 onions, chopped
⅓ cup (3 fl oz/90 ml) dry white wine, Madeira, sherry or port
1 tablespoon chopped sage or 2 teaspoons ground dried sage
2 garlic cloves, finely chopped
1½ tablespoons drained capers, coarsely chopped
2 salted anchovies, rinsed in running water then coarsely chopped
1 cup (8 fl oz/250 ml) chicken broth (stock)
salt and freshly ground black pepper
12 small slices Italian country-style bread or French bread
parsley sprigs for decoration

Heat oil in a skillet and brown the beef and chicken livers together with the onions for about 3 minutes. Add the wine. When nearly evaporated, add the sage and garlic. Cook for 3 minutes, cool slightly, then put the mixture quickly through a food processor or blender. Return the coarse paste to the skillet. Add the capers, anchovies and half the broth. Season with salt and a generous amount of pepper.

Toast the bread in the oven. Either serve the toast alongside the pâté or spread with it. Decorate with parsley and capers and serve hot.

SERVES: 6

Acquacotta dell' Umbria

Tomato Soup

A simple and tasty thick soup from Cascia, this is another dish that incorporates leftover bread.

2 lb (1 kg) tomatoes, peeled and quartered, or 2 cans peeled tomatoes
4 onions, thinly sliced
8 or 10 fresh mint leaves
1 cup (8 fl oz/250 ml) vegetable broth (stock) made with a bouillon cube
6 thick slices Italian country-style bread or French bread, preferably stale, toasted
12 tablespoons extra virgin olive oil
salt and freshly ground black pepper
½ cup (2 oz/60 g) freshly grated Parmesan cheese

In a saucepan over moderate heat, simmer the tomatoes with the onions, mint, half the vegetable broth and a pinch of salt for about 30 minutes. Should the mixture become too dry, add the remaining broth.

Place a slice of toast in each soup bowl. Cover each slice with 2 tablespoons of oil and season with salt and pepper. Pour the tomatoes into the bowls, sprinkle with Parmesan and serve.

SERVES: 6

Left: Tomato Soup, Salad of Raw Vegetables and Bread, Chicken Liver Croutons, Spaghetti with Garlic, Oil and Chili Peppers

Spaghetti Aglio Olio e Peperoncino

Spaghetti with Garlic, Oil and Chili Peppers

This simple and quickly prepared dish is a favorite in Italy as a late snack after a night out at the movies or the theater.

4 garlic cloves, finely sliced
3 dried hot red chili peppers, crushed
½ cup (4 fl oz/125 ml) extra virgin olive oil
1¼ lb (625 g) spaghetti
3 tablespoons chopped parsley

Sauté the garlic and chili in the oil until the garlic is golden. Pour the mixture into a warm serving bowl.

Cook the spaghetti in a large pot of boiling salted water until *al dente*. Drain well, place in the serving bowl and sprinkle with the parsley. Toss and serve at once.

SERVES: 6

Polletti alla Diavola in Padella

Spatchcock with Chili, Tuscan Style

The successful preparation of this dish will depend on your capacity to keep the birds well and truly flat against the cooking surface.

3 spatchcock or Cornish hens, halved
extra virgin olive oil
salt
3 large dried hot red chili peppers, crushed
1½ tablespoons ground dried sage or 18 sage leaves
6 garlic cloves, halved and lightly crushed
2 onions, chopped
3 tablespoons chopped parsley

Beat the spatchcock halves flat with a meat mallet, removing the larger bones, if desired. Brush them all over with olive oil and sprinkle with salt, the chili and ground sage, or position 3 sage leaves on each serve.

Take 1 or 2 wide heavy skillets or shallow saucepans and heat enough oil to cover the bottoms. Spread the garlic evenly in the skillets then position the spatchcock pieces in a single layer, skin side up. Cover with lids slightly smaller than the skillets, weighing them down with bricks or pots filled with water to keep the spatchcock flat.

Cook over moderate heat for 10 minutes then remove the weights and covers. Spread the onions over the top of the spatchcock, turn them over, sprinkle with the parsley and replace covers and weights. Cook a further 10 to 15 minutes.

Serve with boiled potatoes, with spinach moistened with the pan juices and a little oil or with a salad.

SERVES: 6

Spatchcock with Chili, Tuscan Style

PETER JOHNSON

PETER JOHNSON

Veal Feet Florentine, Florentine Beef Stew with Pasta, Mullet Livorno Style

Stracotto alla Fiorentina colla Pasta

Florentine Beef Stew with Pasta

This substantial dish takes some time to prepare, but should be served as a *piatto unico*, needing only a salad and a dessert to complete the meal.

2½ lb (1.25 kg) beef rump or round, well marbled, in 1 piece
⅓ cup (3 fl oz/90 ml) virgin olive oil
2 tablespoons butter
1 pork chop
2½ oz (75 g) salt pork or bacon, sliced thickly and diced
2 onions, finely chopped
1 celery stalk, finely chopped
2 carrots, finely chopped
2 tablespoons tomato paste
¾ cup (6 fl oz/180 ml) dry red wine, preferably Chianti
salt and coarsely cracked black pepper
1½ cups (12 fl oz/375 ml) beef broth (stock)
1 lb (500 g) short pasta, such as pennette, pipe *or* tortiglioni
½ cup (2 oz/ 60 g) freshly grated Parmesan cheese

Brown the beef in a large heavy pot with the oil and butter. Add the pork chop, salt pork, onions, celery and carrots. Stir until vegetables are golden brown, then add the tomato paste dissolved in the red wine. Let the wine evaporate then season the meat with salt and pepper. Add the broth. Cover well and let simmer for 2½ hours. Remove the beef and cover with aluminum foil in order to keep it warm. After 5 or 10 minutes, when it has firmed, slice it.

Meanwhile, remove the pork chop, debone it and pulp the meat in a food processor or blender. Cook the pasta in plenty of boiling salted water until *al dente*. Drain and mix with half the sauce, to which the pork paste has been added. Place on half a large serving dish and sprinkle with Parmesan. Lay the beef slices alongside and cover them with the rest of the sauce. Serve immediately.

SERVES: 6 to 8

Zampetti alla Fiorentina

Veal (or Pork) Feet Florentine

The rich flavor of this old Florentine dish is ample compensation for the time it takes to cook.

6 veal or pork feet (trotters), scraped and well cleaned
3 tablespoons butter or margarine
2 onions, finely chopped
salt and freshly ground black pepper
$1\frac{1}{4}$ cups (10 fl oz/310 ml) strong beef broth (stock), made with 3 bouillon cubes
1 rosemary sprig, chopped
$\frac{1}{2}$ cup (4 fl oz/125 ml) dry white wine
2 tablespoons virgin olive oil
5 tomatoes, peeled and chopped, or 1 can peeled tomatoes
3 egg yolks
generous pinch of ground cinnamon
$\frac{1}{2}$ cup (2 oz/60 g) freshly grated Parmesan cheese

Boil the feet in enough salt water to cover them well for about $2\frac{1}{2}$ hours or until well cooked. Remove from the liquid and carefully discard the bones.

Heat the butter in a saucepan and sauté the onions until golden brown. Brown the foot flesh with the onions, seasoning with salt and pepper. Add the broth, rosemary, wine, oil and tomatoes. Bring to a boil then simmer, uncovered, until the liquid is well reduced.

Beat together the egg yolks, cinnamon and Parmesan. Pour this mixture in with the feet, mix well and serve immediately.

SERVES: 6

Triglie alla Livornese

Mullet Livorno Style

A traditional, delicate way to cook red mullet, snapper or other varieties of reef fish with firm flesh.

$\frac{1}{2}$ cup (4 fl oz/125 ml) virgin olive oil
2 small onions, finely chopped
1 celery stalk, sliced
3 garlic cloves, peeled
3 tablespoons finely chopped parsley
$1\frac{1}{2}$ lb (750 g) tomatoes, peeled and coarsely chopped
salt and freshly ground black pepper
6 small or 3 medium red mullet, gutted and scaled

Heat the oil in a saucepan and sauté the onions, celery, garlic and $\frac{2}{3}$ of the parsley until the onions are golden brown. Add the tomatoes and season with salt and pepper. Cover the pan and simmer for 30 minutes. Sieve into a shallow flameproof tureen large enough to accommodate the fish. Check the seasoning. If the sauce is a little thick, stir in a few tablespoons of hot water.

Rinse and dry the mullet and place in tureen, head to tail. Simmer over low heat until cooked (15 to 20 minutes), basting frequently. Serve hot, in the tureen, sprinkled with parsley.

SERVES: 6

Funghi e Zucchine alla Nepitella

Mushrooms and Zucchini with Mint

The unusual blend of flavors in this dish is reminiscent of the Tuscan countryside.

3 tablespoons virgin olive oil
2 oz (60 g) butter
$\frac{1}{2}$ lb (250 g) champignon mushrooms, cleaned and sliced
3 garlic cloves, peeled and lightly crushed
1 tablespoon chopped mint
salt and freshly ground black pepper
5 medium zucchini (courgettes), sliced

Heat the oil and butter in a saucepan and sauté the mushrooms with the garlic and mint. Season with a little salt and pepper. Cover and cook for 10 minutes over moderate heat. Add the zucchini and stir well. Cover and cook for a further 10 minutes. Remove garlic and serve hot.

SERVES: 6

Baggiana

Broad Beans Umbrian Style

To test broad beans for freshness, bend a pod. If it feels rubbery and does not snap promptly, it left the field some time ago.

$2\frac{1}{2}$ lb (1.25 kg) large fresh broad beans
3 tablespoons virgin olive oil
5 oz (155 g) lean bacon, cut in strips $\frac{1}{4}$ in x $1\frac{1}{2}$ in (5 mm x 4 cm)
10 to 12 basil leaves, coarsely chopped
salt and freshly ground black pepper
12 oz (375 g) tomatoes, peeled and quartered, or 1 can peeled tomatoes

Pod the beans. Heat oil in a saucepan and sauté the bacon. Add the broad beans and basil and season with a little salt and pepper.

Cover and cook over moderate heat for 8 to 10 minutes. Add the tomatoes. Let cook a further 30 minutes, uncovered, on low heat, stirring occasionally, until the sauce is reduced and the beans are cooked. Serve hot.

SERVES: 6

Right: Mushrooms and Zucchini with Mint, Broad Beans Umbrian Style

Glistening fresh trout for sale.

RAY JOYCE

PETER JOHNSON

PETER JOHNSON

Zuccotto

Almond and Chocolate Cake

This rich and famous cake is similar in shape to a halved pumpkin, *zucco*, hence its name.

8 oz (250 g) sponge cake or savoiardi *sponge fingers*
Alchermes or Maraschino liqueur
4 cups (2 pt/1 l) heavy (double) cream
2½ oz (75 g) superfine (caster) sugar
1 teaspoon vanilla extract (essence)
¼ cup (1½ oz/45 g) candied mixed fruit, in small pieces
¼ cup (1 oz/30 g) toasted almonds, crushed
2½ oz (75 g) semisweet (plain) chocolate
½ cup hot water
1 tablespoon rum or brandy
¼ cup (1 oz/30 g) walnuts, coarsely crushed
4 oz (125 g) strawberries

Line a large round bowl with wedge-shaped strips of sponge cake or *savoiardi* sponge fingers moistened with a mixture of Alchermes liqueur and water. (Start with equal amounts of Alchermes and water and add water until you consider the flavor to be the right intensity.) Whip ⅓ of the cream and when stiff stir in 1½ oz (45 g) of the sugar and the vanilla extract. Gently fold in the candied fruit and almonds. Spread the mixture in an even layer over the sponge lining and place the bowl in the freezer.

In a double boiler melt 2 oz (60 g) of the chocolate, broken in pieces, with the hot water. Stir in the rum. Whip another ⅓ of the cream and fold into the cooled chocolate sauce, with the walnuts. Spread this mixture evenly over the previous cream layer, and place the bowl again in the freezer.

Mash the strawberries, whip the remaining cream and mix together gently, along with the remaining sugar. With this mixture fill the center of the mold. Store the cake in the freezer, moving it to the fridge 1 hour before serving.

To serve, unmold the cake onto a chilled dish, grating the remaining chocolate over the top.

SERVES: 6 to 8

Almond and Chocolate Cake

Pignoccate alla Perugina

Pine Nut Fondants

These fondants are a specialty from Perugia. They are sold widely during the festive season between the end of November and 6 January.

2 cups (14 oz/440 g) pine nuts
2½ cups (1 lb/500 g) sugar
1 cup (8 fl oz/250 ml) water
1 tablespoon cornstarch (cornflour)
grated rind of 1 lemon or 2 oz (60 g) semisweet (plain) chocolate
rice paper cut in circles about 2 in (5 cm) in diameter (optional)
waxed paper to wrap the fondants

Spread the pine nuts in a baking dish and dry them in an oven set at 150°F (70°C). Dissolve the sugar in the water in a saucepan over moderate heat then bring to a boil, stirring occasionally with a wooden spoon.

Keep cooking the syrup until it becomes white and opaque. (It will be ready when a drop pressed between thumb and forefinger forms a thin bridge of syrup when they are parted.)

Remove the syrup from the heat and add the pine nuts, cornstarch, and lemon rind. (To make chocolate fondants, melt the chocolate in a double boiler with 2 tablespoons of water, then add it to the mixture instead of the lemon rind.)

Using your hands, form the fondant into walnut-sized balls. Place each ball on a rice paper circle, then flatten it to about ½ in (1.5 cm) thick. Let them harden before trimming the rice paper.

If not using rice paper, spread the fondant evenly over a table, preferably marble, to a thickness of about ½ in (1.5 cm) and cut it in diamond shapes before it cools. Wrap the fondants in waxed paper like bonbons.

Serves: 10

Crostata di Pere alla Livornese

Pear Tart from Livorno

This treat of a tart is also know as "the cake with the spirit of Livorno", containing as it does a generous quantity of the well known Galliano liqueur.

5 medium pears, firm and sweet
½ cup (4 fl oz/125 ml) Galliano liqueur
⅔ cup (5 oz/155 g) superfine (caster) sugar
4 oz (125 g) unsalted butter
3 eggs
2 cups (8 oz/250 g) all purpose (plain) flour
salt
1 cup (8 fl oz/250 ml) heavy (double) cream (optional)

Peel the pears and slice thinly. Steep them for several hours in Galliano mixed with half the sugar, turning occasionally.

Soften the butter with the remaining sugar. Stir in 1 egg, the yolk of a second one, the flour and a pinch of salt. Knead the dough well then wrap it in a slightly damp cloth and put it in the fridge for 30 minutes. Butter and flour a 9-in (23-cm) pie pan. Roll the dough out and use ¾ of it to line the pan.

Drain the pears (reserving the liqueur) and fill the pastry case with the slices, partly overlapping them on each concentric circle.

Divide the remaining dough into several pieces and roll these to form "spaghetti" about ¼ in (6 mm) in diameter. Intertwine these in a lattice on top of the pears, gently pressing down at every point where dough meets dough.

Brush the surface of the tart with a whole beaten egg, then bake in oven preheated to 300°F (150°C) until the pastry turns golden. Pour the reserved Galliano evenly over the top and bake a further 3 minutes. Serve lukewarm, with whipped cream if desired.

Serves: 6

Cenci o Nastrini di Monaca

Tuscan Fried Pastries

These little "rags" of pastry, also known as nuns' ribbons or lovers' knots, are a particular favorite at Carnevale.

2 cups (8 oz/250 g) all purpose (plain) flour
1 tablespoon fresh yeast
2 eggs
2 tablespoons superfine (caster) sugar
1 teaspoon aniseed (optional)
pinch of salt
grated rind of 1 orange
1 teaspoon vanilla extract (essence)
3 tablespoons Vin Santo, other sweet white wine or sherry
3 tablespoons unsalted butter, softened
lard or oil for deep frying
powdered (icing) sugar

PETER JOHNSON

In a bowl, mix together the flour, yeast, butter, eggs, sugar, aniseed, salt, orange rind, vanilla extract and Vin Santo until the dough becomes elastic. If it is too stiff, add more wine.

Wrap the dough in a cloth and store in the fridge for 1 hour.

On a work bench sprinkled with flour, roll the pastry until quite thin, then cut it in ribbons ¾ in x 5 in (2 cm x 12 cm.) If you wish, tie the ribbons in lovers' knots.

Heat plenty of lard in a deep fryer and fry 2 or 3 ribbons or knots at a time. When they are golden and puffed-up, drain them well on paper towels and let them cool. Sieve powdered sugar over them and serve either on their own with a dessert wine, or with ice cream or portions of fruit.

SERVES: 6 to 8

Pine Nut Fondants, Pear Tart from Livorno, Tuscan Fried Pastries

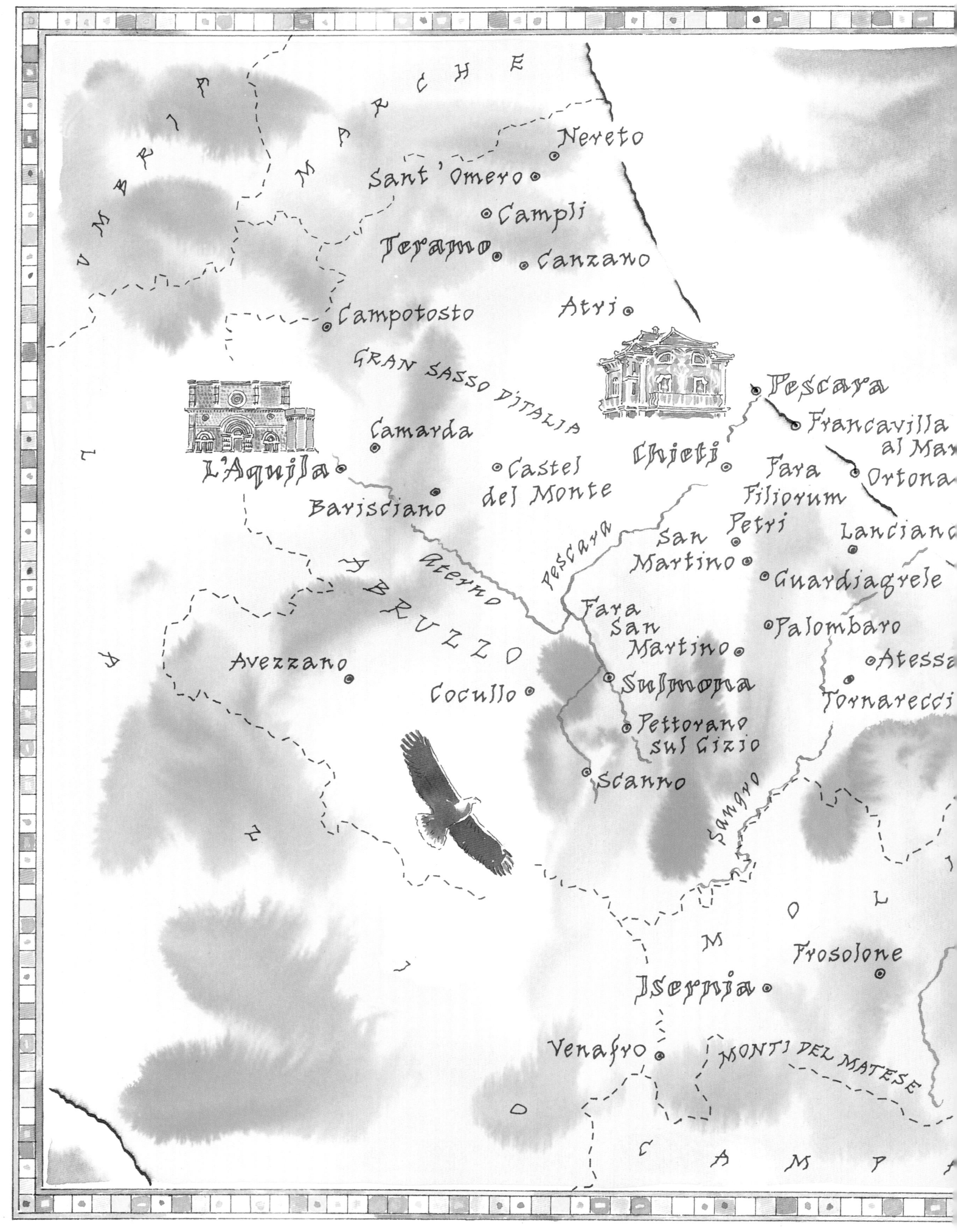

U M B R I A
M A R C H E
Nereto
Sant'Omero
Campli
Teramo
Canzano
Atri
Campotosto
GRAN SASSO D'ITALIA
Pescara
Francavilla al Mare
L'Aquila
Camarda
Castel del Monte
Chieti
Fara Filiorum Petri
Ortona
Barisciano
Pescara
Aterno
San Martino
Lanciano
Guardiagrele
A B R U Z Z O
Fara San Martino
Palombaro
Avezzano
Cocullo
Sulmona
Atessa
Tornareccio
Pettorano sul Gizio
Scanno
Sangro
L A Z I O
M O L I
Frosolone
Isernia
Venafro
MONTI DEL MATESE
C A M P

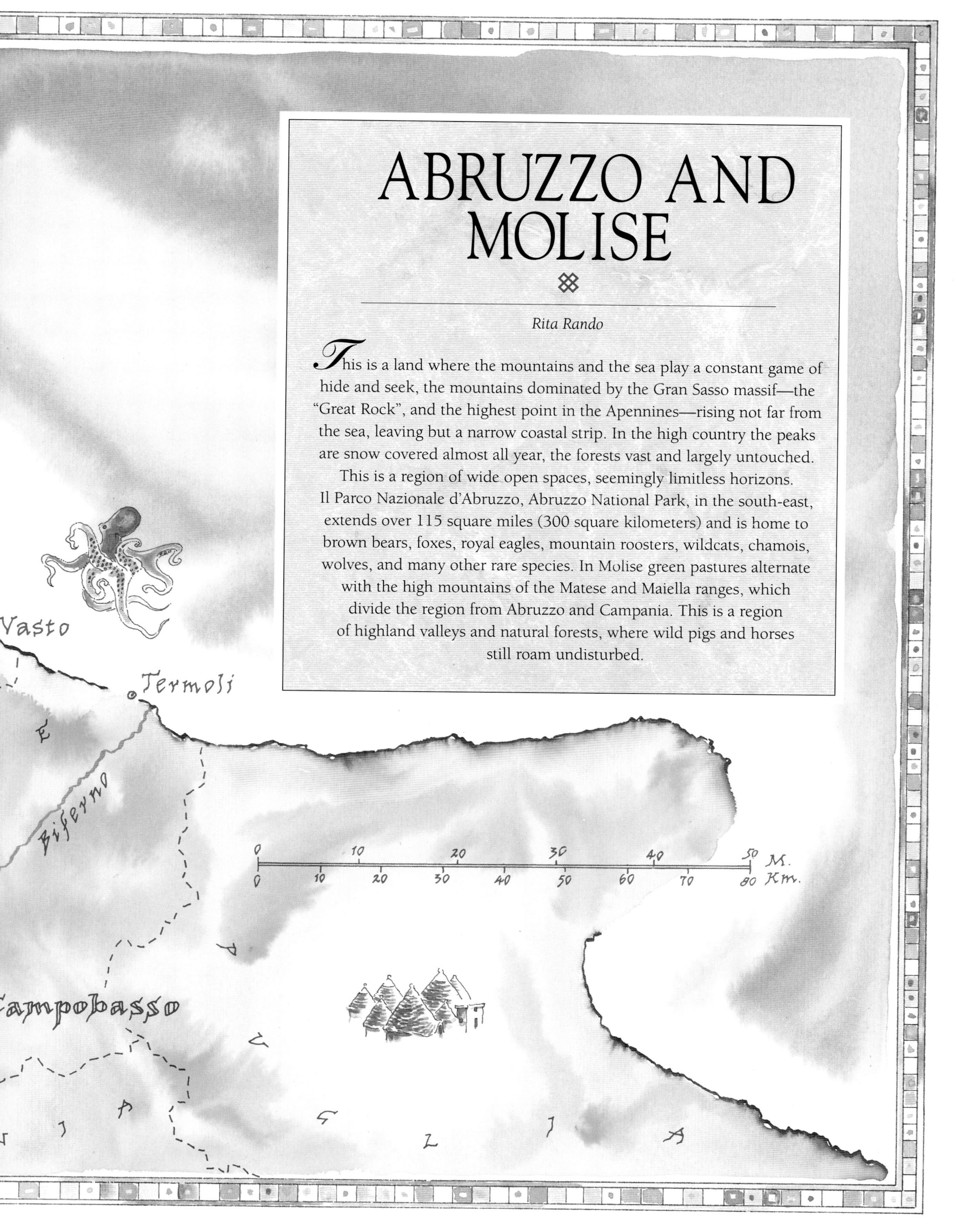

ABRUZZO AND MOLISE

Rita Rando

This is a land where the mountains and the sea play a constant game of hide and seek, the mountains dominated by the Gran Sasso massif—the "Great Rock", and the highest point in the Apennines—rising not far from the sea, leaving but a narrow coastal strip. In the high country the peaks are snow covered almost all year, the forests vast and largely untouched. This is a region of wide open spaces, seemingly limitless horizons. Il Parco Nazionale d'Abruzzo, Abruzzo National Park, in the south-east, extends over 115 square miles (300 square kilometers) and is home to brown bears, foxes, royal eagles, mountain roosters, wildcats, chamois, wolves, and many other rare species. In Molise green pastures alternate with the high mountains of the Matese and Maiella ranges, which divide the region from Abruzzo and Campania. This is a region of highland valleys and natural forests, where wild pigs and horses still roam undisturbed.

S.FIORE/FIOREPRESS

A flock of sheep in the remote mountain country of Abruzzo. In this region the Apennines are at their highest, culminating in the Gran Sasso d'Italia, the Great Rock of Italy.

Historically, socially, economically, and culturally Abruzzo and Molise evolved as one and were considered so until 1963, when they were officially separated and L'Aquila became the capital of Abruzzo, while Campobasso was made the capital of Molise. Abruzzo is derived from the Latin *Aprutium*, while Molise was named after one of its many landlords, the Count of Molise.

After the fall of the Roman Empire, the region suffered a severe cultural and spiritual decline, barbaric invasions forcing the population to take refuge high in the mountains. Conditions began to improve only with the advent of Christianity and the establishment of abbeys and monasteries. In 1140, Ruggero II, king of the two Sicilies, conquered the area and thereafter the region followed this kingdom's fate, until Italy's unification in 1860. Until recently there was little industry and earlier this century it was common for the younger generation to leave home in search of work, some settling in the industrialized regions of Italy, others trying their luck in the Americas, Canada, and Australia.

Today things have changed. Industry, commerce, and tourist activities are on the increase throughout the region. L'Aquila exports saffron, cheeses, truffles, mushrooms, cereals, and meats, its arts and crafts are flourishing, tourists are plentiful and there are are a variety of cultural activities, based mainly on its university. The provinces of Teramo and Chieti export agricultural goods, including wine, olive oil, pasta, and industrial products. There is fishing the length of the coast, with sea trade based in Pescara, which is also an industrial, commercial, and tourist center. All through the summer the port's foreshores are dotted with multicolored umbrellas, and the restaurants, cafés, *gelaterie*, and *trattorie* are buzzing with customers.

BRUCE COLEMAN LTD

Salami, prosciutto, cookies, and cheeses hang together outside a shop in the most mouthwatering display. The people in this part of Italy are particularly fond of cheese.

Straightforward Cooking with Plenty of Chili

Writers of the stature of Ovid, Petronius, and Pliny have attempted to describe the quality of the local cooking. The regions boast a straightforward, tasty cuisine using simple local ingredients, including plenty of chili. Gastronomic training began in 1390 at Villa Santa Maria, between Sulmona and Vasto, when the Lords of Altavilla encouraged some of the local peasants to learn how to cook game. Prince Ferrante Caracciolo purchased the villa in 1560 as his summer house. Hunting was his favorite pastime and after the hunt those who had taken part, the servants, and the cooks all used to get together to hone their game cooking skills. The prince founded a cooking school which to this day continues to produce chefs of international standard trained to keep gastronomic traditions alive.

In Abruzzo and Molise there is a great reverence for the old ways and each family tends to jealously preserve its own recipes. Famous is the collection written by the family of the Duke of Acquaviva, who owned the town of Atri in the fifteenth century. Intended for the not-so-young, the recipes are full of aphrodisiacs, and are guaranteed to perform miracles.

Abruzzo is the country of the *panarda*, a colossal banquet held on special occasions of between thirty-five and forty courses which, understandably, lasts for hours. The *panarda*, the origins of which lie in antiquity, is not so much a meal as a cultural experience. A mixture of hospitality, eroticism, fantasy, and gastronomy, it is intended to stimulate all five senses. Guests are expected to taste at least a bit of each dish, washing it down with local wines, soups, and juices and completing the meal with a glass of Centerbe, an extremely powerful digestive.

Pasta "Perfumed like Flowers"

Undoubtedly the best known dish of the region is *maccheroni alla chitarra*, macaroni guitar style. More than just a dish, these *maccheroni* are supposed to be "fine like hair, light like feathers and perfumed like flowers". Once the dough has been worked to perfection it is rolled flat and cut into sheets the size of the "guitar"—a rectangular wooden box fitted with numerous fine steel strings. Spread over the "guitar", with the help of a rolling pin, the dough is pressed between the wires. The pasta is then cooked and served with one of a variety of sauces, such as *ragù di pecora,* mutton sauce; *all'amatriciana,* bacon, olive oil, and plenty of grated pecorino; *alle polpettine,* with meat balls; and with *aglio, olio e peperoncino,* garlic, oil, and chili. Fish and shellfish sauces are favored in coastal areas.

The *antipasto,* considered an essential overture, is usually composed of: *fellata,* well seasoned ham, at least one year old, produced in Campotosto; *capelome,* a local pork sausage that is seasoned by the fireplace and smoke darkened; *salsicciotto,* a sausage made with twice-ground lean pork; *antipasto di mare,* mixed seafood; and *bruschetta,* thickly sliced bread, toasted on the open fire and served with *olio santo* and chopped garlic and herbs.

Following pages: Scanno, high in the mountains of central Abruzzo, lies blanketed in snow. The town lies on the western border of the Abruzzo National Park.

M. PEDONE/THE IMAGE BANK

Finding Local Specialties

Here are where some of the best regional specialties of Abruzzo and Molise can be found: Saffron from L'Aquila province, around Navelli; pecorino cheese from Atri; cheese with chili from Castel del Monte; *porchetta* from Campli; smoked ham from Canzano; pickled sausages (very spicey!) from Sant'Omero; dried fig sweets and *sanguinaccio* (sausage made with pig's blood) from Chieti; honey from Atessa; preserved olives from Palombaro; confetti from Sulmona; *scamorze* from Tornareccio; pasta from Fara San Martino, and the hot *diavulilli* chilies (little devils) from Lanciano.

Quantities of high quality fruit are produced in the region, available fresh and dried: of particular note are the apples from Camarda, the pears from Scanno, the grapes from Barisciano, the peaches from Piazzano di Atessa, the hazelnuts from the Gran Sasso, and the dried figs from around Teramo and Chieti.

CHARLES C. PLACE/THE IMAGE BANK

Olio santo is extra virgin olive oil seasoned with plenty of hot chili, left to infuse for a week. It can be used on meat, fish, cereals, and salads. This powerful condiment is served everywhere in these regions, but the inexperienced should use it with caution! *Agliata*, garlic oil, is prepared by blending garlic, walnuts, parsley, and basil in a mortar. *Salsa all'aquilana,* made with egg yolk, a pinch of cinnamon, and a few drops of vinegar, is used on boiled meats, and *salsa agli agrumi* is a citrus sauce served with duck.

Scrippelle 'mbusse originated in the area around Teramo, famous for its gastronomy. They are pancakes stuffed with grated pecorino, served in hot chicken consommé. Other superb dishes made with pancakes are *timballo di scrippelle,* pancake lasagna; *scrippelle al forno,* baked pancakes; and *sformato di scrippelle,* which is a pancake pie.

As in all other Italian mountain regions, the people of Abruzzo and Molise eat quantities of polenta, especially in winter. It is generally served with *ragù di maiale,* a pork sauce; *con la lepre,* with hare; *stufata,* with sausages; with chickpeas or with beans. *Polenta con le vongole*, a seaside specialty, is served with clam sauce and *polenta al latte,* cooked in milk, is a variety eaten during Lent.

Soups are popular in winter, lentils, *cannellini* beans, chickpeas, chicory, and chestnuts being common ingredients. The most famous soup of all is the *virtù*, "virtue", traditionally made at the beginning of May. It takes ages to prepare, but is truly delicious. It is made with all available spring vegetables and cereals mixed together with pork cuts, and is served with a variety of home-made pasta.

Pork Lamb and Game

Porchetta, roast piglet, is another local delicacy the origins of which go back to Roman times. Its preparation must be left in the capable hands of a *porchettaro,* a *porchetta* cook, who will know exactly how to "marry" the piglet with the right aromatic herbs from the local mountains. Pork meat holds a place of honor in the Abruzzo and Molise gastronomy, being used for ham, bacon, salami, lard, *coppa, lonza, soppressa,* and many different kinds of sausages (a visit to any local butcher's shop, a *norcinerie,* will provide ample illustration). Every part of the animal is used for one thing or another: liver with the addition of chili makes a sausage called *fegato pazzo,* crazy liver, while a touch of honey turns it into *fegato dolce,* sweet liver. *'Ndocca 'ndocca* is a winter-time Teramo specialty, consisting of various parts of the pig, including the feet and the ears, boiled with herbs and tomato.

Lamb is cooked in a variety of ways, seasoned with local herbs and spices. Famous dishes include *agnello cacio e uova,* lamb stew with cheese and eggs; *bracioline d'agnello,* baby lamb chops; *agnello in fricassea,* fricassee of lamb, and *agnello alla pecorara,* lamb casserole. *Castrato,* mutton, once considered an inferior meat, has now gained respect and is used to prepare many tasty dishes including the famous *ragù abruzzese*, a perfect accompaniment to *maccheroni alla chitarra.*

Game of all sorts is popular, made particularly flavorsome through the aromatic herbs they eat. Goat meat is generally roasted, cooked on the spit, or casseroled with plenty of olive oil and white wine. Turkeys are fed with walnuts, and attended to with tender loving care until they are ready to eat. *Tacchino alla canzanese* is cooked with oil, salt, pepper, laurel leaves, rosemary, and sage and served cold; *tacchino alla nerese* is roasted open on the spit to let the inside cook to perfection. Ducks are cooked simply with lard and lemon juice or with local

JOHN BULMER/SUSAN GRIGGS AGENCY

A farmer's wife busy making pasta. In the country home-made pasta is still common, using eggs from the family chickens.

truffles and bacon. *Coniglio affogato alla molisana*, skewered rabbit with sausages; *coniglio uova e limone,* rabbit with eggs and lemon; *coniglio ripieno alla chietina,* stuffed rabbit; and *pollo all'abruzzese,* chicken with tomatoes and bell peppers, are all dishes with a typically local flavor.

Frittate, omelettes, are made with a variety of ingredients such as carrots, spinach, *scamorza*, and bacon. *Frittata pazza,* crazy omelette, is a specialty of Fontavignone in which milk and flour are added to the eggs in order to give the dish more bulk. *Frittata maritata* is a tasty mixture of eggs, sausages, *scamorza*, pieces of tuna, and chopped anchovies, and there is the *frittata al basilico,* basil omelette, from Teramo. *Frittata con le cipolle,* onion omelette, is a hearty breakfast for those who work in the fields.

Fish and seafood abound along the Abruzzo and Molise coastline, Vasto being famous for its *scapece,* fish steaks with vinegar and saffron—the only local dish to use saffron—and *polpi in purgatorio,* octopus stew. In the interior freshwater fish such as trout and tench can be found, generally served broiled or baked, and you can have *rane fritte*, fried frogs. Dried cod, *stoccafisso*, imported from Norway since ancient times, is used according to equally old recipes.

From the Past

In praise of the local cheese, the famous writer Gabriele d'Annunzio, who was born in Pescara, once wrote "the flavor of the Maiella [a local mountain] is all in our cacio pecorino".

Quajata is a form of junket made in Abruzzo, and on Ascension Day morning a festive version of this called *cacio ricotta* is made and religiously eaten before anything else. Milk is at its best at this time of year, and the *quajata*, considered auspicious, is offered to friends, neighbors, and notables. Locals once believed that Christ came back on the night before Ascension Day to bless the land, and they would leave all the things they wanted blessed out on the window-sill.

Local sausages are very tasty and around Epiphany, children once went from house to house asking for presents, singing: *"Se me la dai la saucicella, te canto la pasquarella"*. ("If you give me the little broiled sausage / I'll sing you a song".)

Another little rhyme the children would have chanted is dedicated to the *bruschetta,* bread baked in *olio santo* and flavored with herbs and garlic.

Quant'è bona la bruschetta
da n'aghittu profumata,
vocca mea! Ma n'accetta
l'arca nostra l'à spaccata.

("How good is the *bruschetta* / flavored with garlic, / mouth, open up / and cut it in two.")

Sweets and Cheeses

The preparation of sweets, unlike the rest of the local cuisine, tends to be extremely elaborate, as can be seen with the *torrone*, king of them all, a delicious chewy concoction of honey, sugar, almonds, and egg whites. *Parrozzo,* a dessert from Pescara, was originally a dish for the poor made from cornmeal, but it is now a sought-after delicacy made with almonds and chocolate bearing little resemblance to the original recipe. The *cicerchiata* of Chieti are sweets shaped like chickpeas, made with honey; *fiadone* and *siffioni* are Easter pastry cakes filled with ricotta; *pizza ripiena alla crema e marmellata di lamponi* is a sweet pizza filled with fresh custard and raspberry jelly; *pane dell'orso,* bear's bread, is a sweet bread made with plenty of honey from Scanno. Teramo is famous for its sweets like the *pepatelli,* which are cookies made with lots of honey, almonds, orange rind, and pepper, which gives them their name. Sulmona produces beautiful sugared almonds and *mostaccioli,* little chocolate-covered cakes.

King of the local cheeses is the pecorino, used as a dessert cheese (it is delicious eaten with pears), a filling for many dishes and grated on pasta. The best pecorino is Gentile di Puglia, produced from sheep which in the summer graze on the highlands of the Gran Sasso and Maiella and in the winter on the plains of Puglia. Among the fresh cheeses are mozzarella, and *scamorza,* a dried version of mozzarella which is roasted on the open fire, and mountain ricotta.

Right: At festival time a rock provides a convenient place for this woman to sit, a tranquil figure in black. Below: Farming country on the coastal plain, not far from the town of Atri.

FOTO MAIRANI/SPERANZA

REGINA MARIA ANZENBERGER

Young women wearing the most elaborate traditional costumes, taking part in festivities in Cocullo in L'Aquila.

DEFILIPPIS/FOREPRESS

Festivals Year Round

The local calendar lists many festivals, celebrations which are not organized just to bring in the tourists, but because the people of Abruzzo and Molise really enjoy food and socializing and wish to keep their traditions alive. The festival year begins on 17 January at Fara Filiorum Petri in Chieti with the Festival of the Farchie, and ends on 31 December in Pettorano sul Gizio where everyone enjoys polenta and sausages. In between there are a variety of saint's day festivals, and festivals commemorating all sorts of produce, such as endive, cherries, grapes, lamb, and turkey. Perhaps the most intriguing of all is the Processione dei Serpari, the Procession of the Snake Charmers, which takes place at Cocullo in L'Aquila on the first Thursday in May. The saint's statue, covered with snakes, is carried in procession followed by shepherds who are also covered with live snakes. Snake-shaped cakes called *cervone* and *serpente dolce* are especially made and sold for the occasion. Whatever the season, the visitor is bound to find celebrations to join and feasts in which to share.

VIGOROUS WINES

The people of Abruzzo and Molise love their vigorous wines, and even on religious occasions it is considered appropriate to indulge. In many centers, on Corpus Domini Day, little wine fountains are set up by households along the way to sustain the people taking part in the long procession. The success of the proceedings is measured by the number of drunks at the end of the day.

The best red wine is without doubt the Montepulciano d'Abruzzo, but the Marsicano is also a good dry red. Cerasuolo d'Abruzzo is a dry, soft rosé, Trebbiano d'Abruzzo, also known as Abruzzo Bianco, yellow in color, is dry and fresh with a certain bitterness. Biferno (white, red, and rosé) and Pentro di Isernia (white and red) are produced in Molise. Among liqueurs Centerbe, meaning "one hundred herbs", is unique and mighty powerful, being 70 per cent proof. It is considered an excellent remedy for colds and other maladies. Another famous specialty is the liqueur Aurum, produced in Pescara. Many households still make their own liqueurs using old family recipes. Similarly, local abbeys and monasteries, as in many other regions in Italy, produce a number of wines, liqueurs and amari.

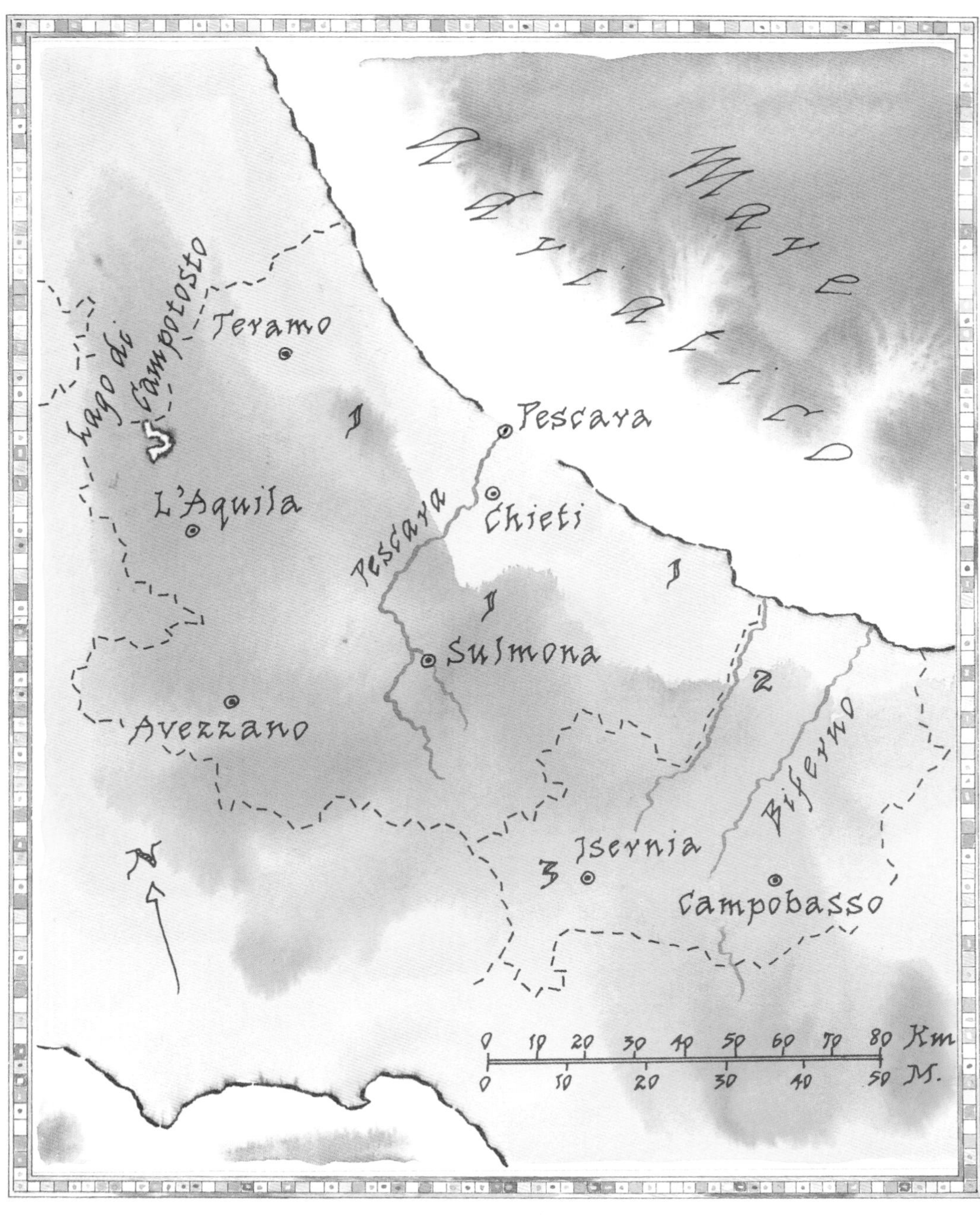

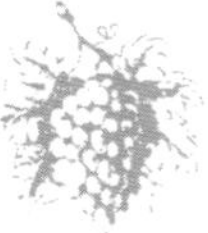

ABRUZZO

DOC WINES

1. Montepulciano d'Abruzzo
1. Trebbiano d'Abruzzo

OTHER WINES

Rubino

MOLISE

DOC WINES

2. Biferno
3. Pentro

OTHER WINES

Bianco del Molise
Montepulciano del Molise
Ramitello

RECIPES OF ABRUZZO AND MOLISE

Don Andrea Scirè Borghese and Donna Marisa Borghese

PETER JOHNSON

Zuppa di Lenticchie alla Montanara

Lentil Soup

This soup has for generations warmed up the nights of Abruzzo highlanders.

2½ cups (1 lb/500 g) lentils
30 to 40 fresh chestnuts
salt and freshly ground black pepper
5 bay leaves
9 tablespoons virgin olive oil
4 oz (125 g) salt pork or streaky bacon, chopped
1 teaspoon dried marjoram, crushed or powdered
3 tablespoons chopped basil
2½ tablespoons tomato paste
6 to 8 slices Italian country-style bread, or French bread, toasted
1 cup (4 oz/120 g) freshly grated Parmesan cheese

Soak the lentils in enough water to cover them for 12 hours. Stir and discard the ones that come to the surface. Drain. With a sharp knife, cut the rounded part of the outer skin of the chestnuts. Spread them in a shallow baking tray and place in oven preheated to 350°F (180°C) for about 30 minutes or until cooked. Peel the outer and inner skins, break the chestnuts into small pieces and set aside.

Place the lentils in a medium pot and fill it with cold water to about 4 times the volume of the lentils. Add a generous pinch of salt, a teaspoon of pepper and the bay leaves. Cover and bring to a boil. Lower the heat and cook until the lentils are tender (30 to 40 minutes). Turn off the heat. Remove and discard the bay leaves. Keep the pot covered.

Heat 3 tablespoons oil in a small pan over a low heat and sauté the salt pork without crisping it. Add the marjoram, basil, chestnuts and the tomato paste dissolved in ½ cup of the water in which the lentils were cooked. Stir well and cook until the sauce has reduced.

Reheat the lentils, add the sauce and cook over moderate heat for 20 minutes. Check the seasoning. Pour the soup into individual bowls over a bed of toast and pour a tablespoon of olive oil into each serving. Serve with grated Parmesan.

SERVES: 6

Lentil Soup, Maccheroni alla Chitarra with Lamb, Spaghettini Abruzzo Style

Maccheroni alla Chitarra con l' Agnello

Maccheroni alla Chitarra with Lamb

This pasta is formed by pressing the rolled dough with a rolling pin through a frame of many parallel steel wires. Excellent commercial varieties are made in Abruzzo and exported world-wide. Traditionally, this dish is served as a *piatto unico*, a meal in one plate.

3 lb (1.25 kg) lean lamb
1¼ cups (10 fl oz/310 ml) dry white wine
salt and freshly ground black pepper
1 cup (8 fl oz/250 ml) virgin olive oil
4 garlic cloves, lightly crushed
5 bay leaves
2 lb (1 kg) tomatoes, peeled and coarsely chopped, or 2 cans peeled tomatoes
6 large bell peppers (capsicums) preferably 2 yellow, 2 green and 2 red, seeded and cut into ½-in (1-cm) strips
2 cups (16 fl oz/500 ml) vegetable or beef broth (stock)
1 lb 6 oz (685 g) pasta alla chitarra
¾ cup (3 oz/90 g) freshly grated Parmesan cheese

Cut out and put aside the less appealing parts of the meat to a total weight of about 1 lb (500 g) and grind in a food processor. Cut the rest of the meat into generous bite-size pieces. Rinse the meat in the wine (which should be reserved) then sprinkle with salt and pepper.

Heat the oil in a wide, heavy saucepan and sauté the garlic and bay leaves over moderate heat. When the garlic is golden brown remove it and set aside. Add the ground meat and the meat pieces and brown evenly, turning as necessary. Add the wine and cook until it evaporates. Remove and discard the bay leaves. Add the tomatoes (or canned ones with their juice), bell peppers and reserved garlic. Season with salt and pepper and cover. Cook for 2 hours over moderate heat, stirring from time to time. Should the sauce become too dry, add a ladle or so of broth.

Cook the pasta in plenty of boiling salted water until barely *al dente*, then drain. Return it to the cooking pot, pour over the sauce and stir gently over moderate heat for 2 minutes. Serve immediately, on a large serving dish, sprinkled with the Parmesan.

SERVES: 6 to 8

Spaghettini all'Abruzzese

Spaghettini Abruzzo Style

The rich flavor of this dish is achieved using simple ingredients that are available in practically every household in the mountains of Abruzzo.

15 to 18 very thin slices of salt pork or streaky bacon cut in squares ¾ in x ¾ in (2 cm x 2 cm)
5 white onions, finely chopped or ground in a food processor
3 garlic cloves, finely chopped or ground in a food processor
1¼ lb (625 g) spaghettini *(a thin variety of spaghetti)*
salt
¼ cup (2 fl oz/60 ml) extra virgin olive oil
½ cup (2 oz/60 g) freshly grated pecorino cheese
½ cup (2 oz/60 g) freshly grated Parmesan cheese
2 tablespoons chopped parsley

Sauté the salt pork in a heavy skillet (without adding any other fat) together with the onion and garlic. Cook over moderate heat, stirring occasionally with a wooden spoon, until the onions and garlic turn light gold. Remove from heat.

Cook the *spaghettini* in plenty of boiling salted water until *al dente*, then drain. Place the sauce in the pan in which the pasta was cooked. Warm it up, then add the *spaghettini*.

Over moderate to high heat, toss the pasta in the sauce for 2 minutes. Remove from heat, mix in the oil and cheeses, then the parsley. Serve at once in warmed soup bowls.

SERVES: 6

Cicoriella a Cacio e Uova

Endive Soup with Cheese and Eggs

The endive (chicory) gives a slightly bitter taste to this soup. In Abruzzo it is made from freshly-picked wild chicory. Good results can also be achieved using the cultivated species, but shop around to find the youngest and freshest available.

2 lb (1 kg) young fresh endive (chicory)
salt
4 oz (125 g) salt pork or streaky bacon, finely chopped or ground in a food processor
4 white onions, finely chopped or ground in a food processor
4 eggs
¾ cup (3 oz/90 g) freshly grated Parmesan cheese, or if stronger taste is preferred, blend ½ Parmesan and ½ pecorino
4 cups (2 pt/1 l) meat and chicken broth (stock)

Place the endive in a pot of lightly salted boiling water. Depending on how young the endive is, it will take between 10 and 25 minutes to cook. Drain in a colander, then squeeze out the excess water with your hands. Cut in small pieces and put to one side.

Sauté the salt pork and onion in a large skillet until the onions become a golden brown color. Over low heat, add the chopped endive and simmer for 5 minutes, stirring constantly.

In a bowl, beat the eggs and add the Parmesan. Bring the broth to a boil in a large pot, pour in the egg and cheese mixture, stirring continuously with a metal whisk. Add the endive, then check the seasoning. Lower the heat a little and keep whisking for a further 2 to 3 minutes. Serve hot, with crusty country-style bread.

SERVES: 6

Endive Soup with Cheese and Eggs

PETER JOHNSON

PETER JOHNSON

Fish Stew Pescara Style

Guazzetto alla Marinara alla Pescarese

Fish Stew Pescara Style

This dish, traditionally cooked in an earthenware pot, is eaten with a spoon, like soup.

1 cup (8 fl oz/250 ml) virgin olive oil
4 garlic cloves, halved
3 tablespoons chopped parsley
salt
pinch of dried crushed hot red chili pepper (optional)
3 tablespoons white wine vinegar
handful of baby clams and/or 12 mussels, in shell, rinsed and cleaned, beards removed
3 lb (1.5 kg) fillets and cutlets of 4 different white fish varieties, such as bass, cod, flounder, mackerel, red mullet, perch, sole and whiting, skinned and boned as much as practicable and cut into large pieces, heads kept for broth (stock)
2 cuttlefish or squid, cleaned and cut into ½-in (1-cm) rings
12 large shrimp (king prawns), peeled and cleaned, heads kept for broth (stock)
1 small lobster (optional), flesh divided into 6 pieces

Place 6 cups (3 pt/1.5 l) water and the oil in a large pot. Add the garlic and parsley (keeping aside 2 tablespoons), a pinch of salt and, if desired, the chili. Rinse the fish and shrimp heads and add them to the pot. Place over low heat, covered, and simmer for 30 minutes, stirring occasionally. Add the vinegar, clams and/or mussels. Cook for 5 minutes then strain the broth into a bowl through a fine sieve or through muslin. Keep aside the clams and/or mussels. Discard the fish and shrimp heads and garlic. Check the broth for seasoning.

Pour broth back into the pot and bring it to a boil. Add the fish pieces, cuttlefish, shrimp, lobster, clams and/or mussels. Cook, covered, over medium heat for 10 minutes. Using a perforated spoon, distribute the fish and seafood evenly between 6 bowls. Place the mollusks and lobster on top. Spoon over the reduced broth and sprinkle with the remaining parsley. Serve at once.

SERVES: 6

Pollo all'Abruzzese

Chicken Casserole

Throughout southern Italy peppers, both sweet and hot, are used in many recipes.

3 large bell peppers (capsicums), preferably yellow or green
1 cup (8 fl oz/250 ml) virgin olive oil
2 large onions, coarsely chopped
4 to 6 lb (2 to 3 kg) chicken pieces
salt
pinch of dried crushed hot red chili pepper
2 large celery stalks, sliced
1½ cups (12 fl oz/375 ml) dry white wine
1 lb (500 g) canned tomatoes, with juice

Broil (grill) the bell peppers under high heat, turning often. When evenly charred remove from heat, cover and cool. Peel, cut in half and discard core and seeds. Wipe clean, if necessary, with a paper towel, but avoid rinsing. Cut in ½-in (1-cm) juliennes. Set aside.

Heat the oil in a large shallow casserole and sauté the onions until pale gold. Add the chicken pieces and brown on both sides. Season with salt and chili. Add the celery and wine and cook, turning the chicken pieces once, until most of the wine has evaporated. Add the tomatoes and juice, breaking the tomatoes open.

Cover and cook over low heat for about 30 minutes. Add the bell peppers. Stir the sauce and turn the chicken pieces over. Check the seasoning. Cook, uncovered, until the chicken is tender and the sauce has reduced (15 to 20 minutes). Serve hot.

SERVES: 8 to 10

Coniglio Affogato alla Molisana

Skewers of Rabbit and Pork Sausage

Aromatic wood on the barbecue gives the meat additional flavor.

1 large rabbit (3 to 4 lb/1.5 to 2 kg)
1½ cups (12 fl oz/375 ml) white wine vinegar
80 to 90 large fresh sage leaves
4 large fresh rosemary sprigs, leaves stripped from 2 and finely chopped
salt and freshly ground black pepper
3 tablespoons chopped parsley
20 large thin slices prosciutto
12 Italian-style pork sausages, not too thick
¾ cup (6 fl oz/180 ml) virgin olive oil

PETER JOHNSON

Chicken Casserole, Skewers of Rabbit and Pork Sausage

Remove the rabbit meat from the bones and cut it into bite-size pieces. In a large bowl mix the vinegar with an equal amount of water. Add 12 sage leaves and the 2 rosemary sprigs. Season with a pinch of salt and a generous amount of pepper and stir well. Add the rabbit to the marinade and leave for 12 to 24 hours in the fridge, turning from time to time. Drain.

Sprinkle the rabbit pieces with salt and pepper, half the parsley and the chopped rosemary. Wrap each piece in a slice of prosciutto. If the prosciutto slices are very long, halve them. Cut each sausage into 3.

Alternate the rabbit and sausage on the skewers, placing a sage leaf between them. Allow at least 2 skewers per person, each with about 3 rabbit pieces and 3 sausage pieces, plus 1 extra to allow you to taste the meat and determine when it is cooked.

Brush the skewers with oil and cook on a barbecue, basting occasionally with oil and turning often. Sprinkle with parsley and serve at once.

SERVES: 6

Peperoni Arrostiti coi Diavoletti

Broiled Bell Peppers with Garlic and Chili

Try these peppers also as a snack, served on toasted slices of country-style bread.

6 large bell peppers (capsicums) preferably mixed yellow, orange, green and red
2 garlic cloves, finely chopped
16 fresh basil leaves, preferably small-leafed variety
salt
2 teaspoons finely sliced rings of fresh hot red chili pepper, or 1 teaspoon dried crushed hot red chili pepper
$\frac{3}{4}$ cup (6 fl oz/180 ml) extra virgin olive oil

Broil (grill) the bell peppers under high heat, turning often. When evenly charred remove from heat, cover and cool. Peel, cut in half and discard core and seeds. Wipe clean, if necessary, with a paper towel, but avoid rinsing. Cut in $\frac{1}{2}$-in (1-cm) juliennes. Place in a mixing bowl. Add the garlic and 10 of the basil leaves, cut in narrow strips. (Place the unused basil leaves in a glass of cold water to prevent them wilting.) Season with salt and chili.

Pour the oil over the peppers and mix well, using your hands. Leave the peppers in the dressing for a few hours to absorb the flavors. Drain the oil through a fine sieve and store it for use in other dishes.

Either serve the peppers in a bowl or arrange them in a circular, shallow serving dish, the strips like rays of the sun emanating from the center, the colors alternating. Over the top spread the garlic and chili recovered from the sieve. Decorate with basil.

SERVES: 6

PETER JOHNSON

Broiled Mushrooms

Funghi alla Brutta

Broiled Mushrooms

The people of Abruzzo use wild mushrooms for this recipe and grill them over charcoal, but good results can be obtained with large cultivated mushrooms, broiled.

1 or 2 very large flat mushrooms per person, stalks removed, cleaned and only peeled if skin is very leathery
3 tablespoons finely chopped parsley
3 garlic cloves, finely chopped
salt
1 teaspoon dried crushed hot red chili pepper
$1\frac{1}{2}$ to 2 fl oz (40 to 60 ml) extra virgin olive oil

Place the mushrooms, stalk side up, in a large shallow baking tray. Mix together the parsley and garlic and spread evenly over the mushrooms. Season with salt and chili.

Pour $1\frac{1}{2}$ teaspoons oil over each mushroom, distributing it evenly. (Use only 1 teaspoon of oil if the mushrooms are quite small.) Place under a preheated broiler (grill) and broil under high heat for about 10 minutes. Serve hot.

SERVES: 6

PETER JOHNSON

Broiled Bell Peppers with Garlic and Chili, Abruzzo Style Salad

Insalata all'Abruzzese

Abruzzo Style Salad

This salad can be served as a side dish or as a main course for a summer lunch. For a main course, increase the quantity of tuna to 1 lb (500 g).

2 white onions, sliced thinly
20 fresh basil leaves, preferably small-leafed variety, cut in narrow strips
3 or 4 tablespoons wine vinegar
6 to 8 tablespoons virgin olive oil
pinch of dried crushed hot red chili pepper
generous pinch of ground oregano
1 small can ($1\frac{1}{2}$ oz/45 g) anchovy fillets, cut in $\frac{1}{2}$-in (1-cm) pieces
5 oz (155 g) canned tuna, in oil
8 oz (250 g) green beans, trimmed
3 or 4 tomatoes, peeled, seeded and cut into discs or wedges
2 large bell peppers (capsicums), yellow, orange or red, seeded and cut in $\frac{1}{4}$-in (5-mm) strips
4 to 6 small to medium zucchini (courgettes), trimmed

Place the onions rings and basil in a bowl of cold water and put in the fridge. Place the vinegar, oil, chili and oregano in a medium-sized bowl. Stir well. Add the anchovies and tuna. Stir gently and put to one side.

Cook the beans in boiling salted water until *al dente* (approximately 10 minutes). Drain and dip in cold water, to retain their color. Place in a large bowl with the tomatoes and bell peppers.

Cook the zucchini in boiling salted water for 6 minutes. Drain, cool and cut them in $\frac{1}{2}$-in (1-cm) slices. Add to the other vegetables.

Drain the onion and basil (reserving 2 tablespoons of basil) and add to the vegetables. Pour the dressing on top and toss gently with your hands.

Transfer to a serving dish and sprinkle with reserved basil.

SERVES: 6

Cassata di Sulmona

Cassata Sulmona Style

The name *cassata* can easily be confused with the well-known ice cream, which should really be called *cassata gelata*.

7 oz (220 g) unsalted butter
4 very fresh egg yolks
1 cup (5 oz/155 g) powdered (icing) sugar
$1\frac{1}{2}$ oz (45 g) unsweetened cocoa powder
$1\frac{1}{2}$ oz (45 g) semisweet (plain) chocolate, chopped to coffee bean size or smaller
2 oz (60 g) torrone *(white nougat with almonds and/or hazelnuts), chopped to coffee bean size or smaller*
1 teaspoon vanilla extract (essence)
2 oz (60 g) croccante *(a crunchy bar of caramelized sugar and almonds), chopped to coffee bean size or smaller*
1 round pan di spagna *sponge cake (see* Zuppa Inglese *recipe page 184)*
$\frac{1}{3}$ cup (3 fl oz/90 ml) Centerbe liqueur from Abruzzo, or Strega combined with 2 teaspoons green mint syrup
powdered (icing) sugar and 12 candied cherries for decoration

Soften the butter a little (leaving it near a heat source) then beat it in a large mixing bowl until creamy. Add 1 egg yolk and mix it well with the butter, then add $\frac{1}{4}$ of the sugar and blend it in. Repeat this procedure 3 times, mixing in the remaining yolks and sugar. It is important not to add an ingredient until the previous one has been perfectly amalgamated. (Using a powerful electric mixer will make this whole process less strenuous.)

Divide the mixture between 3 mixing bowls. Into the first stir the cocoa powder. Into the second stir the chocolate and *torrone*. Into the third stir the vanilla extract, then the *croccante*. In an additional bowl place 2 generous tablespoons of each flavored mixture. Blend well and set aside. (This will be used as the topping.)

Slice the sponge cake to obtain 4 discs and put the bottom one on a serving dish. Dilute the liqueur to your taste and sprinkle ¼ of it on this slice, covering it evenly with the vanilla and *croccante* cream. Place the second slice of sponge on top and press down lightly. Sprinkle with ¼ of the liqueur and cover it evenly with the cocoa cream. Place the third slice on top and press down lightly. Sprinkle with ¼ of the liqueur and cover it evenly with the chocolate and *torrone* cream. Place the final slice on top and sprinkle with the remaining liqueur.

Evenly cover the top and sides of the cake with the reserved topping cream, smoothing it with a spatula repeatedly dipped in hot water.

Cover the cake and store in the fridge overnight, or at least for several hours. (If you have no cake cover a loose-fitting one made with aluminum foil will do.) Before serving, sieve some powdered sugar over the cake and decorate it with candied cherries.

SERVES: 6 to 8

Castagne al Cucchiaio

Chestnut and Chocolate Pudding

A glass of brandy is an ideal accompaniment to this rich cold dessert.

2 lb (1 kg) shiny chestnuts (shiny ones are easier to peel)
salt
3 bay leaves
6 oz (185 g) semisweet (plain) chocolate, broken up and melted
¾ cup (6 oz/185 g) superfine (caster) sugar
6 oz (185 g) unsalted butter
1 cup (8 fl oz/250 ml) heavy (double) cream
½ oz (15 g) semisweet (plain) chocolate for grating

Place the chestnuts in a saucepan and cover with cold water. Season with a generous pinch of salt and the bay leaves. Bring to a boil. Cover and simmer, over low heat, until cooked (about 1 hour). Drain, peel whilst still hot, then purée them, rubbing them through a fine sieve or using a mouli.

Warm the purée in a saucepan, stirring constantly, and add the chocolate, sugar and butter. Remove from heat and work the paste well with a wooden spoon.

Butter and flour a medium-sized rectangular cake pan and line it with buttered waxed (greaseproof) paper.

LEO MEIER

Chestnuts prior to harvesting.

Spoon the mixture into the mold, taking care not to leave any air pockets. Store in the coldest part of the fridge (but not in the freezer) for at least 4 hours.

Turn the pudding out onto a serving dish and, using a forcing bag, surround it with whipped cream. If you wish, decorate with grated chocolate.

SERVES: 6

Parrozzo Abruzzese

Almond and Chocolate Cake

This simple and delicate cake from Pescara is delicious served with sweetened whipped cream flavored with Amaretto liqueur.

¾ cup (4 oz/125 g) blanched almonds
6 bitter almonds (optional)
⅔ cup (5 oz/155 g) superfine (caster) sugar
¾ cup (3 oz/90 g) all purpose (plain) flour
½ cup (2 oz/60 g) potato flour
4 oz (125 g) unsalted butter
5 large eggs, separated
2 teaspoons vanilla extract (essence)
5 oz (155 g) semisweet (plain) chocolate

Put the almonds (making sure they are dry) in a blender with 3 tablespoons sugar and pulverize them. Mix this powder with the flour and potato flour.

Melt butter in a small saucepan over very low heat and let it cool a little. Preheat the oven to 350°F (180°C).

Place the egg yolks, vanilla extract and remaining sugar in a large mixing bowl and beat vigorously with a wooden spoon until they treble in volume. In a second bowl beat the egg whites, using a metal whisk, until stiff. Gradually combine the nut mixture with the yolks, stirring continuously with a wooden spoon. Stir in the melted butter, then gently fold in the egg whites. Pour the mixture into a buttered and floured 9-in (23-cm) cake ring or pan and bake until it has risen and the top is firm and golden (about 40 minutes). Let the cake cool then turn out onto a serving dish.

Break the chocolate in pieces and melt it, with a tablespoon of water, in a double boiler, then stir in the remaining tablespoon of butter. Spread evenly over the top and sides of the cake. Top with whipped cream.

SERVES: 6

Pepatelli Ricche

Pepper Cookies

These chewy cookies have quite a fiery flavor and are not recommended for children. They make an excellent accompaniment to a glass of dessert wine.

3¼ cups (2 lb/1 kg) honey
2 cups (10 oz/315 g) blanched almonds, slivered or sliced
1¼ cups (5 oz/155 g) pine nuts
1¼ cups (5 oz/155 g) walnuts, coarsely crushed
grated rind of 2 oranges
1 tablespoon vanilla extract (essence)
3 to 6 teaspoons ground white pepper
3½ cups (1 lb/500 g) stoneground wholewheat (wholemeal) flour
1½ tablespoons butter or margarine to coat mold and baking tray

Warm the honey in a saucepan over moderate heat and stir occasionally until it boils. Lower the heat and add the almonds, pine nuts, walnuts, orange rind, vanilla extract and pepper. (Vary the amount of pepper to suit your taste.) Stir well. Gradually add enough flour, stirring continuously, to obtain a firm mixture.

Lightly butter a baking tray 8 in (20 cm) square. In this spread out the dough, flattening the surface with a wet spatula. When cold unmold and cut into slices 2 x 1½ in (5 x 4 cm), using a knife moistened in hot water.

Place the cookies on a large buttered baking tray and cook in oven preheated to 350°F (180°C) for about 30 minutes. Serve cold. Store in an airtight container.

SERVES: 10

Following pages: Chestnut and Chocolate Pudding, Cassata Sulmona Style, Pepper Cookies, Almond and Chocolate Cake

PETER JOHNSON

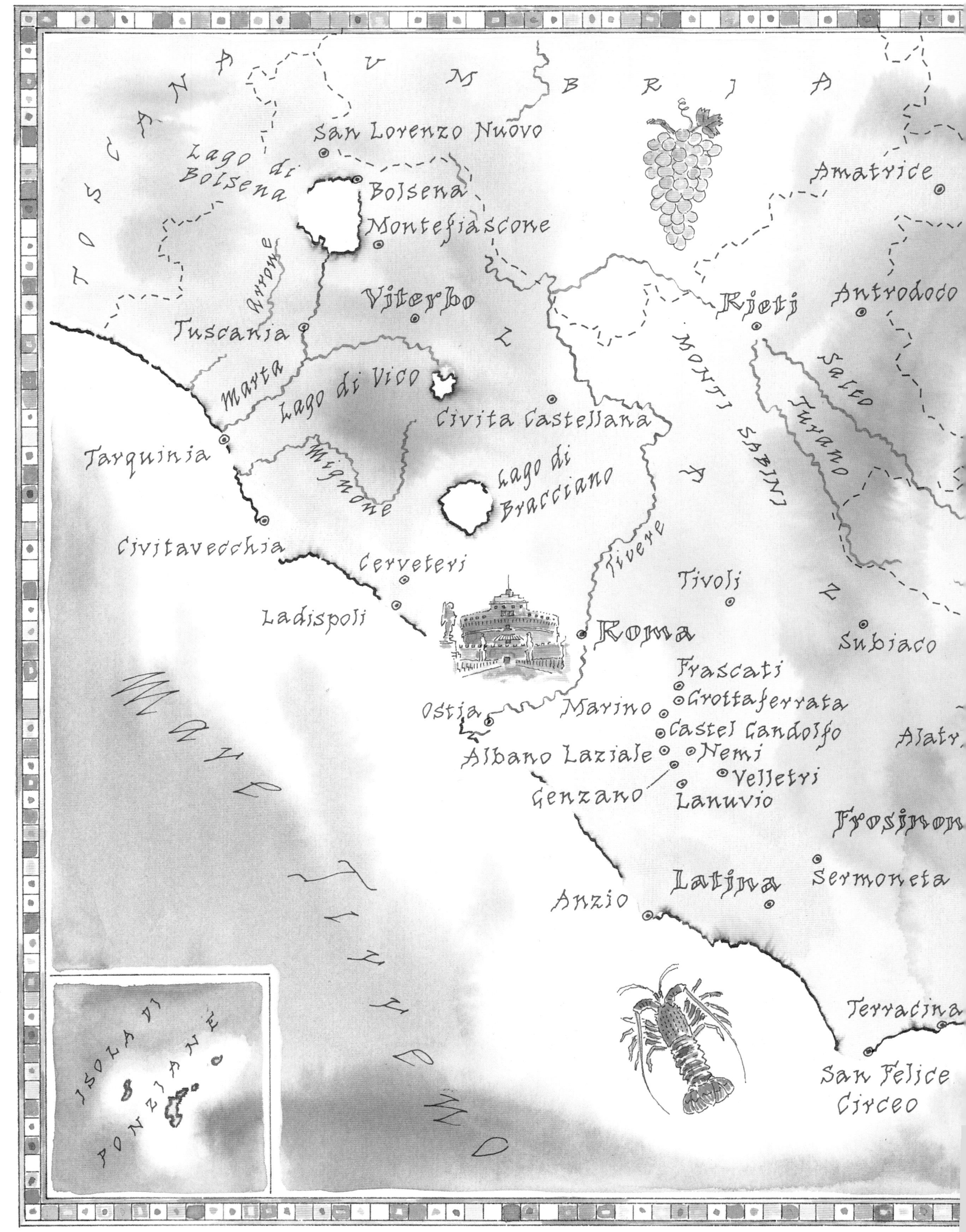

T O S C A N A
U M B R I A
L A Z
San Lorenzo Nuovo
Lago di Bolsena
Bolsena
Montefiascone
Amatrice
Arrone
Viterbo
Tuscania
Rieti
Antrodoco
Marta
Lago di Vico
Monti Sabini
Salto
Turano
Civita Castellana
Tarquinia
Mignone
Lago di Bracciano
Civitavecchia
Cerveteri
Tevere
Tivoli
Ladispoli
Roma
Subiaco
Frascati
Grottaferrata
Ostia
Marino
Castel Gandolfo
Albano Laziale
Nemi
Velletri
Genzano
Lanuvio
Alatr
Frosinon
Anzio
Latina
Sermoneta
Terracina
San Felice Circeo
Mare Tirreno
Isola di Ponziane

LAZIO

Gaetano Rando

South from Toscana and bordered by Umbria and Abruzzo to the east, Lazio is a region of rich coastal plains, green undulating hills, and harsh mountain country. Rising in the mountains in Emilia-Romagna, the River Tiber flows down through Umbria, across the Lazio plain to the national capital Roma, and from there to the sea.

RAY JOYCE

An angel musician from a fragment of a fresco by Melozzo da Forlì, which is now in the Vatican Museum.

The variety of Lazio's terrain permits a wide range of food production, the rich volcanic soil being particularly well-suited to grape growing. There are pastures for livestock, hills for olive growing, plains for cereals and vegetables. In the mountains, in amongst the larch and chestnut, mushrooms grow, and there are lakes, rivers, and the sea for fish.

Administratively Lazio is divided into five provinces, the main one being Roma, with Viterbo and Rieti to the north and Frosinone and Latina to the south. The presence of the nation's capital, Roma, at its center, which is also the site of the Vatican, the world's smallest but by no means least powerful independent state, has a significant demographic and economic effect on the region, substantially affecting agricultural production. The wide variety of fruit, vegetables, and other produce available may be seen at the markets spread throughout the city. With the capital's population now over three million, it is not surprising that Lazio cannot produce sufficient food for all its people, so considerable quantities are imported. Wine, however, is a major export.

The virtually treeless sun-drenched belt of land around Roma is noted for the excellence of its vegetables. Marino is famous for onions, San Lorenzo Nuovo for garlic, Nemi for strawberries, and Onano for lentils. The best tomatoes come from the Sperlonga area, Rieti is the province for lamb and kid, and Latina for artichokes, while Frosinone is renowned for the production of cheeses such as ricotta, pecorino, *caciocavallo,* and a type of *provola* made from buffalo milk.

Home Cooking

RAY JOYCE

Little shops can be found around almost every corner in the older parts of Roma. Here a butcher's shop has been built into an ancient Roman ruin at Portico d'Ottavia.

Lazio's is a commonsense cuisine based on home cooking, and many *trattorie* lay claim to this tradition by displaying the sign "*cucina casareccia*".

Some of the region's gastronomic traditions can be traced back to Roman times. Legend has it that *porchetta*, suckling pig flavored with rosemary, aniseed, and garlic, traditionally spit-roasted over a wood fire, was originally eaten during the religious festivals held at the temple of Jupiter in the Alban Hills near present-day Ariccia, before spreading to other parts of central Italy and Sardegna. Despite claims by other parts of Italy regarding its invention, pasta was known to the ancient Romans and was probably widely eaten by the lower classes.

Pasta continues to be an important feature of Lazio cuisine, a typically Roman specialty being *bucatini all'amatriciana* with a sauce made from salt pork, chili, onions, and tomato and sprinkled with grated pecorino cheese. *Spaghetti alla carbonara*, made with streaky bacon, oil, eggs, pepper, and pecorino, is reputed to have been originally a dish made by the *carbonari*, charcoal burners, in the Lazio forests. Other typical pasta dishes are *spaghetti* and *penne all'arrabbiata*, made with chili, tomato, and Parmesan cheese; *spaghetti alla pestinara*, made with olive oil, garlic, and black pepper; *spaghetti a cacio e pepe*, made with pecorino cheese and black pepper; and *rigatoni con pagliata*, made with oxen and sheep entrails.

A popular first course is *gnocchi alla romana*, usually eaten on Thursdays, made from yellow potatoes and flour. The various soups include the delicate *stracciatella*, a consommé into which eggs, lemon juice, and cheese is poured, and the tasty *minestra di pasta e lenticchie,* pasta and lentil soup. Polenta and rice, typical of the north, are used to prepare two local dishes—*polenta laziale,* served with the tips of pork ribs, local sausages, and tomato sauce, a traditional winter dish, and *supplì* the local specialty *par excellence*, rice croquettes filled with a variety of stuffings, often eaten as a snack.

A. EDGEWORTH/THE IMAGE BANK

In central Roma there are any number of vantage points from which to view the city's classical domes and façades, and the gentle terracotta colorings of walls and tiles.

One of the most characteristic second courses is *abbacchio*, baby lamb, eaten in spring, which is prepared in a variety of ways from simply roasting to dishes such as *abbacchio alla cacciatora*, with olive oil, herbs, garlic, and anchovies, or *abbacchio brodettato*, with an egg sauce containing prosciutto, onions, and lemon. The heart, liver, and lungs of the *abbacchio*, fried with artichokes, are used to prepare another delicacy, the *coratella.*

Among other popular meat dishes are *stufatino col sedano*, a beef stew, a variant being *coda alla vaccinara,* which uses oxtail. The famous *saltimbocca* (literally "jump in the mouth") are veal *scaloppine* with prosciutto and sage, cooked in butter. *Scaloppine* are also used in *frittura piccata,* flour coated and fried with butter, prosciutto, and lemon juice. Chicken is featured in the exquisite *pollo coi peperoni*, chicken with peppers and tomatoes fried in oil, butter, garlic, and white wine (*pollo alla romana* being a variant without peppers); tripe in *trippa alla romana,* with onions, carrots, celery, tomato paste, and Parmesan (traditionally eaten on Saturdays); kidneys in *rognone di manzo in umido*, stewed with butter, olive oil, lard, tomatoes, onions, and wine; and lamb's or calf's brains in *frittura di cervella,* fried with eggs, onion, lemon, flour, and oil.

Perhaps the most famous of all Roman dishes are *carciofi alla romana,* artichokes stuffed with bacon, garlic, and mint, and *carciofi alla giudia,* flattened out and fried in olive oil, a name which shows the recipe's Jewish origin. Other vegetable dishes of note include spinach with pine nuts and raisins; stuffed tomatoes; peas with

Est! Est!! Est!!!

Montefiascone, overlooking the lake of Bolsena, produces a famous straw-yellow muscat wine that has a strange name, Est! Est!! Est!!! and a most unusual story.

In the twelfth century the German bishop, Johann Fugger, while traveling down the length of Italy towards Roma, sent a servant ahead of him to sample all the local wines and write "*Est*" (Latin for "[here it] is") with a piece of chalk on the doors of the taverns which served the best. On reaching Montefiascone the servant found a wine so good that he wrote "*Est*" not once but three times on the tavern door. The bishop, on reaching the town, apparently agreed with his servant's verdict and drank so much that he died. On his tomb, located in the church of St Flaviano, the following Latin epitaph can still be read today: "My lord, John De Foucris, died here because of too much *Est*".

Fugger willed all his belongings to the town council on condition that each year a barrel of wine be poured over his tomb, a practice observed until about a century ago.

onions and prosciutto; broad beans or peppers with bacon; mushrooms with garlic and mint; fried marrow flowers; and zucchini stuffed with ground lean beef. Celery is indispensable in Roman cooking, used not only in *stufatino* and *coda,* but also in *involtini al brodo* and in bean and lentil soups. Lentils are a star feature of the New Year's Day lunch: eaten with *cotechino* (a type of pork sausage), it is believed that the more lentils you eat, the more money you will make the coming year.

In the Carnevale period before Lent, *frappe* and *castagnole,* fried pastries dusted with powdered sugar, are traditional sweets. *Crostate,* tarts, are also typical of the area, particularly *crostata di visciola*, with sour cherry jelly. Ricotta is used to make ricotta pudding and ricotta fritters.

Festivals and Feast Days

Festivals and feast days are intertwined with gastronomic traditions, be they family or public occasions. The Festa del Giocattolo is held in the splendid Baroque piazza Navona in Roma between Christmas and the feast of the Befana. Traditionally it was the Befana, a kindly old woman, not Santa Claus, who brought Italian children presents on 6 January, and this festa enables Romans to buy these gifts. As well as toy stalls, there are booths offering traditional sweets, such as *pangiallo,* a dense yellow Christmas cake, *pignolata*, almonds cooked in sugar and honey, and *torrone*. One sweet looks like a lump of coal, but is really made from sugar and black coloring, a reminder that traditionally the Befana would give naughty children coal rather than toys.

And then there is the Sagra della Polenta, the Polenta Festival, held at Sermoneta, on the second to last Sunday in January. It is said that a local nobleman, Guglielmo Caetani, exiled to the Americas for several years by the Borgias, introduced the maize from which polenta is made.

Another occasion for celebration is the feast of St Joseph on 19 March, when the streets of the Trionfale district of Roma, which has St Joseph as its patron saint, are crowded with stalls decorated with his picture, piled with *porchetta,* hot appetising *frittelle*, pancakes, and *bignè di San Giuseppe*, a variety of fritter.

The evening before the feast of St John the Baptist, on 24 June, there is a procession of floats, and songs are sung in Roman dialect in piazza San Giovanni in Laterano, one of Roma's four basilicas, while the local *trattorie* offer the traditional dishes of snails, frogs, and *porchetta*, washed down with vino dei Castelli. Traditionally St John's day was an occasion for families to gather to reconcile the past year's enmities. Since snails' horns were considered symbols of discord, what better way to bury the hatchet than to eat snails?

Perhaps the best known Roman festival, the Festa de' Noantri, "Our Festival" is held in Trastevere for one week from 16 July, which is the feast of the Madonna del Carmine. A much more modern event, the Fiera di Roma, is held in the EUR district of Roma at the end of May and features a gastronomic village offering food from all over Italy.

Ferragosto, the feast of the Assumption, on 15 August, is celebrated in piazza Calamatta in the coastal town of Civitavecchia, where a squad of cooks fries literally tons of fish in a gigantic pan, which are then eaten and washed down with Orvieto wine. Civitavecchia is the most important port of the region and is noted for, among other things, the production of the famous Sambuca Molinari liqueur, a colorless anisette.

GUIDO ALBERTO ROSSI/THE IMAGE BANK

ROBERT HARDING PICTURE LIBRARY

WINES

Lazio is one of the country's most productive wines regions, with Roma province contributing the major portion. Wines that were valued in antiquity, such as Falerno and Cecubo, are still produced, but their style has changed, for the Roman's liked their wines syrupy.

The best known wines of Lazio are those of the Castelli Romani, so called because of the castles that proliferate among the towns in the Colli Albani, southeast of Roma, an area that is now almost part of the city itself because of the suburban sprawl. These hills, once volcanoes, are well-suited to growing wine grapes, and each of the towns in the region (Frascati, Grottaferrata, Marino, and Velletri being among the more prominent) produces wines of repute. As well as the golden-yellow Frascatis there are the dry whites known as Colli Albani made at Albano Laziale, Ariccia, and Castelgandolfo (where the Pope has his summer residence), the full-bodied wines of Lanuvio and Genzano, known as Colli Lanuvini, and the excellent full-flavored white wines of Marino.

As for dessert wines, the Aleatico of Gradoli in the Viterbo district, a sweetly aromatic red, is recommended, as are the Cesanese of the Sabina and Ciociaria areas west of Roma, and the Maccarese wines produced near the city itself.

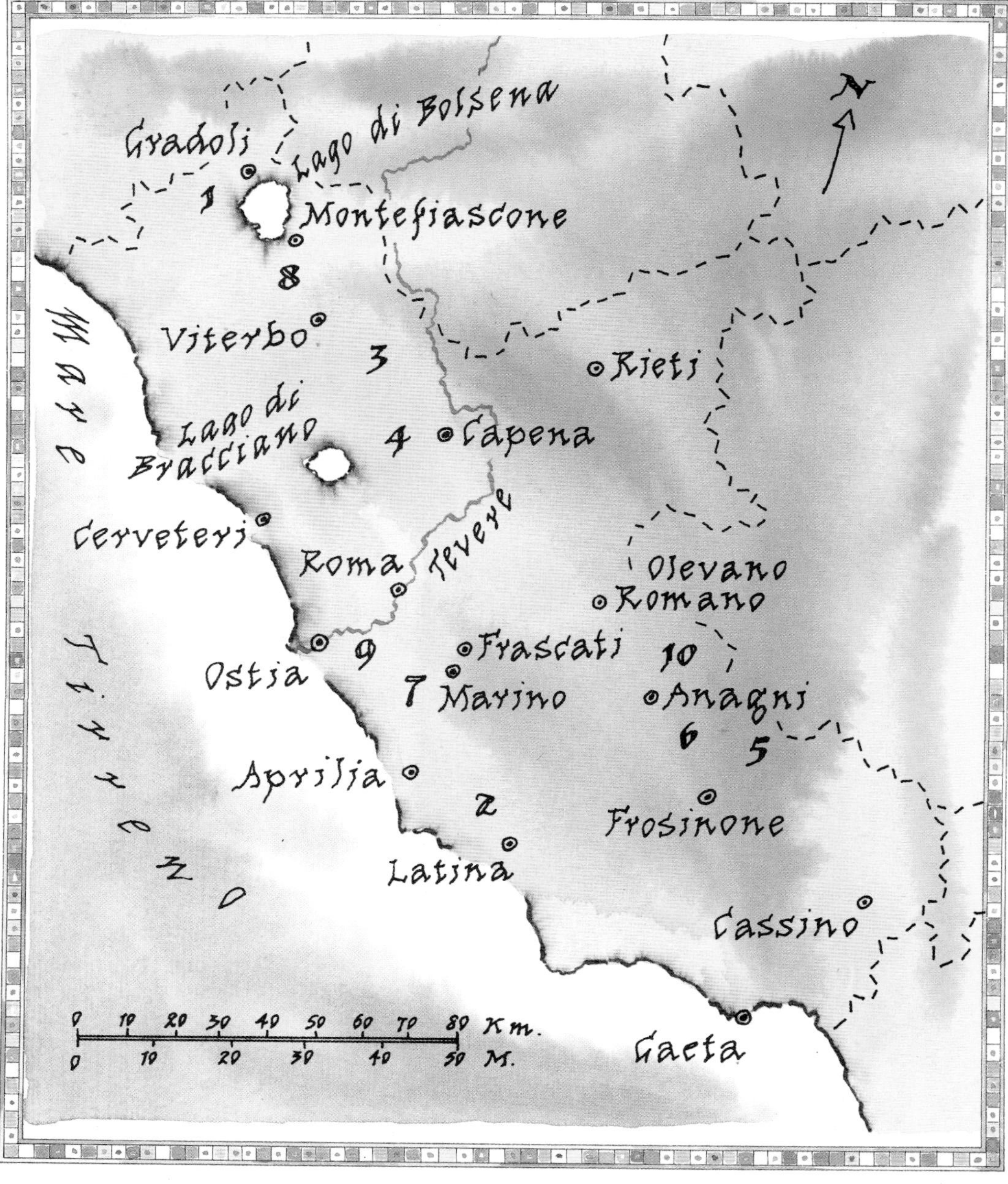

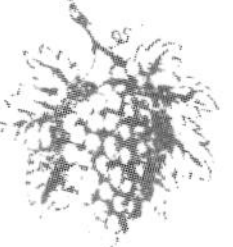

LAZIO WINES

DOC WINES

1. Aleatico di Gradoli
2. Aprilia
3. Bianco Capena
4. Cerveteri
5. Cesanese del Piglio
5. Cesanese di Affile
6. Cesanese di Olevano Romano
7. Colli Albani
7. Colli Lanuvini
7. Cori
8. Est! Est!! Est!!! di Montefiascone
9. Frascati
9. Marino
7. Montecompatri Colonna
7. Velletri
10. Zagarolo

Left: Crowds gather in the piazza di Spagna for the festivities to mark Ascension Day.

Page 173: Shoppers busy at the markets, making their selections from tempting displays of produce.

PETER JOHNSON

Recipes of Lazio

Don Andrea Scirè Borghese and Donna Marisa Borghese

Supplì al Telefono

Rice Croquettes

When these delicious croquettes are cut and lifted from the plate, the melted cheese filling forms "telephone wires".

Risotto:
4 tablespoons olive oil
2 garlic cloves, lightly crushed
6 fresh basil leaves, chopped
2 tablespoons chopped parsley
2 lb (1 kg) canned tomato pieces (pulp)
salt and freshly ground black pepper
$2\frac{1}{2}$ cups (1 lb/500 g) Arborio rice
3 cups (24 fl oz/750 ml) strong broth (stock) made from bouillon cubes
2 eggs, well beaten
2 oz (60 g) butter
$\frac{3}{4}$ cup (3 oz/90 g) freshly grated Parmesan cheese
Filling:
1 tablespoon tomato paste
$1\frac{1}{2}$ oz (45 g) dried porcini *mushrooms, broken up and soaked in $\frac{1}{2}$ cup hot water*
$\frac{1}{3}$ cup (3 fl oz/90 ml) dry red wine
oil for frying
1 onion, chopped
8 oz (250 g) lean ground (minced) beef
3 chicken livers, coarsely chopped
salt and freshly ground black pepper
To complete the supplì:
10 oz (315 g) mozzarella cheese, cut into $\frac{1}{3}$-oz (10-g) strips
fine dry breadcrumbs
oil for frying

For the risotto: Heat oil in a large, heavy saucepan and sauté garlic until golden, then discard. Add the basil, parsley and tomatoes. Season with salt and pepper and simmer for 30 minutes. Increase heat to moderate and when sauce is boiling, gradually add the rice, stirring continuously. The rice will gradually absorb the sauce, so keep it moist by adding broth, a ladle at a time. Keep stirring for 15 minutes, or until rice is cooked. Remove from heat. Mix in the eggs, butter and Parmesan and put aside.

For the filling: Dissolve the tomato paste in the soaking water with the mushrooms. Mix in the wine. Heat a little oil in a skillet over moderate heat and brown the onion with the beef and chicken livers. Season with salt and pepper. Add the mushroom mixture, stir well and cook until all the liquid has evaporated. Put aside.

To make the *supplì*: Take a spoonful of rice and flatten it a little in the palm of your hand. Curl your hand to shape the rice like a boat, using a teaspoon. Place some filling in the recess, topping it with a strip of mozzarella. Close the "boat" by covering it with another spoonful of rice. Shape the croquettes into ovals and roll in breadcrumbs.

Heat oil in a deep fryer until nearly smoking. Fry the croquettes, 2 or 3 at a time until golden. Drain on paper towels, keep warm until all are cooked, then serve.

SERVES: 6 to 8

Bucatini all'Amatriciana

Bucatini with Salt Pork, Tomatoes and Cheese

This simple pasta dish comes from Amatrice, on the Lazio–Abruzzo border.

3 tablespoons lard or virgin olive oil
1 small dried crushed hot red chili pepper
2 garlic cloves, lightly crushed
2 onions, thinly sliced
5 oz (155 g) salt pork or lean streaky bacon, diced
$\frac{1}{2}$ cup (4 fl oz/125 ml) dry white wine
1 lb (500 g) ripe tomatoes, peeled and chopped, or 1 can tomatoes, chopped
salt and freshly ground black pepper
2 tablespoon chopped parsley (optional)
$1\frac{1}{4}$ lb (625 g) bucatini *(a long hollow pasta)*
$\frac{1}{2}$ cup (2 oz/60 g) freshly grated Parmesan cheese
$\frac{1}{4}$ cup (1 oz/30 g) freshly grated pecorino cheese

Heat the lard in a shallow saucepan and sauté the chili and garlic. Discard the garlic when brown. Add the onions and sauté over moderate heat. Add the salt pork as soon as the onion is golden. After 2 minutes add the wine and cook until it evaporates. Add the tomatoes. Check the seasoning. Stir well and cook over high heat for 5 minutes. At the last minute, if desired, stir in the parsley.

Break the *bucatini* into 4-in (10-cm) pieces and cook in plenty of boiling salted water until *al dente*. Drain and toss well with the sauce and cheeses. Keep some cheese to sprinkle on top of the pasta before serving.

SERVES: 6

Left: Bucatini with Salt Pork, Tomatoes and Cheese, Fusilli with Eggs and Bacon, Rice Croquettes, Rice-stuffed Tomatoes, Roman Egg Soup

Fusilli alla Carbonara

Fusilli with Eggs and Bacon

This recipe is a refined version of the pasta once eaten by the charcoal burners in the forests.

5 tablespoons virgin olive oil
1 garlic clove, lightly crushed
5 oz (155 g) streaky bacon, diced or cut in ¼ x ¾-in (5 x 15-mm) strips
3 tablespoons dry white wine
3 eggs
3 egg yolks
½ cup (2 oz/60 g) freshly grated Parmesan cheese
⅓ cup (1½ oz/40 g) freshly grated pecorino cheese
1 heaped teaspoon freshly ground black pepper
grated rind of ½ lemon
½ cup (4 fl oz/125 ml) heavy (double) cream
3 tablespoons chopped parsley (optional)
1 lb 2 oz (560 g) fusilli *(spiral pasta) or spaghetti*

Heat the oil in a small saucepan and sauté the garlic until golden, then discard. Add the bacon and cook for about 2 minutes over moderate heat. (It should not become crisp.) Add the wine and cook until evaporated. Remove from heat.

In a large mixing bowl lightly beat the eggs and egg yolks. Add the Parmesan and pecorino, a generous teaspoon of pepper, the lemon rind, the cream and the parsley (if desired). When the oil and the bacon have cooled sufficiently not to cook the eggs, stir them well into the mixture. Transfer the mixture into a saucepan large enough in which to toss the pasta when cooked.

Cook the *fusilli* in plenty of boiling salted water until *al dente*. Drain and toss in the sauce. The heat of the pasta will partly cook the eggs. Serve at once.

SERVES: 6

Pomodori col Riso

Rice-stuffed Tomatoes

A popular summer dish in Lazio, using ripe but firm tomatoes.

6 large, firm, round tomatoes
salt and freshly ground black pepper
1¼ cups (8 oz/250 g) Arborio rice
2 small garlic cloves, finely chopped
1 tablespoon drained capers
2 teaspoons dried oregano, crushed
1½ tablespoons currants
¾ cup (6 fl oz/180 ml) virgin olive oil

Slice the tops off the tomatoes to make caps. With a teaspoon hollow out each tomato and sieve the flesh into a bowl. Sprinkle salt inside the tomatoes and leave them upside down for 30 minutes to drain.

Add the rice, garlic, capers, a heaped teaspoon of oregano, the currants and 3 tablespoons of oil to the tomato pulp. Season with salt and pepper and mix well. Spoon into the tomatoes, filling them just over half way as the rice will swell. Replace caps.

Place the tomatoes in a shallow oiled baking dish and pour the rest of the oil over them. Sprinkle with salt and pepper and oregano. Cook in oven preheated to 350°F (180°C) until the tomatoes are soft (about 1 hour) basting them occasionally. Serve lukewarm or cold.

SERVES: 6

Stracciatella

Roman Egg Soup

This classic Roman soup is now found in many regions of Italy.

4 eggs
few drops lemon juice
½ cup (2 oz/60 g) freshly grated Parmesan cheese
freshly grated nutmeg
salt
¾ oz (20 g) fresh breadcrumbs or durum semolina (optional)
4 cups (2 pt/1 l) home-made chicken broth (stock)
1 tablespoon finely chopped parsley

In a mixing bowl, beat the eggs with the lemon juice, then add the Parmesan, a sprinkle of nutmeg and a pinch of salt. If you wish, you can also add fresh breadcrumbs or semolina. Dilute the mixture with a ladle of cold broth and add the parsley.

Bring the broth to a boil. Pour in the egg mixture and stir with a metal whisk. Lower heat and keep whisking for a further 2 minutes. Serve hot. Croutons of bread toasted in the oven can be sprinkled on each serving.

SERVES: 6

Trippa alla Romana

Tripe Roman Style

In the traditional cuisine there are quite a number of dishes that make good use of the entrails.

2¾ lb (1.35 kg) veal or ox tripe, washed and cut into large pieces
salt
2 bay leaves, fresh or dried
2½ oz (75 g) lard
1 large celery stalk, finely sliced
2 large carrots, finely sliced
2 large onions, finely sliced
3 oz (90 g) prosciutto, finely chopped
2 tablespoons finely chopped parsley
2 garlic cloves, finely chopped
5 tablespoons tomato paste
3 teaspoons pure meat extract
1 teaspoon freshly ground black pepper
6 to 8 fresh mint leaves, chopped
1¼ cups (5 oz/150 g) freshly grated Parmesan cheese, or if stronger taste is preferred, blend ½ Parmesan and ½ pecorino

Place the tripe in a large pot of cold water. Bring to a boil, then drain. Refill the pot with cold water, add a good pinch of salt and the bay leaves. Bring to a boil, cover and cook slowly over moderate heat for at least 3 hours.

Heat the lard in a large saucepan and sauté the celery, carrots, onions, prosciutto, parsley and garlic over moderate heat until the onions turn golden. Dissolve the tomato paste and 2 teaspoons of meat extract in a cup of hot water. Add to the saucepan and cook for 15 to 20 minutes.

Drain the tripe and cut into finger-wide strips up to 4 in (10 cm) long. Discard the bay leaves. Place the tripe in the sauce. Season with pepper, stir well with a wooden spoon and cook over low heat for 30 minutes. (If necessary, to preserve moistness, occasionally add a few tablespoons of hot water flavored with a touch of meat extract.) Remove the saucepan from the stove. Add the mint, keeping 1 teaspoon aside, and roughly ¾ of the Parmesan. Stir well and serve. Pass around a bowl containing a mixture of the remaining cheese and mint to be used as a garnish.

SERVES: 6

Tripe Roman Style

PETER JOHNSON

Polenta sulla Spianatora alla Brigida

Polenta with Pork Sausage, Pork Ribs and Tomato Sauce

This is quite a substantial meal and should not be preceded by an *antipasto* or a first course.

Sauce:
1/3 cup (3 fl oz/90 ml) olive oil
2 large onions, finely chopped
1 celery stalk, finely chopped
1 large carrot, finely chopped
2 garlic cloves, finely chopped
9 to 12 Italian-style pure pork sausages
8 pork ribs cut in half, giving 16 pieces
3/4 cup (6 fl oz/180 ml) dry red wine
2 lb (1 kg) tomatoes, peeled and coarsely chopped, or 2 cans peeled tomatoes, reserving 1 cup (8 fl oz/250 ml) juice
salt and freshly ground black pepper
2 tablespoons chopped parsley
Polenta:
7 cups (3 1/2 pt/1.75 l) water
salt
4 oz (125 g) lard
3 1/2 cups (1 lb 3 oz/600 g) cornmeal
1 1/4 cups (5 oz/150 g) freshly grated Parmesan cheese

For the sauce: Heat the oil in a large saucepan and sauté the onions, celery, carrot and garlic until golden. Reduce heat to moderate. Peel 3 sausages, add them to the pan and break them up with a wooden spoon while they are browning. With a fork, thoroughly puncture the remaining sausages and add them to the pan, together with the ribs. Turn the sausages and ribs occasionally to let them brown well.

After 10 minutes pour in the wine and let it evaporate. Add the tomatoes with 1 cup of hot water. (If using canned tomatoes, use 1 cup of the juice from the can.) Season with salt and pepper. Reduce heat to moderate, cover the pan and let the mixture cook for 1 1/2 hours, until sauce is well reduced. Stir in the parsley and keep warm.

For the polenta: In a large, heavy saucepan (preferably a copper pot), bring to a boil salted water, to which the lard has been added. While continuously stirring with a wooden spoon, pour a thin, consistent stream of cornmeal into the boiling water. Keep stirring slowly for about 50 minutes or until cooked. (The polenta is cooked when it comes away easily from the sides of the pot whilst stirring.)

Pour the polenta onto individual plates, flattening the mixture to a thickness of about 3/4 in (2 cm) with a spatula. Reheat the sauce and pour over the top of the polenta. Either place the meat in a dish in the center of the table, so that the diners can help themselves, or place a sliced sausage and 2 ribs in the center of each plate. Sprinkle servings generously with Parmesan.

SERVES: 6 to 8

PETER JOHNSON

Polenta with Pork Sausage, Pork Ribs and Tomato Sauce

Saltimbocca alla Romana

Veal Scallops with Prosciutto and Sage

A side dish of creamy mashed potatoes makes a particularly good accompaniment to *saltimbocca.*

12 veal scallops (escalopes), about 2 to 3 oz (60 to 90 g) each
1 teaspoon ground dried sage (optional)
6 slices prosciutto, halved
2½ oz (75 g) butter
½ cup (4 fl oz/125 ml) dry white wine
salt

Flatten each scallop well with a meat mallet then, if you wish, dust them on both sides with ground sage. On each slice place a prosciutto slice and a sage leaf, secured with a toothpick.

Heat the butter in a large heavy skillet and brown the scallops, prosciutto-side up, over moderate to high heat for 3 minutes. Turn gently and cook for 2 minutes. Sprinkle the wine over the meat and cook for 2 minutes.

Arrange the veal on a serving dish, prosciutto-side up. Stir 2 tablespoons water into the pan juices and let boil for 1 minute. Check the seasoning and add salt if necessary. Spoon the sauce over the meat and serve at once.

SERVES: 6

Baccalà in Guazzetto

Dried Salt Cod in a Sauce of Tomatoes, Golden Raisins and Pine Nuts

Once respectfully called "sea hen", *baccalà* has been favored by the Romans for a long, long time.

2 lb 11 oz (1.35 kg) baccalà *or* stoccafisso *(dried salt cod)*
3 or 4 tablespoons all purpose (plain) flour
¾ cup (6 fl oz/180 ml) virgin olive oil
3 garlic cloves, chopped
2 lb (1 kg) tomatoes, peeled and quartered, or 2 cans peeled tomatoes
salt and freshly ground black pepper
2 tablespoons golden raisins (sultanas)
2 tablespoons pine nuts
2 tablespoons chopped parsley

If not using pre-soaked salt cod, soak the fish in water for at least 24 hours, changing the water frequently. Blanch it for 3 to 5 minutes in boiling water.

PETER JOHNSON

Veal Scallops with Prosciutto and Sage, Dried Salt Cod in a Sauce of Tomatoes, Golden Raisins and Pine Nuts

Remove the skin and the bones and cut the fish into pieces about 2½ in (6 cm) square. Dust the fish in flour and fry in very hot oil in a deep, wide skillet. Turn the pieces carefully and when cooked drain them on paper towels.

When all the fish pieces have been fried, lower the heat and sauté the garlic until golden. Add the tomatoes. Season with salt and pepper.

Add the golden raisins, pine nuts and half the parsley. Stir well. Let the sauce cook for 10 to 15 minutes, then gently lay the fish pieces in it, covering them with the sauce.

Allow 2 or 3 minutes for them to absorb the flavors, sprinkle with the remaining parsley and serve.

SERVES: 6

Broccoletti Strascinati in Padella

Turnip Tops Fried with Oil, Garlic and Chili

Broccoli is a good substitute for the turnip tops, if they are unavailable.

¾ cup (6 fl oz/180 ml) virgin olive oil
2 garlic cloves, sliced
3 small dried hot red chili peppers
3½ lb (1.75 kg) young turnip tops, chopped, woody stems discarded
salt
½ cup (4 fl oz/125 ml) dry white wine
5 oz (155 g) prosciutto, cut in strips
1½ cups (12 fl oz/375 ml) broth (stock) made from 1 vegetable bouillon cube

Heat oil in a large, heavy skillet and sauté the garlic and chili until garlic is golden. Add the turnip tops and season with a pinch of salt.

Pour in the wine, stir well and let evaporate. Lower heat, mix in the prosciutto and cover the skillet. Add a few tablespoons of broth whenever turnip tops seem to be drying out a little, stirring well. Cook for about 30 minutes, or until tender. Serve hot.

SERVES: 6

PETER JOHNSON

Cauliflower with Anchovies, Turnip Tops Fried with Oil, Garlic and Chili, Artichokes Roman Style

Carciofi alla Romana

Artichokes Roman Style

In Roma *carciofoli*, as the locals call them, are a great delicacy, sold in every *rosticceria*, snack bar. Use two artichokes per person if this dish is to be served as a first or main course.

6 young artichokes, chokes removed
juice of 1 lemon
5½ oz (170 g) lean bacon, chopped
3 garlic cloves, chopped
1 or 2 fresh mint sprigs, chopped, or 2 teaspoons dried mint, crushed
⅔ cup (5 fl oz/150 ml) virgin olive oil
salt and freshly ground black pepper
1 tablespoon chopped parsley

Discard the outer leaves of the artichoke and the hard parts of the stalks, leaving about 2 in (5 cm) of stalk attached. Peel the stalks. Remove the hard top parts of the leaves by laying each artichoke on a chopping board and cutting them all at once with a sharp knife. Applying gentle pressure with your thumbs, spread open the leaves. Place the artichokes in a bowl of cold water, to which the lemon juice has been added, and let soak for 30 minutes.

Mix together the bacon, garlic and ⅔ of the mint. Drain the artichokes. Separate the leaves a little with your fingers and fill as many gaps as possible with the mixture, pushing it in deep. Place the artichokes close together in a saucepan, stalks upwards. Pour over the oil and sprinkle with salt, pepper and the remaining mint.

Cook for a few minutes over moderate heat then add 1 cup hot water. Cover and cook over low heat until artichokes are tender (test by puncturing with a fork) and the liquid is well reduced (about 30 minutes).

Carefully transfer the artichokes to a serving dish, lying them side by side. Pour over the sauce and sprinkle with parsley. Serve hot or cold.

SERVES: 6

Cavolfiore con le Acciughe

Cauliflower with Anchovies

This dish goes well with a main course of stewed or boiled meats.

2 lb (1 kg) cauliflower florets
3 or 4 tablespoons wine vinegar
1 teaspoon salt
¼ cup (2 fl oz/60 ml) virgin olive oil
2 large garlic cloves, finely sliced
10 or 12 anchovies, mashed

Rinse the cauliflower in a bowl of cold water to which the wine vinegar has been added. Drain. Fill a large saucepan with water, add salt and bring to a boil. Cook the cauliflower, uncovered, until barely *al dente* (10 or 12 minutes).

Heat the oil over moderate heat and sauté the garlic. When golden, add the anchovies and the cauliflower. Stir gently and let the flavors blend for 2 or 3 minutes. Serve hot.

SERVES: 6

Dolci di Ricotta

Roman Cheesecake

Ricotta, used in many Roman dishes, from first courses to desserts, forms the base of this delicious crustless cheesecake.

1 lb 5 oz (655 g) very fresh ricotta
⅔ cup (6 oz/185 g) superfine (caster) sugar
4 very fresh eggs
¼ cup (2 fl oz/60 ml) white rum
1 teaspoon vanilla extract (essence)
1¾ cups (14 fl oz/430 ml) heavy (double) cream
1 oz (30 g) semisweet (plain) chocolate, grated
8 to 12 candied cherries

In a large bowl mix together well the ricotta, sugar, eggs, rum and vanilla extract. Whip the cream then gently fold ¾ of it into the ricotta mixture. Moisten the inside of a plain cake mold with water (a salad bowl could be used) and transfer the mixture into it, pressing it down firmly. Store for at least 6 hours in the coldest part of the fridge, but not in the freezer.

Turn the cake upside down onto a serving dish. Decorate with the remaining whipped cream, using a piping bag. Sprinkle with the grated chocolate and decorate with cherries.

SERVES: 6

PETER JOHNSON

Roman Cheesecake

Castagnole alla Romana

Fried "Chestnuts" of Pastry with Rum or Aniseed Liqueur

These small cakes are often served after a meal or as an afternoon snack with a sweet wine called Cannellino.

5 cups (1¼ lb/625 g) all purpose (plain) flour
6 eggs
5 oz (155 g) butter
¼ cup (2 fl oz/60 ml) rum or aniseed liqueur
grated rind of 1 lemon
pinch of salt
1½ cups (12 fl oz/375 ml) oil for deep frying
1 teaspoon finely ground cinnamon
½ cup (3 oz/90 g) powdered (icing) sugar

Sift the flour in a large mixing bowl. Beat the eggs and pour them into the center of the flour. Melt the butter in the liqueur with the lemon rind and salt and pour into the flour. Mix to form a dough then knead thoroughly until smooth and rubbery.

Divide the dough into small pieces then roll them between your hands to form little chestnut-sized balls.

Fry the balls, a few at a time, in very hot oil in a large heavy skillet or a deep fryer, retrieving them promptly when golden and draining them well on paper towels.

Mix the cinnamon with the powdered sugar and sift about ¾ of this mixture over the "chestnuts". Arrange them on a serving dish in layers, to form a pyramid, and sift the remaining sugar and cinnamon mixture on top. Serve either hot or cold.

SERVES: 6

Zuppa Inglese

Trifle

Literally translated, the name of this dish means "English soup". This is a cake, not a soup, and it is not English at all. On the contrary, it is the original creation that inspired the English when they "invented" English trifle.

Pan di Spagna *(Sponge Cake):*
Either buy a ready-made sponge cake large enough to obtain 3 discs about 8 to 10 in (20 to 25 cm) in diameter and 1 to 1½ in (2.5 to 3.5 cm) thick, or prepare one using the following ingredients:
6 eggs, separated
⅔ cup (5 oz/155 g) superfine (caster) sugar
grated rind of 1 lemon
1¼ cups (5 oz/155 g) all purpose (plain) flour
1 oz (30 g) butter to coat cake pan
Egg Custard:
3 eggs, separated
⅓ cup (3 oz/90 g) granulated sugar
½ cup (2 oz/60 g) all purpose (plain) flour
1 teaspoon vanilla extract (essence)
2 cups (16 fl oz/500 ml) milk
1 oz (30 g) butter
Zuppa Inglese:
1 fl oz (30 ml) Alchermes liqueur: if unavailable, use Cointreau with a few drops of red food coloring
¼ cup (2 fl oz/60 ml) rum
¾ cup (4 oz/125 g) powdered (icing) sugar
¾ cup (4 oz/125 g) candied fruit, including orange peel or cherries

For the sponge cake: In a large mixing bowl, using a wooden spoon, vigorously beat the egg yolks with the sugar until they treble in volume. Whilst mixing, add the lemon rind. Set aside.

In a second bowl, beat the egg whites, using a metal whisk, until stiff and standing in peaks, then gently fold into the yolk mixture. Whilst stirring gently with the wooden spoon, gradually sprinkle in the flour.

Transfer the mixture to a 9-in (23-cm) round baking pan, lightly coated with butter and flour. Bake 30 minutes in oven preheated to 350°F (180°C). Cool, then remove from pan.

For the egg custard: In a saucepan, using a wooden spoon, mix together the egg yolks and sugar. Stir in the flour and vanilla extract. Heat the milk and when near boiling add it gradually to the egg mixture, using a metal whisk to prevent lumps forming.

Place the saucepan over moderate heat and stir the mixture continuously. Simmer for 5 minutes, always stirring. Remove from the heat and add butter. The custard should be slightly runny: if necessary whisk in a few tablespoons of very hot milk.

For the *zuppa inglese*: Slice the sponge horizontally to give 3 discs. Place them on 3 separate plates. Trim the perimeter of one, to make it look like a flattened dome. Dilute the Alchermes with a little water then spoon it over an untrimmed cake layer. Dilute the rum in the same way, spooning the liquid over the remaining 2 layers.

Take a large ovenproof serving dish, about 12 in (30 cm) in diameter, and over it spread 3 tablespoons of custard to cover an area about 1 in (2 or 3 cm) larger than the discs. Lay the untrimmed, rum-flavored disc on the custard base.

Stir the candied fruit into the custard (keeping aside some orange peel or cherries for decoration) and spread half on top. On this place the sponge soaked in Alchermes. Cover this with the shaped top piece, sandwiching the layers with the remaining custard.

Beat the egg whites until stiff and standing in peaks and then mix in the powdered sugar. Coat the cake evenly, top and sides, using a spatula. Decorate with peel.

Bake the cake for a short time in oven preheated to 275°F (140°C) to dry the meringue and give the cake an all-over straw color. Serve cold.

SERVES: 6 to 8

Trifle,
Fried "Chestnuts" of Pastry with Rum or Aniseed Liqueur

PETER JOHNSON

LAZIO
MOLISE
Volturno
Sessa Aurunca
Mondragone
Capua
Caserta
Benevento
Ariano
Golfo di Gaeta
Marcianise
Maddaloni
Tufo
Aversa
Acerra
Cardito
Nola
Avellino
Bagnoli
ISOLA DI PROCIDA
Pozzuoli
Napoli
VESUVIO
Ercolano
POMPEI
M. EPOMEO
Torre Annunziata
Pagani
ISOLA VIVARA
ISOLA D'ISCHIA
Castellammare
Ravello
Salerno
Eboli
Golfo di Napoli
Sorrento
Positano
Amalfi
Sele
PIANA DEL SELE
Golfo di Salerno
GROTTO AZZURA
ISOLA DI CAPRI
Paestum
Agropol
Mare Tirreno
Golfo
0 10 20 30 M.
0 10 20 30 40 50 Km.

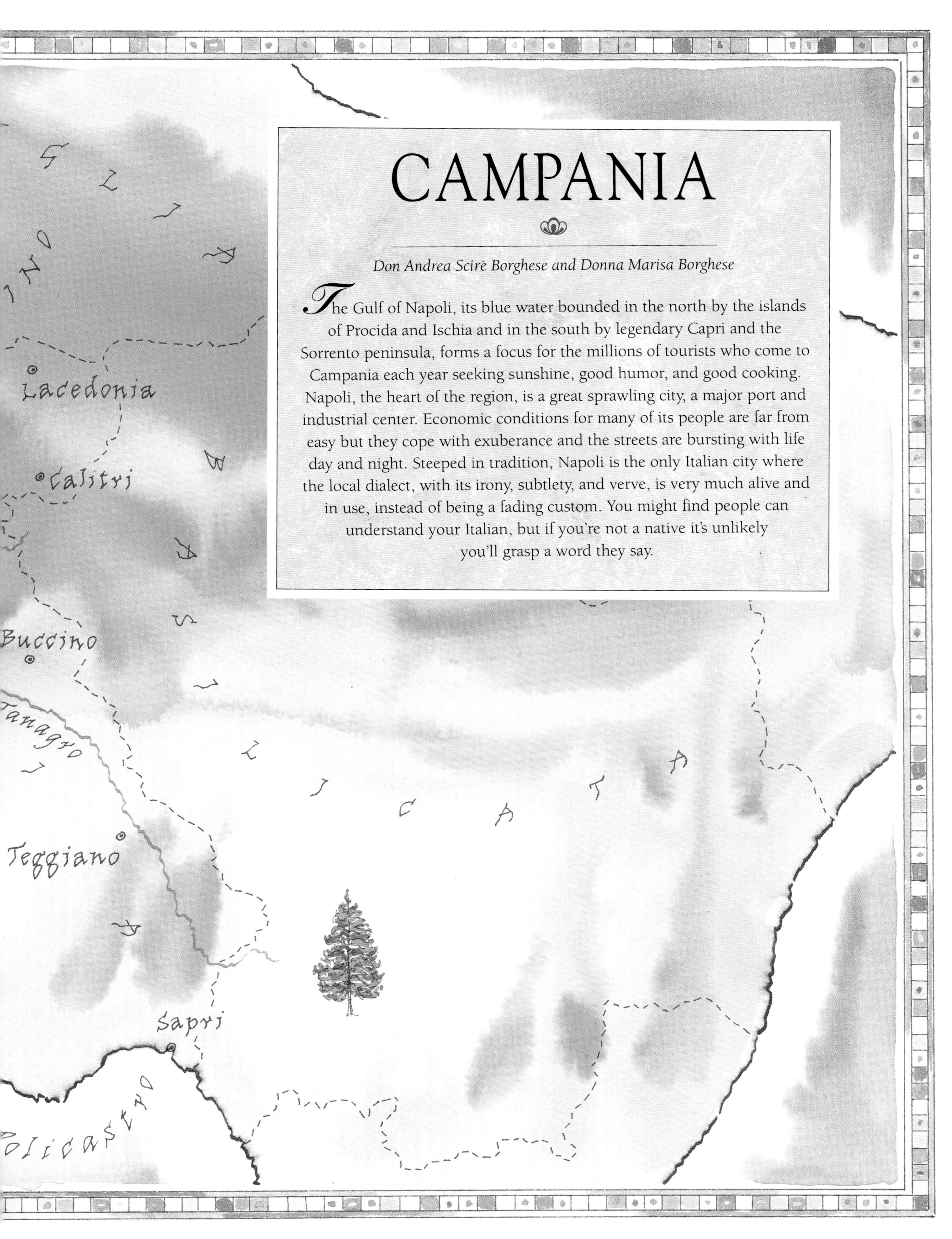

CAMPANIA

Don Andrea Scirè Borghese and Donna Marisa Borghese

The Gulf of Napoli, its blue water bounded in the north by the islands of Procida and Ischia and in the south by legendary Capri and the Sorrento peninsula, forms a focus for the millions of tourists who come to Campania each year seeking sunshine, good humor, and good cooking. Napoli, the heart of the region, is a great sprawling city, a major port and industrial center. Economic conditions for many of its people are far from easy but they cope with exuberance and the streets are bursting with life day and night. Steeped in tradition, Napoli is the only Italian city where the local dialect, with its irony, subtlety, and verve, is very much alive and in use, instead of being a fading custom. You might find people can understand your Italian, but if you're not a native it's unlikely you'll grasp a word they say.

GUIDO ALBERTO ROSSI/THE IMAGE BANK

A street performance in Napoli, with music and clowning to entertain the locals. Not a place to go for peace and quiet, the city pulses with activity day and night.

Pasta and Pizza

The cooking of Campania and of Napoli are largely all one, with the exception of a few area-specific dishes. Food is of great importance, frugal but not poor, and people are meticulous about even the simplest ingredients. For centuries Neapolitans were called *mangiafoglie*, leaf eaters, because of the predominance of vegetables in their diet, then, with the advent of *pastasciutta*, dried pasta, they became known as *mangiamaccheroni*, macaroni eaters. And today, when you say "pasta" you are nearly as close to defining *the* Neapolitan dish as when you say "pizza".

The best pasta is made from *grano duro*, durum wheat, a variety that grows particularly well in the south. The high gluten content in this wheat gives the pasta an elasticity that prevents it from becoming mushy when it is cooked. Some of Italy's largest pasta factories are in this region, mainly in the Salerno area. The yearly production of one of these factories is over eighty million pounds (forty million kilograms), with a range of well over one hundred different shapes. The best sellers are the short, tubular, and ridged varieties, such as macaroni, *rigatoni,* and *penne*, and of course spaghetti. These types of pastas are considered to be the best recipients for all the sauces.

And the sauces? The majority contain the *pomodoro*, golden apple—the humble tomato. With only a little oil, an onion, a few basil leaves, a sprig of parsley, salt, and pepper to complement sun-ripened tomatoes, preferably the oblong San Marzano variety, *salsa alla napoletana* is created. And of course tomatoes are central to *pizzaiola* sauce. *Vermicelli con le cozze e le vongole*, *vermicelli* with a sauce of tomato, mussels, and cockles is one of the many seafood, tomato, and pasta dishes that proliferate along the coast.

The *ragù* is one of Campania's more important dishes, for which tomatoes are also an essential ingredient. The northern sauce *ragù alla bolognese* shares with it the name and certain ingredients, but the southern *ragù* provides a tasty meat dish as well as a rich pasta sauce. The pasta and the meat can, of course, be served together, as a *piatto unico*. A *ragù* takes time to make. The variant named *ragù del guardaporta* alludes to this: it means the sauce of the doorkeeper, referring to the caring cook who must keep a watchful eye on the pot as it simmers.

Another notable *piatto unico* is the *sartù*, a ring-shaped rice dish with an immense array of ingredients: bacon, breadcrumbs, chicken livers, mushrooms, eggs, garlic, ground meat, mozzarella, olive oil, onion, Parmesan, parsley, pork sausage, stock, and tomato paste. Then there is *lasagna imbottita*, stuffed lasagna, in which the pasta is layered with other preparations, requiring more than twenty ingredients, and *minestra maritata*, a heavy winter soup in which vegetables are married with a broth made from pork entrails. Substantial dishes such as these need only be followed by a salad or a light dessert, such as *granita di caffè,* coffee water ice, or *coviglie al cioccolato*, chocolate mousse.

A visitor to Napoli must call at a *friggitoria*, a snack bar that sells deep-fried tidbits. These can be found all over the city, selling all the delicious bits and pieces that make up the famous *fritto alla napoletana*. Among these piping hot and crunchy bite-sized morsels are vegetables such as artichokes, eggplant, seaweed, zucchini flowers, and fennel; rice and potato croquettes; fish and seafood of every kind, including tiny fish eaten whole; pieces of polenta called *tittoli*; bread and pastry; and all sorts of cheese delicacies, including the famous *mozzarella in carrozza*, a deep-fried mozzarella sandwich.

S. FIORE/FIOREPRESS

The heart of Campania, Napoli is a major port and industrial center.

Pizza is Napoli's greatest gustatory success story, but a Neapolitan *pizzeria* with its proud pizza maker busy throwing dough in the air to make a circle of the correct size and thickness, maybe loudly praising his product or singing as he works, is a far cry from the fast food world of pizza parlors. There is a huge range of pizza toppings from the simple *napoletana*, with tomato, mozzarella, basil, garlic, oil, and oregano, to the *quattro stagioni*, four seasons, which on a tomato and mozarella base has one of the following combinations on each quarter: sliced mushrooms and/or artichoke hearts preserved in oil; prosciutto and/or sliced pork sausage; mussels and/or fillets of anchovies; and finally pitted black olives.

Throughout Campania, particularly in Napoli, one sees stalls with *pizze* of all sorts prepared in large rectangular trays. These *pizze* are cut to order and each portion is folded in two, *a libretto*, like a book, making it easier to handle—a flavorsome and economical meal or an impromptu snack to be eaten as you stroll along.

Complex Sweet Creations

A few words must be said, too, about the delights of Neapolitan cakes. A classic is *pastiera napoletana*, filled with a mixture of macerated wheat (at times rice or barley are subsituted), eggs, the freshest ricotta, candied peel, and orange flower water. *Sfogliatelle* are made from crunchy ribbons of *pasta riccia* around a moist filling of ricotta, semolina, sugar, candied fruit, and cinnamon—complex creations that are quite delicious. Don't miss a visit to one of Napoli's many *pasticcerie* or coffee bars to sample some of these delicacies. Nor should you miss the frozen desserts. Neapolitan ice creams are famous the world over.

Una "Tazzulella 'e Cafe"

A particular rite for Neapolitans is the *tazzulella 'e cafè*, the small cup of coffee. Few will dispute that they make the best *espresso* in the country, and of this they are justly proud.

In Napoli one has a cup of coffee early, to wake up, one later in the morning to stay alert, another after lunch as a digestive, various cups in the afternoon to relax, and a few more, just for the pleasure of it. The coffee is good almost everywhere.

Making an excellent cup of coffe is not a simple process. Undoubtedly the quality of the water is important, but so is blending the various Arabica and Robusta coffee beans, and gauging the correct grinding, the quantity of powder to use, the water temperature, the filtering time...

Domenico Modugno, a famous Italian singer, wrote a "hymn" to Neapolitan coffee. It loses somewhat in translation, but the message remains:

Ah, what beautiful coffee!
Only in Napoli do they know
How to make it
And no one understands why
It's so very good...
But a million Neapolitans
Don't want to know a thing
...the coffee keeps them going.

One of the region's many fishing villages. In the heat of the day few people can be seen in the streets or on the harbor foreshore.

S. FIORE/FIOREPRESS

Wines for the Romans

Many delightful wines are produced in Campania, some of which were keeping up the spirits of the Romans over 2000 years ago, like the Greco di Tufo, a dry white, an ideal complement to saucy fish dishes like *purpetielle affocate*, baby octopus "drowned" in tomato sauce, or *zuppa di cozze*, mussel soup. Falerno, a wine praised by the poet Horace, is still produced today by the Fattoria Villa Matilde in Cellole, a dry white of medium strength. The same winery produces a rosé and a red, the latter being soft and balanced and excellent with red meats, game, and strong cheese. Generally Campania's wines are not suited to lengthy cellaring, with the exception of the best Taurasi reds, produced in the Avellino region.

Other good local wines include the whites Ischia and Capri, bearing the names of the islands that make them, and reds like Rosso di Procida, Vesuvio, and Monte di Procida. These wines go well with the richer local dishes.

The Romans exported wine and other goods from Campania, mainly from the port of Puteoli, known now as Pozzuoli. This town is a shadow of what it once was, largely because earthquake activity has forced people to move. Between 1982 and 1984 alone the soil lifted nearly six feet (two meters). Pozzuoli's most notable recent export has been Sophia Loren.

Offshore from Pozzuoli lie the jewel-like islands of Procida, Vivara, and Ischia, set in the blue enamel of the Tyrrhenian Sea. Ischia is known as the green island because of its citrus trees, pines, and vineyards. It has much to offer the visitor—curative springs, fine hotels, beautiful beaches, sophisticated restaurants, and simple *trattorie*, and a beautiful mountain to climb, Mount Epomeo.

Preceding pages: Holidaymakers soak up the sun in comfort on the waterfront at Positano, on the Gulf of Salerno.

SLIM AARONS/FOCUS

A specialty of the island is *coniglio all'ischitana*, rabbit cooked in the local style. In Ischia Porto there is an enoteca, a wine boutique, where you can taste some of the local produce as well as some of the best wines of Campania. Don Alfonso and Epomeo, available in red, white, and rosé, and the white Ischia are all recommended.

Mount Vesuvio and Southwards

Not far south of Napoli lie Ercolano, Pompei, and majestic Vesuvio. An excursion to the top of this volcano, which dominates the landscape, will give you an excellent view from Capri to your left across to Procida and Ischia to your right. On 24 August 79 AD Vesuvio erupted and a gigantic flow of volcanic mud engulfed Herculaneum, the flourishing Roman town near its lower slopes, from which most of the inhabitants had fortunately fled. A greater part of this city has yet to be excavated as modern Ercolano has been built on top of it. From a nearby hill you can see the contrast between the well-ordered Roman streets which have been exposed, and the ugly conglomerate of "boxes" of the new city.

Pompei, a little farther south, was completely submerged by lava from the eruption that destroyed Herculaneum. Archaeological excavations were begun in 1748, gradually uncovering the 10 000 inhabitants and their city. With the help of a map from the local tourist bureau you can stroll in the streets of this ancient city feeling as if you are actually in the great time of the Caesars, whilst admiring the villas, frescoes, statues, mosaics, and all sorts of everyday objects, down to the loaves of bread and the dried figs in a shop window.

"Come back to Sorrento" says the song, an invitation that is superfluous once you have seen this peaceful small town built on cliffs high above the sea offering glorious views over the Gulf of Napoli and the nearby island of Capri. The sea

CHARMET/MARY EVANS PICTURE LIBRARY

A painting showing how one of the shops in Pompeii originally appeared. Archeologists have been able to reconstruct a detailed picture of the residents' daily lives.

Nets studded with corks are looped over poles and piled all around in readiness for the next day's fishing.

JOHN CALLANAN/THE IMAGE BANK

MOZZARELLA

Mozzarella cheese is considered almost synonymous with Campania, as are "tomato sauce" and "pizza". Indeed, what would a pizza be, without its generous topping of mozzarella?

This soft and juicy white cheese, made from either cow or buffalo milk (the latter is far superior in taste) has little in common with the rubbery and flavorless industrial product sold under the same name that is found all over the world.

Mozzarella can be found throughout the year and is made in a number of shapes—spheres, ovals, and forms like cottage loaves. Its flavor is mild and creamy. A smoked version is available which has a stronger taste.

Throughout Italy you can find good mozzarella, but the people of Campania are adamant that it is the quality of their soil, their air, even the incline of their pastures, and the influence of the moon where their herds graze that contribute to the superiority of their mozzarella, and the many local cheeses— *treccia, burriello, provola,* and *scamorza*.

The best areas for these cheeses are around Aversa, Cardito, and Capua, and the region commonly known as Piana del Sele, which lies between Salerno and Paestum.

MELINDA BERGE/BRUCE COLEMAN LTD

The houses seem to almost grow out of the cliffs along the Amalfi coastline.

breeze carries the bouquet of the lemon and orange groves and of the many flowers that bloom here. It is said that the dance of the tarantella originated here. The town boasts some good restaurants and is known for its fresh cheeses and its walnuts.

In Sorrento you can board a ferry, as you can from Napoli, to reach Capri, certainly one of the most elegant and sought-after holiday resorts on earth. For four centuries Capri was the private playground of Roman emperors and patricians, but was then largely neglected until the seventeenth century. It has never since lost its prestige and allure, having, over the years, a particular attraction for jet-setters and playboys. The island is blessed with incomparably beautiful spots, such as the Grotta Azzurra, the Blue Grotto, and the harbor of Marina Piccola, often crowded with yachts from around the world, but if you do not enjoy hordes of holidaymakers, stay well away in mid-summer. The piazzetta is the island's open air "lounge" where one can watch the people passing whilst sipping an aperitif and deciding where to go to sample some of the excellent local food: fish and seafood, game, pasta with tomato and basil, rabbit, goat cheese and ricotta, fine vegetables, and fruit, all washed down with Capri wine.

Back on the mainland, traveling towards Salerno, is the glorious coastline around Positano, Amalfi, and Ravello. The multicolored houses of Positano form an amphitheater looking out over the iridescent water, and the peace and beauty of this little town is palpable. After wandering along the town's one narrow lane and up and down the wide-stepped stairs, there is nothing more pleasant than to eat in a restaurant by the waterside. Sitting under a pergola covered with bougainvillea you could enjoy a variety of freshly-caught grilled fish; a *riso alla pescatora*, rice with seafood; *alici in tortiera*, layers of fresh anchovies cooked in the oven with breadcrumbs, garlic, parsley, olive oil, and vinegar; some omnipresent mozzarella, even some tempting almond cake. Suggested wines would be a white and fruity Caruso di Ravello, made near Amalfi, and a red Taurasi, softened by age. An elegant Aleatico would complement the dessert.

Further down the coast, past the Gulf of Salerno, is the Gulf of Policastro, shared by Campania with neighboring Basilicata. All along the seaboard, its cliffs frequently rising straight from the sea, there are places of great beauty and fascinating monuments from the times of Greek and Roman occupation. Conditions are difficult, however, for those who struggle to wrest a living from the mountainous rocky country. It is easy to understand why people from the hinterland have for so long been losing heart and setting off in search of more reliable sources of income. Many have emigrated to the rich industrial centers of the north and overseas; other have gone no further than the slums of Napoli. Despite all their difficulties, however, the people of Campania are resourceful and spirited, and for the endless flow of tourists there is always a fine welcome.

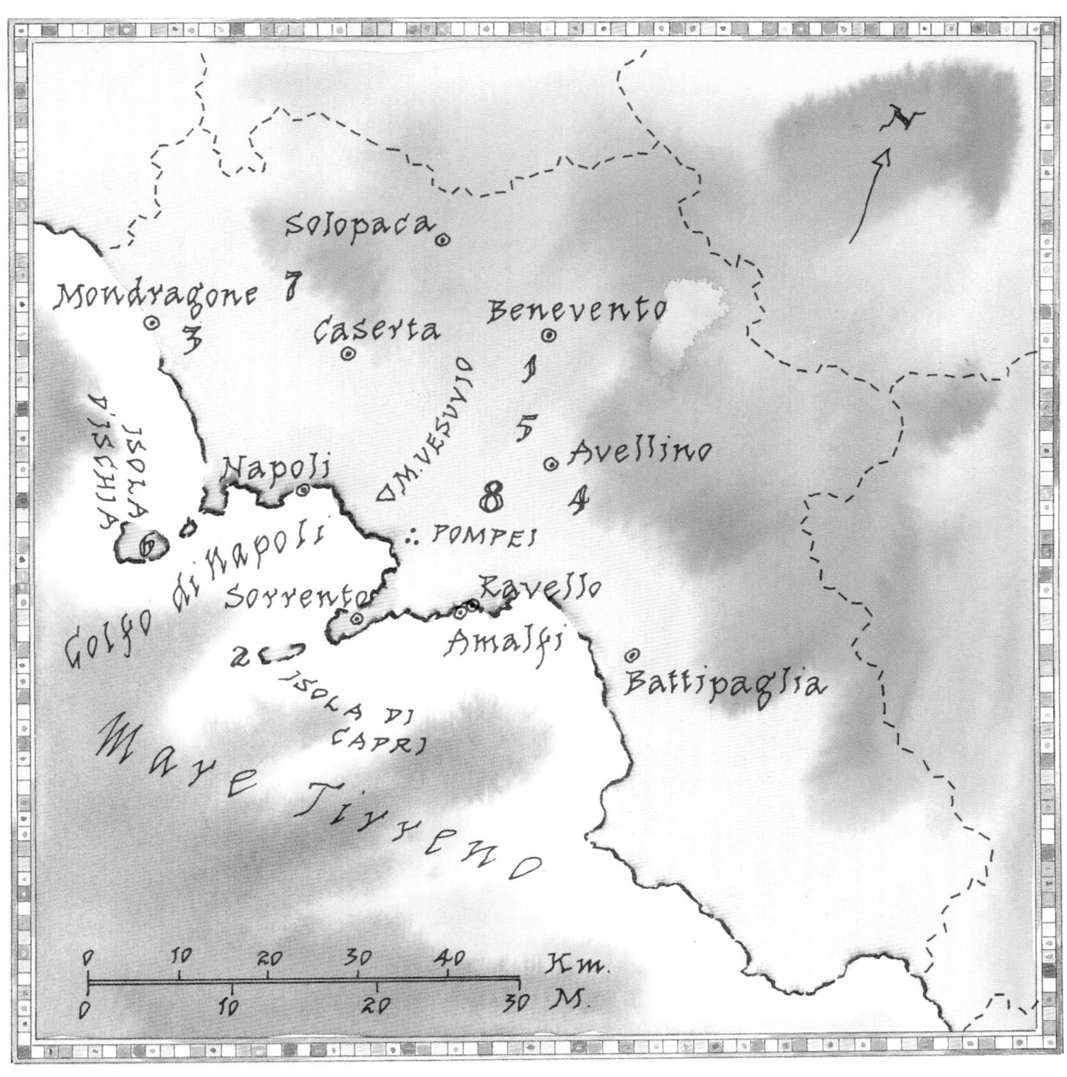

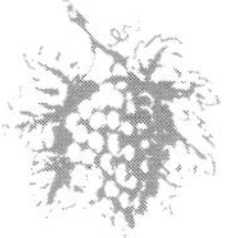

CAMPANIA

DOC Wines

1. *Aglianico del Taburno*
2. *Capri*
3. *Falerno del Massico*
4. *Fiano di Avellino*
5. *Greco di Tufo*
6. *Ischia*
7. *Solopaca*
1. *Taurasi*
8. *Vesuvio*

Other Wines

Cilento
Don Alfonso
Epomeo
Falerno
Procida

RECIPES OF CAMPANIA

Don Andrea Scirè Borghese and Donna Marisa Borghese

PETER JOHNSON

Vermicelli con le Cozze e le Vongole

Vermicelli with Mussels and Clams

Pasta, tomatoes and seafood: the main ingredients of this dish are indisputable Neapolitan favorites.

2½ lb (1.25 kg) black mussels (buy only closed ones)
2½ lb (1.25 kg) small clams or cockles (buy only closed ones)
6 tablespoons salt
¾ cup (6 fl oz/180 ml) virgin olive oil
4 garlic cloves (1 crushed, 3 finely chopped)
6 anchovy fillets, chopped
1 large onion, chopped
1½ lb (750 g) ripe tomatoes, peeled and chopped, or 1 can peeled tomatoes, chopped with ½ cup (4 fl oz/125 ml) juice retained
salt and freshly ground black pepper
1¼ lb (625 g) vermicelli *(a thin variety of spaghetti) or spaghetti*
3 tablespoons chopped parsley

Scrub the mussels and clams, removing the mussel beards. Rinse well then place for about 1 hour in a large bowl of cold water with 5 tablespoons salt, stirring occasionally. Rinse under running water.

Heat 2 tablespoons oil in a large saucepan and sauté the crushed garlic and anchovies. Discard the garlic when brown. Add the mussels and clams. Cover and cook over moderate heat for 5 minutes, shaking the pan occasionally. Remove from heat and discard unopened shells. Remove ⅔ of the mollusks from their shells. Place the shelled and unshelled mollusks in a covered container and keep warm. Strain the pan juices and put aside.

Heat the remaining oil in a large saucepan and gently sauté the onion and 2 cloves of chopped garlic. When the onions are golden add the tomatoes. Cook over moderate heat for 6 to 8 minutes, stirring frequently. Stir in the retained pan juices, a generous pinch of pepper and a pinch of salt, if required. Lower heat, cover the pan and simmer for 30 minutes.

Cook the *vermicelli* in a large pot of boiling salted water until barely *al dente*. While the pasta is cooking, add the remaining garlic, the parsley and the mollusks to the sauce. Stir gently and cook for 2 minutes only.

Drain the pasta and place it in a large mixing bowl. Pour the sauce on top and mix well.

Place in a serving dish with the mollusks in their shells on the top and around the sides. Sprinkle with the remaining parsley and serve at once.

SERVES: 6 to 8

Zuppa di Cozze

Mussel Soup

When serving, have a bowl or two on the table into which the empty shells can be discarded. Finger bowls and bibs are also a good idea, as the mussels should be eaten with the fingers.

4 lb (2 kg) black mussels (buy only closed ones)
⅓ cup (3 fl oz/90 ml) virgin olive oil
pinch of dried hot red chili pepper, crushed
4 garlic cloves, finely chopped
2 lb (1 kg) canned peeled tomatoes, preferably Italian, with juice
3 heaped tablespoons tomato paste
salt
¾ cup (6 fl oz/180 ml) dry white wine
4 tablespoons chopped parsley, preferably flat-leafed
6 large slices Italian country-style bread or French bread, toasted

Scrub the mussels and remove the beards. Rinse well in cold water and set aside. Heat the oil in a large saucepan over moderate heat and sauté the chili and half the garlic for less than a minute. Add the tomatoes, breaking them open, and the juice. Mix in the tomato paste and a generous pinch of salt. Cook for 15 minutes, stirring occasionally.

Place the mussels in the saucepan, cover and cook until they open (10 to 12 minutes). Discard any unopened ones. Add the wine and cook, uncovered, for 5 minutes. Stir in the remaining garlic and the parsley. Check the seasoning. Pour into soup bowls, over a slice of toast, and serve at once.

SERVES: 6

Left: Mussel Soup, Vermicelli with Mussels and Clams

PETER JOHNSON

Deep-fried Mozzarella, Neapolitan Savories

Mozzarella in Carrozza

Deep-fried Mozzarella

The people of Napoli named these crispy, fried sandwiches "mozzarella traveling in a coach".

1¼ lb (625 g) mozzarella cheese in ¼-in (5-mm) slices
12 slices from a white sandwich loaf, preferably 1 or 2 days old
5 eggs
4 tablespoons milk
pinch of salt
1 cup (4 oz/125 g) all purpose (plain) flour
olive oil for frying

Trimming the mozzarella as necessary, cover 6 slices of bread. Top with the remaining 6 slices. Trim and discard the crusts, then cut sandwiches in half.

In a mixing bowl lightly beat the eggs with the milk and salt. Pour into a dish slightly larger than the sandwiches. Spread the flour on a plate and place each sandwich in it, pressing down lightly on each side. Then gently lay each sandwich in the batter, pressing down for some of the mixture to soak in. Turn the sandwich over and repeat the process. Drain over the dish and put to one side.

Heat ½ in (1 cm) oil in a skillet. When it is almost smoking add the sandwiches and fry them on both sides until golden. Drain well on paper towels. Keep warm until all portions have been cooked, then serve at once.

SERVES: 6

Crostini alla Napoletana

Neapolitan Savories

These cheese savories go well with drinks at a cocktail party.

9 slices from a white sandwich loaf, preferably 1 or 2 days old
½ cup (4 fl oz/125 ml) virgin olive oil
1¼ lb (625 g) mozzarella cheese in ¼-in (5-mm) slices
1½ oz (45 g) anchovy fillets in oil, each fillet halved lengthwise
6 small ripe tomatoes, sliced
freshly ground black pepper
1 tablespoon dried and crushed oregano or marjoram
18 small basil leaves, rinsed and wiped dry

Trim the crusts from each bread slice and cut each slice diagonally. Coat a large baking tray with oil and place the bread triangles on it.

Cover each triangle with a slice of mozzarella slightly smaller than the bread, followed by a piece of anchovy and a slice of tomato. Sprinkle with pepper and oregano. Dribble over each *crostini* 1 teaspoon of olive oil.

Bake in oven preheated to 350°F (180°C) until the cheese is golden (about 8 to 10 minutes). Place on a warmed serving dish, decorate each of the *crostini* with a basil leaf and serve at once.

SERVES: 6

Calamaretti alla Napoletana

Neapolitan Baby Squid

In this dish the sea-taste of baby squid is blended with pine nuts and black olives.

3 lb (1.5 kg) baby squid
⅓ cup (3 fl oz/90 ml) virgin olive oil
3 garlic cloves, chopped
1 lb (500 g) canned peeled tomatoes, preferably Italian, with juice
salt and freshly ground black pepper
1½ oz (45 g) golden raisins (sultanas)
1½ oz (45 g) pine nuts
8 oz (250 g) black olives, pitted and halved
½ cup (4 fl oz/125 ml) dry white wine
12 slices Italian country-style bread or French bread, toasted
2 tablespoons chopped parsley, preferably flat-leafed

Skin the squid and remove the ink sac and the guts. Keep the external body and the tentacles, discarding the rest. Wash thoroughly in cold running water. Place in a bowl of cold salted water and put to one side.

Heat the olive oil in a medium saucepan and sauté the garlic over a moderate heat until light gold. Add the tomatoes, breaking them open, and the juice. Season with salt and pepper. Stir well and simmer for 10 to 15 minutes.

Put the golden raisins in a small bowl of lukewarm water for about 10 minutes. Drain and add to the sauce. Add the squid, pine nuts, olives and wine. Stir well. Cover the saucepan and let simmer gently for 30 minutes, stirring occasionally. Check the seasoning.

Place the toast on a warmed serving dish and spoon the squid and sauce over the top. Sprinkle with parsley and serve at once.

SERVES: 6

Neapolitan Baby Squid

PETER JOHNSON

Stewed Octopus

Purpetielle Affocate

Stewed Octopus

In place of a pressure cooker some traditionalists use a terracotta pot sealed with parchment secured with string to keep the flavors from escaping.

3 lb (1.5 kg) small octopus (say 5 or more per pound) preferably with 2 rows of suckers on the tentacles
¾ cup (6 fl oz/180 ml) virgin olive oil
1 lb (500 g)ripe tomatoes, preferably plum, peeled, seeded and chopped, or 1 can peeled tomatoes, chopped
salt and freshly ground black pepper
3 large garlic cloves, chopped
4 tablespoons chopped parsley (optional)

Clean the octopus, removing the sac, eyes and mouth. Rinse thoroughly in cold running water and tenderize well using a meat mallet.

Place the oil in a pressure cooker. Add the octopus and tomatoes. Season with salt and pepper and stir well. Cook on moderate to high heat until the cooker whistles. Lower the heat and cook for 50 minutes. Stir in garlic and parsley, reserving a little parsley for decoration. Cook, uncovered, a further 5 minutes. Check the seasoning.

Transfer the octopus to a warmed serving dish and sprinkle with parsley, if desired. Serve hot, warm or cold.

SERVES: 6 to 8

Fettine alla Pizzaiola

Beef Rump with Pizzaiola Sauce

This recipe for "the sauce with the flavors of pizza" can be used to give a Neapolitan flavor to ribs, steaks and meat balls. It can also be used for cooking fish fillets or cutlets *"alla Pizzaiola"*.

Pizzaiola Sauce:
4 tablespoons virgin olive oil
4 large garlic cloves, crushed with a garlic press
2 lb (1 kg) ripe peeled, seeded and chopped tomatoes, or 2 cans peeled tomatoes, strained and quartered
salt and freshly ground black pepper
½ cup (4 fl oz/125 ml) dry white wine
3 fresh oregano sprigs, chopped, or 3 teaspoons dried crushed oregano
Fettine:
3 tablespoons virgin olive oil
6 thin rump steaks, trimmed and flattened with a meat mallet
salt and freshly ground black pepper
2 tablespoons chopped parsley

For the sauce: Heat the oil in a medium saucepan and sauté the garlic until light gold. Add the tomatoes, season with a pinch of salt and pepper, then stir in the wine and oregano. Lower heat and simmer until the tomatoes are soft, but not pulped (8 to 10 minutes for fresh tomatoes, 5 minutes for canned ones), stirring occasionally. Put aside.

For the *fettine*: Heat the oil in a large heavy skillet and fry the meat until brown on each side, but only half cooked. Spread the sauce generously over each slice, cover the pan, reduce the heat and cook 5 to 7 minutes.

Check the seasoning, adding salt and pepper if necessary. Sprinkle with parsley and serve.

SERVES: 6

PETER JOHNSON

Beef Rump with Pizzaiola Sauce, Veal Rolls with Tomato Sauce and Pasta

Ragù del Guardiaporta

Veal Rolls with Tomato Sauce and Pasta

Traditionally this dish is eaten as a *piatto unico*, a meal in one dish, but the sauce can equally well be eaten with the pasta, and the veal rolls served as a main course, or even at another meal.

1/3 cup (2 oz/60 g) golden raisins (sultanas)
4 garlic cloves
4 or 5 parsley sprigs
1/4 cup (2 oz/60 g) pine nuts
1 cup (4 oz/120 g) freshly grated Parmesan cheese
salt and freshly ground black pepper
3/4 cup (6 fl oz/180 ml) virgin olive oil
2 lb (1 kg) large thin slices of veal rump (9 or more), flattened with a meat mallet
3 oz (90 g) salt pork or streaky bacon, thickly sliced then cubed
3/4 cup (6 fl oz/180 ml) dry red wine
5 heaped tablespoons tomato paste dissolved in 1 cup (8 fl oz/250 ml) water
1 1/4 lb (625 g) tubular pasta, such as ziti tagliati *or* penne

Soak the golden raisins in a bowl of lukewarm water for 20 minutes. Drain, pat dry with a towel and set aside. In a food processor or blender, pulp together the garlic and parsley, then add the raisins and pine nuts, keeping aside 1 tablespoon of each for decoration. Add the Parmesan, a teaspoon each of salt and pepper and 3 tablespoons oil. Spread this paste on the top of the veal slices, roll tightly and secure with toothpicks or cotton string.

Place the salt pork and the remaining oil in a shallow saucepan large enough to accommodate the meat rolls and set over moderate to high heat. As soon as the pork starts to fry add the rolls to the pan and brown them all over. Pour in the wine, let it evaporate almost completely.

Add the diluted tomato paste. Lower the heat, cover and cook gently for at least 2 hours, turning the rolls frequently. Should the sauce start to dry up, stir in a ladle of hot water.

Cook the pasta in a large pot of boiling salted water until *al dente*. Drain then toss with the meat sauce, keeping 3 tablespoons of the sauce aside.

Place pasta in a large warmed serving dish, levelling the top to accommodate the veal rolls (after removing the toothpicks or string). Spread the reserved sauce evenly over the rolls, decorate with the reserved raisins and pine nuts and serve at once.

SERVES: 6

Parmigiana di Melanzane

Baked Eggplant with Mozzarella

This versatile dish can be served as a first course, a main course or a side dish. Quantities here will serve 12 as a side dish, or 6 as a main course. It is a complex dish and making smaller quantities is not worthwhile. It is also delicious cold. The sauce can be used for *Spaghetti alla Napoletana* and to give a Neapolitan flavor to a variety of fish, meat and vegetable dishes.

Neapolitan Tomato Sauce:
3 tablespoons virgin olive oil
2 garlic cloves, peeled
1 onion, finely sliced
2 lb (1 kg) ripe tomatoes, peeled, seeded and coarsely chopped
salt and freshly ground black pepper
10 to 12 basil leaves, preferably small-leafed
3 tablespoons coarsely chopped parsley
Eggplant Parmesan:
3½ lb (1.75 kg) eggplant (aubergine)
salt
olive oil for frying and to coat the baking dish
1¾ cups (7 oz/220 g) all purpose (plain) flour
1½ cups (6 oz/180 g) freshly grated Parmesan cheese
10 oz (315 g) mozzarella cheese in ¼-in (5-mm) slices
2 or 3 eggs, hard cooked and sliced

For the sauce: Heat the oil in a saucepan over moderate heat. Sauté the garlic until it starts to brown, then discard. Add the onions and tomatoes. Season with salt and pepper. Cook over moderate heat for 20 minutes, stirring occasionally, then add the basil and parsley. Cook for 2 more minutes and remove from heat.

For the Eggplant Parmesan: Rinse and trim the eggplant, slice lengthwise, sprinkle lightly with salt and leave in a colander to drain for at least 30 minutes. Rinse and pat dry.

Heat a generous amount of oil in a heavy skillet. Dip the eggplant in flour and fry, a few slices at a time, until golden brown on both sides. Drain thoroughly on paper towels.

Oil an"oven to table" dish. On the bottom spread a few tablespoons of sauce. On this place a layer of eggplant, sprinkle with Parmesan, then a layer of mozzarella and a few slices of egg. Repeat the procedure, reserving sauce, mozzarella and Parmesan for the top, in that order.

Cover with aluminum foil and bake in oven preheated to 350°F (180°C) for 30 minutes. Remove foil and place under broiler (grill) for a few minutes until cheese starts to brown. Serve either warm or cold.

SERVES: 12

PETER JOHNSON

Neapolitan Salad, Potato Croquettes Stuffed with Mozzarella, Baked Eggplant with Mozzarella

Insalata alla Napoletana

Neapolitan Salad

In Napoli this salad is traditionally served between the rich main courses of the Christmas dinner and the desserts, in the belief that it will aid the digestion.

5 oz (155 g) bell peppers (capsicums) in vinegar, cut in ½-in (1-cm) strips, or 2 small bell peppers, preferably 1 yellow and 1 red, seeded and cut in ½-in (5-mm) strips
1 cup (8 fl oz/250 ml) wine vinegar
1 medium-large cauliflower, broken in florets
1 level teaspoon salt
½ cup (4 fl oz/125 ml) extra virgin olive oil
½ teaspoon freshly ground black pepper
2 tablespoons drained capers
1 garlic clove, finely chopped
3 oz (90 g) continental style gherkins, thinly sliced
3 oz (90 g) soft bland green olives, pitted
2 oz (60 g) black olives, pitted
8 anchovy fillets, coarsely chopped
2 tablespoons coarsely chopped parsley

If you are using fresh bell peppers, in a small saucepan boil ¾ cup (6 fl oz/180 ml) vinegar with half as much water and in it cook the peppers over moderate heat, turning frequently, for 8 to 10 minutes. Drain them well and put to one side.

Cook the cauliflower in boiling salted water until *al dente* (4 to 6 minutes). Drain, cool under cold running water, shake dry and set aside.

In a mixing bowl with a fork beat

together the oil, 2 tablespoon vinegar, salt and pepper. Place the capers, garlic and gherkins in a salad bowl. Add the olives, anchovies and parsley. Pour in the salad dressing and toss. Add the cauliflower and bell peppers.

Toss carefully and let stand for at least 1 hour before serving.

SERVES: 8

Crocchè di Patate

Potato Croquettes Stuffed with Mozzarella

Possibly the best-loved of all the fried foods available in Napoli, these croquettes are also ideal as a snack with drinks.

2 lb (1 kg) potatoes
salt
5 eggs
½ cup (2 oz/60 g) freshly grated Parmesan cheese
1 teaspoon ground white pepper
generous pinch of ground nutmeg
all purpose (plain) flour
12 oz (375g) fresh mozzarella cheese, cut in ¾-in (2-cm) cubes
fine breadcrumbs
olive oil for deep frying

Cook the potatoes in boiling salted water until tender. Drain, cool and mash them. Place the purée in a large mixing bowl.

Beat 3 eggs with a pinch of salt, the Parmesan, pepper and nutmeg. Stir the mixture into the potatoes, adding just enough flour, 1 tablespoon at a time, to obtain a malleable dough.

Spread some flour on a work top and roll the dough into 1 or more long cylinders about 1 in (2.5 cm) in diameter. Cut the cylinder into 2-in (5-cm) sections. Coating your fingers in flour, make a cavity in each croquette and into it push a mozarella cube. Fill in the cavity and work the croquette into a round-ended cylinder.

Beat the remaining eggs in a soup bowl and fill another with breadcrumbs. Roll each croquette in eggs, then breadcrumbs.

Heat the olive oil in a deep fryer or skillet and when smoking fry the croquettes, a few at a time, until they are golden brown. Drain on paper towels and keep warm until they are all cooked. Serve immediately.

SERVES: 6 to 8

Pastiera Napoletana all' Orzo

Shortcrust Cake with Ricotta and Barley

The preparation of this cake requires patience and time. To better justify the effort, this recipe is for 10 to 12 people.

Pasta Frolla *(Italian Shortcrust Pastry):*
5 oz (155 g) unsalted butter
2½ cups (10 oz/315 g) all purpose (plain) flour
½ cup (4 oz/125 g) superfine (caster) `sugar
3 large egg yolks
finely grated rind of ½ orange
Filling:
1¼ cups (8 oz/250 g) pearl barley
2 cups (16 fl oz/500 ml) full cream milk
1½ cups (11 oz/345 g) superfine (caster) sugar
3 teaspoons vanilla extract (essence)
pinch of salt
1 lb (500 g) very fresh ricotta
2 tablespoons orange flower water or 2 teaspoons lemon extract (essence) diluted in 6 teaspoons water
1 teaspoon ground cinnamon
3 oz (90 g) candied lemon and orange peel, chopped finely
finely grated rind of 1 lemon, preferably green
finely grated rind of 1 orange
6 egg yolks
4 egg whites
butter to grease the cake pan
powdered (icing) sugar to dust the cake

For the pastry: Melt the butter. Sift the flour and sugar together in a heap and make a well in the center. In this place the egg yolks, butter and orange rind. With your fingers gradually work in the flour. When you have a firm smooth ball of dough, wrap it in a slightly damp towel and put it in the fridge for an hour.

For filling and cake assembly: Soak the barley in water for 24 hours. Drain and place in a saucepan. Cover with water, bring to a boil and simmer for 20 minutes. Drain and return to saucepan. Heat milk to near boiling and pour over barley. Add 2 tablespoons sugar, vanilla extract and salt. Stir well. Bring to a boil then simmer, stirring occasionally, until the barley has absorbed all the milk (about 1½ hours). Put aside to cool.

Sieve the ricotta into a large mixing bowl. Stir in the remaining sugar, the orange flower water, cinnamon, candied peel and the lemon and orange rind. Add the egg yolks, blending each well in before adding the next, then the barley mixture. Beat the egg whites until stiff then fold gently into the mixture.

Butter a 12-in (30-cm) cake pan. Divide the dough in two, one piece twice the size of the other. Roll out the larger piece and line the bottom and sides of the pan. Spoon in the filling, levelling it well. Roll out the other piece of dough to form a circle slightly larger than the pan then cut it in ½-in (1-cm) strips. Position these like lattice over the filling, pressing the ends onto the pastry at the edge. Roll over the edge protruding above the filling and pinch it gently all around. Place in oven preheated to 350°F (180°C) and bake for 1½ hours. Allow cake to cool before turning out. Dust with powdered sugar.

SERVES: 10 to 12

Coviglie al Cioccolato

Chocolate Mousse

For a more "spirited" mousse, perforate the cherries with a fork and leave them in rum overnight, then place a tablespoon of this rum marinade on top of each serve.

⅓ cup (1½ oz/45 g) all purpose (plain) flour
1¼ cups (8 oz/255 g) superfine (caster) sugar
¾ cup (3 oz/90 g) unsweetened cocoa powder
3 cups (1½ pt/750 ml) milk
1½ oz (45 g) unsalted butter, cubed
2½ cups (1¼ pt/625 ml) heavy (double) cream
6 candied cherries

In a bowl, using a wooden spoon, mix together the flour, sugar and cocoa powder. Slowly add the milk, stirring continuously with a metal whisk to prevent lumps forming. Pour into a saucepan and cook over moderate heat stirring continuously until mixture starts to thicken. Add the butter and blend. Return mixture to the bowl and leave to cool, stirring occasionally to prevent a skin forming.

When the mixture is cold, whip ¾ of the cream. Fold it gently into the mixture. Spoon into dessert bowls and place in the coldest part of the fridge, but not the freezer. Whip the remaining cream and curl it over the mousse, using a forcing bag. Decorate with candied cherries.

SERVES: 6

Struffoli

Honey Sweets

This is a traditional Neapolitan Christmas dessert which has a wonderfully festive appearance.

3 oz (90 g) butter
5 cups (1¼ lb/625 g) all purpose (plain) flour
8 eggs
2 egg yolks
4 tablespoons superfine (caster) sugar
3 teaspoons vanilla extract (essence)
finely grated rind of 4 oranges
pinch of salt
light oil for deep frying
¾ cup (9 oz/280 g) honey
1¾ cup (9 oz/280 g) candied lemon and orange peel, finely chopped
1 cup (4 oz/125 g) slivered almonds
2 teaspoons lemon extract (essence)
1 teaspoon ground cinnamon
colored sugar dots

Melt the butter. Sift the flour in a heap on the work top and make a well in the center. In this place the butter, the 8 eggs and 2 yolks, 1 tablespoon of sugar, the vanilla extract, ¼ of the orange peel and the salt. With your fingers work in the surrounding flour. When you have a smooth elastic ball of dough, wrap it in a slightly damp towel and put it in the fridge for an hour.

Divide the dough into lemon-sized pieces and roll them under the palms of your hands on a floured surface to form "spaghetti" the thickness of your little finger. Cut these diagonally and roll out to form little diamonds of pastry no more than ½ in (1 cm) long.

Heat a generous amount of oil in a deep fryer until smoking. Fry the diamonds, a few at a time, until golden. Drain on paper towels.

Heat the honey and 3 tablespoons of sugar in a large saucepan over medium heat until liquefied. Lower the heat and gently stir in the diamonds, half the candied peel, the remaining orange rind, the almonds and lemon extract. Stir gently and frequently with a wooden spoon until the diamonds have absorbed nearly all the honey.

Transfer the contents to a large round serving bowl previously sponged with cold water. Wet your hands and shape to form a ball like a giant donut. Sprinkle over the ball the remaining candied peel, the cinnamon and some colored sugar dots. Leave for a few hours, or overnight, before serving. If properly sealed in foil the *struffoli* will keep for up to 10 days.

SERVES: 8 to 10

Granita di Caffè con Panna Stregata

Coffee Water Ice with Strega Cream

The intense flavor of Italian coffee results from the coffee beans being roasted for longer than they are elsewhere.

1⅓ cups (4 oz/125 g) freshly ground coffee, preferably Italian espresso blend
½ cup (4 oz/125 g) superfine (caster) sugar
2 tablespoons unsweetened cocoa powder
9 cups (4½ pt/2.25 l) water
2 cups (16 fl oz/500 ml) heavy (double) cream
2 tablespoons Strega or Chartreuse liqueur

Rinse 6 long drinking glasses and place them, wet, in the freezer to frost up.

Put the coffee, sugar (reserving 2 tablespoons) and cocoa powder in a large saucepan. Bring the water to a boil and add to the coffee, sugar and cocoa, stirring well. Place over moderate heat, bring to a boil, lower heat and simmer for 15 minutes.

Remove from heat, leave until cold then strain through fine muslin. Pour into freezing trays and place in the freezer. Freeze without stirring until a fairly solid mush (about 1½ to 2 hours).

In a large bowl whip the cream, adding the reserved sugar when the cream becomes opaque. Continue to whip and when the cream is holding its shape add the Strega. Whip a further minute.

Fill the frosted glasses ¾ full with the *granita*. Top with enough whipped cream to stand up above the rims.

SERVES: 6

Shortcrust Cake with Ricotta and Barley, Honey Sweets, Coffee Water Ice with Strega Cream, Chocolate Mousse

PETER JOHNSON

Rodi Garganico
Candelaro
San Severo
Manfredonia
Lucera
San Ferdinando di Puglia
Foggia
Cervaro
Barletta
Cerignola
Trani
Andria
Molfetta
Corato
Bari
Terlizzi
Polignano a Mare
Bitetto
Ofanto
Bitonto
Monopoli
Napoli
Campania
Gravina in Puglia
Putignano
Fasano
Altamura
Alberobello
Basilicata
Salerno
Potenza
Matera
Noci
Ostuni
Martina Franca
Basento
Grottaglie
Mesagne
Taranto
Agri
Manduria
Mare Grande
Roccanova
Sinni
Porto Cesareo
Aradeo
Maratea
Calabria
Corigliano Calabro
Rossano
Cosenza
La Sila
Neto
Nicastro
Crotone
Catanzaro
Mare Ionico
Golfo di Squillace
Vibo Valentia
Stretto di Messina
Messina
Reggio di Calabria

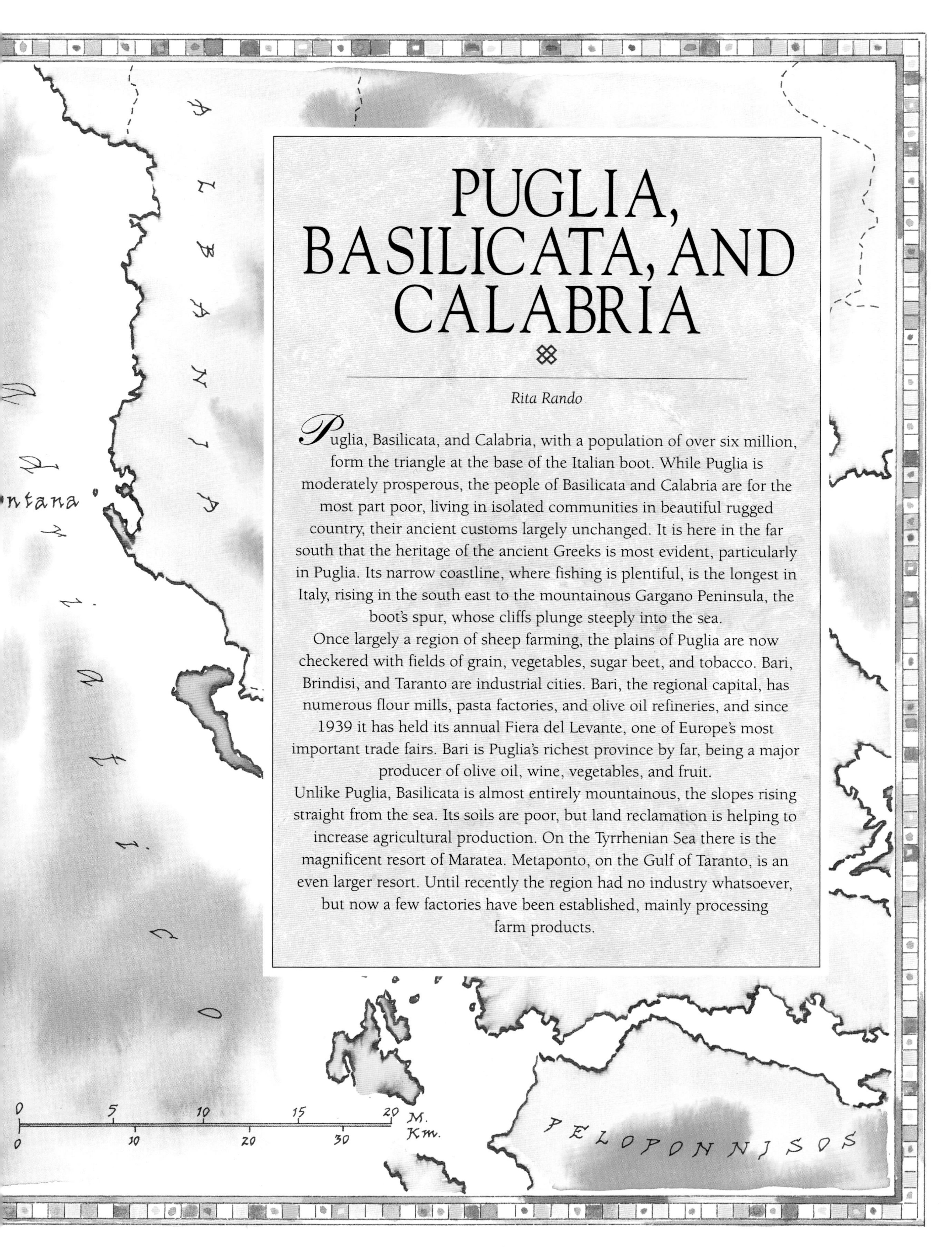

PUGLIA, BASILICATA, AND CALABRIA

Rita Rando

Puglia, Basilicata, and Calabria, with a population of over six million, form the triangle at the base of the Italian boot. While Puglia is moderately prosperous, the people of Basilicata and Calabria are for the most part poor, living in isolated communities in beautiful rugged country, their ancient customs largely unchanged. It is here in the far south that the heritage of the ancient Greeks is most evident, particularly in Puglia. Its narrow coastline, where fishing is plentiful, is the longest in Italy, rising in the south east to the mountainous Gargano Peninsula, the boot's spur, whose cliffs plunge steeply into the sea.

Once largely a region of sheep farming, the plains of Puglia are now checkered with fields of grain, vegetables, sugar beet, and tobacco. Bari, Brindisi, and Taranto are industrial cities. Bari, the regional capital, has numerous flour mills, pasta factories, and olive oil refineries, and since 1939 it has held its annual Fiera del Levante, one of Europe's most important trade fairs. Bari is Puglia's richest province by far, being a major producer of olive oil, wine, vegetables, and fruit.

Unlike Puglia, Basilicata is almost entirely mountainous, the slopes rising straight from the sea. Its soils are poor, but land reclamation is helping to increase agricultural production. On the Tyrrhenian Sea there is the magnificent resort of Maratea. Metaponto, on the Gulf of Taranto, is an even larger resort. Until recently the region had no industry whatsoever, but now a few factories have been established, mainly processing farm products.

JOHN BULMER/SUSAN GRIGGS AGENCY

Harvest time in Calabria, a pair of oxen yoked to a cart piled high with hay.

The golden sheaves spread across this field outside Alberobello seem to echo the shapes of the trulli *clustered in the distance.*

Calabria in the south west forms the toe of the Italian boot and is, like Basilicata, largely mountainous. It is an area of great beauty, with one coastline on the Ionian Sea, the other on the Tyrrhenian. To the north is the remote forest-covered Sila plateau, parts of which are snow-covered for six months of the year. The richest agricultural land is around Reggio Calabria, where citrus fruit of every description are grown. It is here that a large proportion of the world's bergamot oil is produced, an essential ingredient in eau de cologne, its sale earning millions of dollars each year.

With its wild mountains, its forests where wolves can still be found, its parched rocky coastline, its beaches, its blue blue sea, and its enduring traditions, the south is becoming increasingly popular with tourists. A particular attraction are the *trulli* between Martina Franca and Monopoli in Puglia. These strange beehive-shaped houses were built from stones without mortar, to enable them, so the story goes, to be quickly dismantled when the tax man came, so that the people, and their homes, could both disappear. There are over 1000 of these whitewashed *trulli* on the outskirts of Alberobello, most of them inhabited, and they present a remarkable fairytale sight.

Greek and Roman ruins, and Medieval, Norman, Renaissance, and Baroque buildings can be found throughout the region. In Otranto cathedral, in Puglia, you can chart what was known of human history in a 1000-year-old mosaic which covers the floor of the entire building.

GIULIANO COLLIVA/THE IMAGE BANK

WEINBERG/CLARK/THE IMAGE BANK

A group of trulli. *Large numbers of these curious domed, dry-stone structures can be seen in the region between Monopoli and Martina Franca in central Puglia. Quite a number continue to be used as homes.*

Southern Cooking

The local cuisine is essentially based on three major ingredients: grain, grapes, and olives. Bread is the most important element of the local diet, and comes in all sizes, shapes, and colors. Some loaves, like the *scanata,* made from boiled potatoes and flour, are large enough to feed a family for a week. Lecce produces two unusual types of bread: *pane purecasiu*, with a sauce of oil, onion, and tomatoes, and *puccia*, made with black olives.

Calabria has its own special bread, *pitta*, meaning painted, which is colored with various ingredients like tomatoes, sardines, and olives. Even pizzas have acquired a local style, such as *pizza calabrese con tonno e pomodoro*, with tuna and tomatoes, and *pizza di patate*, potato pizza. In Puglia they make *pizza di cipolle*, using thinly sliced onions that have been marinated in olive oil, and *pizza puddica*, its little holes filled with tomatoes and garlic, olive oil, and oregano.

Antipasti include a wide variety of tasty salami, olives, vegetables preserved in oil, seafood, and delicious *calzoni*, stuffed pizzas. *Calzone pugliese* generally has a filling of tomato, onion, olives, anchovies, capers, and parsley; *u cutturidde* is a *calzone* typical of Terlizzi, filled with onion, anchovies, and fried cod, while the *pettue* or *popizze* are large ravioli filled with ricotta, quickly fried. *Lampasciuni*, a wild onion which grows in Puglia and Basilicata, is used to accompany many regional dishes. A Bitetto specialty, *lampasciuni alla vetrettese*, is a purée of *lampasciuni* with vinegar, spread on bread as an *antipasto*.

MUNZIG/SUSAN GRIGGS AGENCY

The air is filled with leaves and twigs as olives are winnowed. The olives are harvested by spreading a sheet beneath the tree, which is then given a vigorous shake that makes the ripe olives fall to the ground.

Soups are common fare, especially in winter. They have imaginative names such as *maritata alla foggiana*, married, Foggia style, using a combination of vegetables, meat, and bacon, and *minestra di castrato*, with mutton and vegetables. Basilicata and Calabria offer *millecosedde*, meaning literally "a thousand things" to refer to the number of vegetables and cereals used, and the simple *pancotto*, bread soup. Puglia and Calabria offer excellent fish soups, such as *zuppa di pesce alla gallipolina*, a fish chowder considered to be a direct descendant of an old Spartan soup, *cozze alla marinara*, a pungent mussel soup with ginger and vinegar, and *zuppa di pesce alla brindisina*, which combines fish with eels.

Pastas and Sauces Galore

All three regions share the same traditions in pasta preparation and, despite being encouraged to consume commercially produced pasta, people continue to favor the home-made variety. Some of the most popular are: *recchie*, ear-shaped, made by pressing the pasta with the thumb; *strascenate* (also called *cavatielli*), square-shaped, pulled along bare boards to give a rough surface; and *fenescecchie*, which are spirals, shaped round a knitting needle. Apulian dishes made with these types of pasta include *recchie ai tre colori*, of three colors, with tomatoes, cheese, and ruchetta, a local herb considered to be an aphrodisiac, and *recchie con cime e acciuga*, with turnip tops and anchovies. Calabria is famous for its *lasagne imbottite e cotte al forno*, a rich baked lasagna pie, and *pasta ammuddicata*, with breadcrumbs and anchovy sauce. Certain pasta sauces deserve particular mention: *ciambotto*, a mixture of fish and seafood; *casseruola di polipetti*, octopus pot; *ragù del macellaio,* made with pork, veal, lamb, and kid; and *bracioline*, consisting of small slices of veal or horsemeat and ham, fried then cooked with tomatoes.

Traditional clothing is still worn by many of the older women in Basilicata, particularly in the more remote villages.

S. FIORE/FIOREPRESS

Facing page: Waves break on the rocks right at the feet of these houses in Rione Chianalea in Calabria. There are few beaches on this harsh coastline.

GIULIO VEGGI

APULIAN LEGENDS

Lecce has an enviable reputation for its *sanguinaccio*, a sausage that is made by mixing pig's blood with pig or veal brain, which is then boiled. This sausage is supposed to be so good that, around three centuries ago, the locals were able to use it as barter to obtain one of the Roman columns at Brindisi which marked the end of the Appian Way.

The sea of the Gulf of Taranto is especially good for the farming of mussels and oysters because on its floor there are several *citri*, natural freshwater springs, around which their cultivation takes place. The biggest of these *citri*, called Anello di San Cataldo, St Cataldo's ring, originates at a depth of about 200 feet (60 meters) and its whirlpool is visible from the surface of the sea. According to legend, St Cataldo, one of the early bishops of Taranto, threw his ring into the sea on a day when a dangerous storm was raging. The storm ceased forthwith and a huge spring appeared on the seabed right at the spot where the ring had fallen.

Locally bred lamb, especially baby lamb, is used extensively, the flesh flavored by the herbs in the pastures on which the flocks graze. When cooked *alla carbonara* it is baked only with salt; *allo squero* means it is spit roasted and *alla brace* is broiled. The dishes *annulieddu a lu furnu*, baked baby lamb and *carducci con l'agnello*, lamb with mushrooms, cooked in the pot, are prepared for Easter. Kid is most commonly eaten in the mountains, perhaps the most famous dishes being *capretto ripieno*, kid stuffed with aromatic herbs and spices, and *capretto ai carciofi*, kid sautéed with artichokes, these being as tender as the kid in springtime and particularly tasty. The combining of the offal of these two animals has produced *gnemeriidde*, small rissoles seasoned with herbs and pecorino, grilled, roasted, or simply sautéed and served with potatoes and bread.

Basilicata has a reputation throughout Italy for its fine preserved meats. Maybe best known are the *luganighe*, long, thin, tasty pork sausages, popular since Roman times, now adopted by northerners as the perfect accompaniment to polenta, and the *sopressate*, large oval sausages seasoned with ginger, often preserved in oil. But there are quantities of others, seasoned variously with pepper, chili, fennel, and other herbs. A sausage which has become popular recently is the *pezzente*, beggar, made with leftovers from the butcher's shop. Other specialties are *cotiche*, made with pig's skin preserved in lard and *tarantello*, from Taranto, a salami filled with tuna fish.

Poultry and game dishes are not widely eaten, but *coniglio alla cacciatora*, rabbit in wine vinegar, or *ai capperi*, with capers, and *pollo ripieno*, stuffed chicken with spices and aromatic herbs, are dishes common to all three regions. *Lepre alla cacciatora*, hare with sage, rosemary, garlic, oil, tomatoes and ginger is a full-flavored specialty of Basilicata.

S. FIORE/FIOREPRESS

Feasts and Festivals

The south boasts the most marvellous variety of feasts and festivals. In Lecce on 17 January there is the feast of Sant'Antonio, and on the following day it is customary to eat a meal of gnocchi, fish, and apple fritters accompanied by Moscato wine. On 5 February Putignano celebrates Carnevale with floats parading through the town as a propitiatory rite to ensure a good harvest. The feast of San Giuseppe is celebrated in March at Cisternino with the Sagra dei Gnemeriidde. Also in March, Reggio Calabria holds its annual Fiera dell'Attività Agrumaria, delle Essenze e degli Olii, the citrus, essence, and oils fair, an international gathering which plays a major part in promoting local produce and wines. In Nemoli the Holy Week rites culminate on Easter Sunday with a *frittata* festival.

In April Lecce holds its Fiera del Vino, a wine fair. On 1 May Taranto holds the Festa di San Cataldo at which the city's patron saint is commemorated with a good deal of sweet eating. On 14 May, the port of Crotone celebrates the feast of the Madonna di Capocolonna with a sea-borne procession and a fish festival. In the same month Rodi Garganico hosts its orange festival, the Festa degli Aranci. On 16 May, Porto Cesareo holds a fish festival. On 15 August Brindisi holds the Melonata Ferragostale, when huge quantities of local watermelons are eaten on the beach. On the same day Roccanova celebrates the feast of San Rocco with plenty of food and entertainment. At Noci the Ferragosto festival comprises a folk festival and a cheese fair.

September is the month when many grape festivals take place in Puglia: they are held at Lecce, Aradeo, San Ferdinando di Puglia, San Severo, and Foggia. During the same month Bari hosts its Fiera del Levante and on 29 September holds the Sagra della Zampina, del Bocconcino e del Buon Vino, an event which offers those who attend the best in local pork, cheese, and wine. On the second Sunday in September Polignano a Mare celebrates the Festa del Cristo with meat rolls, spit-roasted lamb, lettuce, and olives, all set out on long tables for everyone to eat.

Bari and Barletta hold their grape festivals in October, while Cosenza has its yearly show of dried fruit, and San Ferdinando di Puglia holds its Sagra del Carciofo e del Vino Barletta, artichokes and Barletta wine festival. The list ends with Natale tra i Trulli, Christmas among the *trulli*, held in Fasano between Christmas and New Year, at which every kind of local gastronomic delight can be sampled.

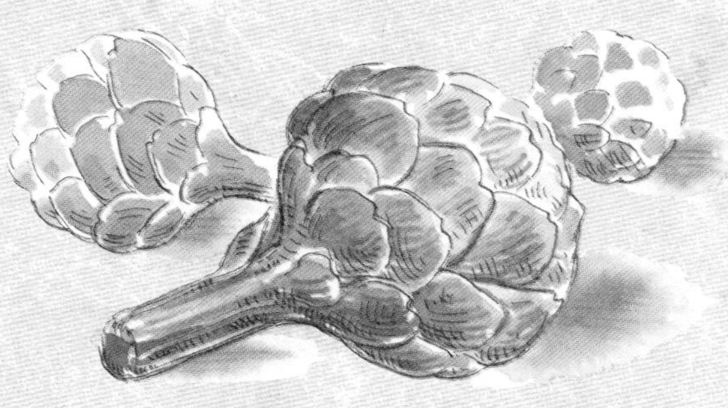

KLAUS D. FRANCKE/BILDERBERG

Winter in Alberobello, when the tourists are largely absent. Two men sit at a streetside café and watch the passers-by.

Facing page: A fisherman at Bisceglie in northern Puglia, absorbed in mending nets.

Of Beans, Macaroni, and Gelati

Apulian people prefer broad beans to all other vegetables and state that "*Di tutti i legumi la fava è regina, cotta la sera, scaldata la mattina*". ("The broad bean is queen of all vegetables, cooked at night-time, warmed up in the morning.") Perhaps the best known dish made from broad beans in this part of the country is *'ncapriata*, a thick soup.

Another saying refers to macaroni, and is in the form of a prayer: "*Christe mi, fa chiove le maccarrune e le chianghe de le logge fatt'a ragù*" ("My Lord, make it rain macaroni, and turn the verandah rails into stew.")

At one time Puglia was known for its *gelati al forno*, baked gelati, a delicious concoction made from two slices of sponge cake filled with gelato, *manteche,* and a mixture of dried fruit, quickly baked before serving. The saying "*Aspiitte ca mo venene le gelate d'o furne*" ("Wait for the baked gelati") is now used when someone seems to be asking for the impossible.

With so much coastline, it is not surprising that Puglia and Calabria are famous for their fish, but freshwater produce such as eels and trout are also available from Basilicata's lakes. Trout and eels can also be caught in Calabria in the rivers of the Sila range. As for saltwater fish, their fine flavor is attributed to the rocky seabed, and to the expertise of the local fishermen who ensure that only fish in season reaches the table. *Orata alla pugliese* is gilthead cooked with potatoes, pecorino, parsley, and olive oil, whereas if prepared *alla San Nicola* (the patron saint of Bari) the fish is washed in sea water, marinated in oil and lemon juice, then broiled. As a sampling of other dishes, there are *sgombri all'aceto*, mackerel in vinegar, *sogliole gratinate*, sole au gratin, *alici recanate*, a kind of anchovy tart, and *polipi arricciati*, curled octopus.

Oysters and mussels have been cultivated in the Mare Piccolo and Mare Grande of Taranto since ancient times. The oysters are commonly served either *arraganati*, crumbed and seasoned with garlic, parsley, oil, oregano, and tomatoes, *bollite*, boiled and served with lemon juice and oil, or in soups. They are best, however, eaten raw with a sprinkling of pepper and a dash of lemon juice. As for the mussels (known in Taranto as *mitili* rather than *cozze*), the locals cook them any number of ways. They are served in soups, they are served *gratinate*, au gratin, *fritte*, fried, and made into a sauce for polenta. A dish named *tielli*, which broadly resembles *paella*, remains in the cuisine as a legacy of Spanish invasion.

Under the Strong Southern Sun

To have an idea of the wonderful range of vegetables that are grown it is essential to visit one of the local markets. Peppers, mushrooms, peas, cardoons, artichokes, olives, broad beans, chickpeas, eggplant, potatoes, tomatoes, cauliflower —appetising fresh vegetables in abundance. Eggplant are a local favorite. Served *ripiene* they are stuffed with anchovies, black olives, and breadcrumbs and baked. In Calabria you can find eggplant soup, eggplant sweet and sour, and even eggplant with chocolate. In Calabria tomatoes are stuffed with pasta; in Puglia they are dried in the sun for four days, then preserved in olive oil to make *pomodori sott'olio*. Potatoes are used in bread, most stews, and in minestrone. In Calabria they are turned into savory cakes called *torta di patate*.

The cheese platter displays the best fresh mozzarella (those from Puglia made with buffalo milk are the finest on the national market), *scamorze, provole, provolone*, fresh and seasoned pecorino and ricotta, and *ricotta sfornata,* baked ricotta. Salted ricotta, used widely, is called *cacioricotta*.

In this part of Italy the hot Mediterranean sun ripens fruit to perfection. Puglia and Calabria export most of theirs, Calabria being particularly famous for its dried fruit. Fresh fruit is eaten at the end of each meal and almonds, nuts, and citrus are used extensively in the preparation of sweets and desserts. *Castagnedde* are made with almond meal, sugar, and flour flavored with lemon peel. *Susamelli* are made with citrus peel mixed with flour and honey. Then there are dishes like *fichi ripieni*, figs stuffed with nuts, chocolate, and honey. There are *carteddate*, little round cakes made with flour, oil, and white wine (a Christmas specialty); *cauciuni*, fried sweets made with chickpea purée mixed with chocolate, *vincotto*, cinnamon, and vanilla; *mostaccioli*, chocolate cookies; and *torta di prugne*, sponge cake with prunes. Particularly delicious specialties are the *confetti mucci*, produced in Andria, which are filled with marzipan, chocolate, and liqueur.

The Wine Cellar of Italy

Viticulture, begun by the Phoenicians, has been most successful in Italy's south, the large variety produced in Puglia causing it to be called "the wine cellar of Italy". Puglia produces eighteen DOC wines and forty-two table wines. Amongst the best are: Aleatico di Puglia, sweet reds; a red, a white, and a rosé from Castel del Monte; Copertino, a red and a rosé; and Locorotondo, a dry, delicate white. Rosso di Barletta and Rosso di Cerignola are also excellent.

Basilicata's three most famous wines are Aglianico del Vulture, a fresh, dry red which is excellent with roasts, Moscato del Vulture, a delicate sparkling wine, and Malvasia del Vulture, a dessert wine.

Wines of particular note from Calabria are Donnici and Savuto, both fine reds; Cirò di Calabria, white, red, and rosé; Esaro Bianco, for fish; and Greco di Gerace, a soft, sweet accompaniment to desserts and pastries.

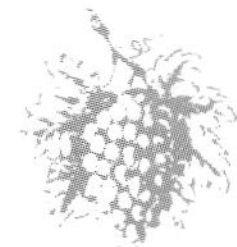

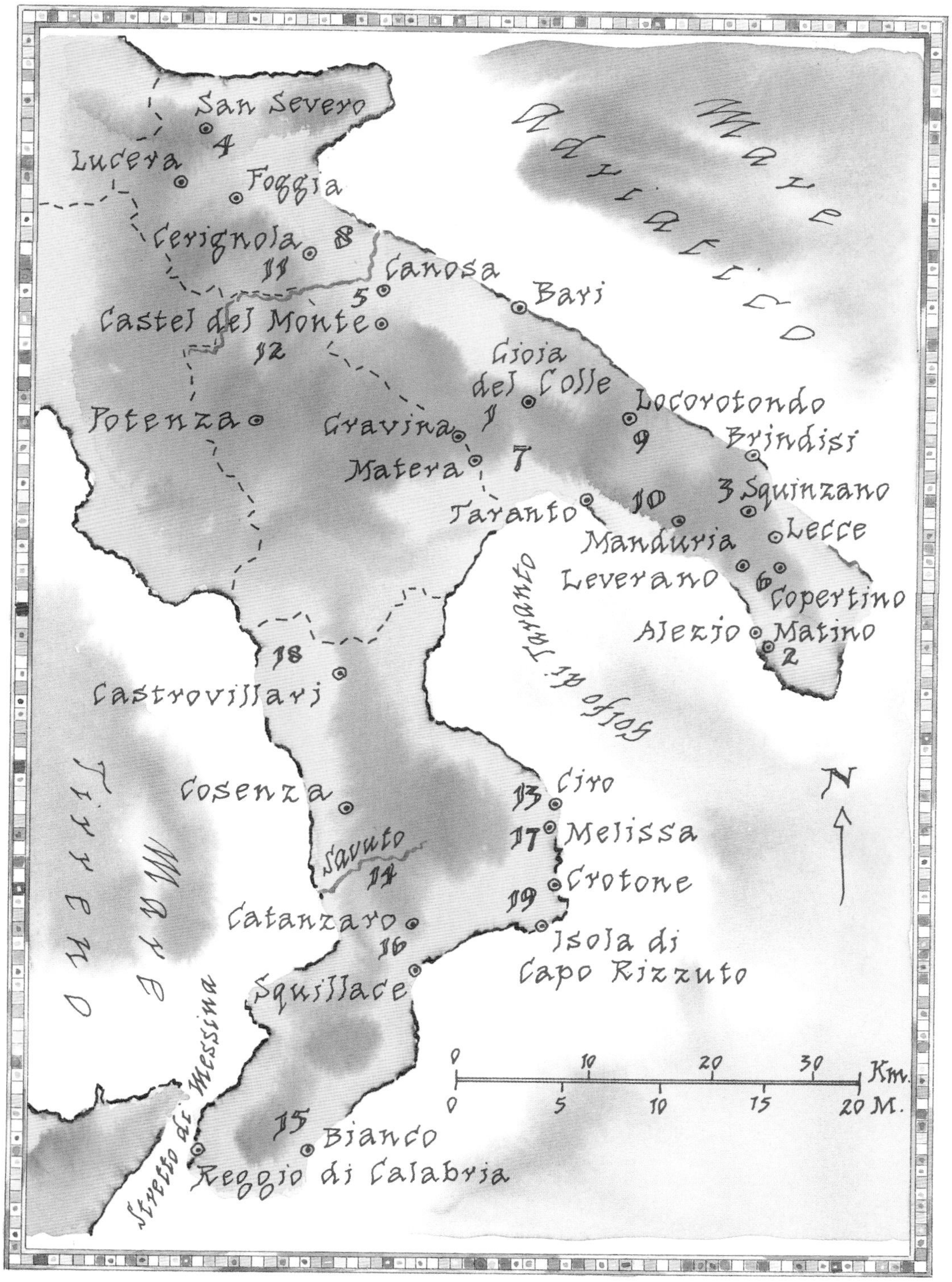

PUGLIA

DOC Wines

1. *Aleatico di Puglia*
2. *Alezio*
3. *Brindisi*
4. *Cacc'e Mmitte di Lucera*
5. *Castel del Monte*
6. *Copertino*
6. *Gioia del Colle*
6. *Gravina*
6. *Leverano*
6. *Locorotondo*
7. *Martina Franca*
2. *Matino*
8. *Moscato di Trani*
2. *Nardò*
3. *Ortanova*
9. *Ostuni*
10. *Primitivo di Manduria*
8. *Rosso di Barletta*
11. *Rosso Canosa*
11. *Rosso di Cerignola*
3. *Salice Salentino*
4. *San Severo*
3. *Squinzano*

BASILICATA

DOC Wine

12. *Aglianico del Vulture*

CALABRIA

DOC Wines

13. *Cirò*
14. *Donnici*
15. *Greco di Bianco*
16. *Lamezia*
17. *Melissa*
18. *Pollino*
19. *Sant'Anna di Isola Capo Rizzuto*
14. *Savuto*

RECIPES OF PUGLIA, BASILICATA AND CALABRIA

Mimmetta Lo Monte

PETER JOHNSON

Morseddu

Savory Morsels

In Calabria, this is often eaten as a breakfast dish.

8 oz (250 g) tripe, precooked
1¼ lb (625 g) veal heart, halved lengthwise
½ cup (4 fl oz/125 ml) olive oil
4 garlic cloves, chopped
6 tablespoons dry red wine
4 oz (125 g) veal liver, sliced ⅓ in (1 cm) thick, cut in 6 pieces
8 large canned peeled tomatoes, seeded and finely chopped
10 3-in (8-cm) sprigs oregano, strip leaves
1 small dried hot red chili pepper, finely chopped
1 teaspoon salt

Parboil and rinse the tripe several times to remove unpleasant odor. Cover with water and boil until tender. Drain and cut in ¼-in (0.5-cm) strips. Set aside.

Boil the heart until tender, about 30 minutes. Drain and cut in ¼-in (0.5-cm) strips. Set aside.

Heat oil and garlic in a large pot. Add heart and cook, stirring, over high heat for a couple of minutes. Add the red wine and let it dissipate briefly. Add liver and all the other ingredients except tripe. Cover and simmer 30 minutes. Add tripe and cook 1 hour. Uncover and cook over high heat until liquid is reduced to barely cover the meat.

Serve hot, beside or on top of thick slices of dense white bread, lightly toasted, or stuffed into pitta bread.

SERVES: 6

Minestra di Verdure

Vegetable Soup

This vegetable soup is a universal dish, not to be confused with *minestrone*. Calabrians add pecorino cheese, garlic and pasta shells to give their local touch.

¼ cup (2 fl oz/60 ml) olive oil
1 oz (30 g) bacon, cut into small pieces
4 tender, small celery stalks, chopped thinly
12 oz (370 g) carrots, cut into ¼-in (0.5-cm) rounds
12 oz (375 g) cabbage, cut into thin strips
1 lb (500 g) broccoli, cut into florets, tender stems sliced ¼ in (0.5 cm) thick
1 clove garlic, finely chopped
1 tablespoon finely chopped parsley
8 oz (250 g) potatoes, diced
2 teaspoons salt
1 teaspoon finely ground black pepper
8 oz (250 g) pasta shells
freshly grated pecorino cheese to taste

Cook oil and bacon over low heat in a large pot, until bacon starts wilting. Add celery and carrots, stir 1 minute over high heat. Add all the other ingredients except the pasta and cheese. Cover barely with water, bring to a boil. Cover and simmer 45 minutes.

Cook pasta in plenty of boiling salted water until *al dente*. Drain and add to vegetables. Mix in pecorino to taste. Serve immediately.

SERVES: 6 to 8

Spaghetti con i Funghi

Spaghetti with Mushrooms

This dish is found throughout Italy, the variety of mushrooms used depending on the locality and the time of year.

1½ cups canned peeled tomatoes, drained (they must be firm)
⅔ cup (5 fl oz/150 ml) olive oil
1 lb (500 g) mushrooms, thinly sliced
1 small onion, finely chopped
1 teaspoon salt
1 tablespoon finely chopped parsley
8 oz (250 g) spaghetti

Seed the tomatoes, reserving the juice. Cut tomatoes into small pieces.

Heat the oil in a very large skillet. Add the mushrooms and the onion and cook over high heat for a few minutes. Mushrooms should not release any liquid. Add tomatoes and salt. Keep cooking over high heat, uncovered, for about 5 minutes. Add reserved juice, cook an additional 5 minutes or until sauce loses excess liquid. Stir only as necessary to prevent scorching. Turn off heat and add parsley.

Cook the spaghetti in plenty of boiling salted water until *al dente*. Drain, toss with the sauce in the skillet and serve immediately.

SERVES: 4

Left: Vegetable Soup, Savory Morsels

Orecchiette con Broccoli

Orecchiette with Broccoli

This delicious dish is best made with home-made pasta. It is quite frequently served cold.

½ cup (4 fl oz/125 ml) olive oil
1 oz (30 g) bacon, finely chopped
1 small onion, finely chopped
3 garlic cloves, coarsely chopped
1½ lb (750 g) broccoli, cut into florets, tender stems sliced ¼ in (0.5 cm) thick
¾ teaspoon salt
1 teaspoon finely ground black pepper
4 anchovy fillets, preserved in olive oil, drained and mashed
6 oz (185g) orecchiette, *or other pasta shells*

Cook olive oil, bacon, onion and garlic in a large pot, over low heat, until the onion begins to wilt. Increase the heat to high and cook briefly, until aromatic.

Add broccoli and stir for a couple of minutes. Add salt, ½ cup water, stir and cook, covered, over low heat for 30 minutes. Turn off heat and add pepper and anchovies.

Cook the *orecchiette* in plenty of boiling salted water until *al dente*. Drain and toss with the broccoli. Serve immediately, or else cold.

SERVES: 4

Orecchiette with Broccoli, Spaghetti with Mushrooms

PETER JOHNSON

Coniglio Brasato

Braised Rabbit

In the south rabbits are quite frequently caught as game.

½ cup (4 fl oz/125 ml) olive oil
4 lb (2 kg) rabbit pieces
4 garlic cloves
1 cup (8 fl oz/250 ml) red wine
12 3-in (8-cm) sprigs fresh oregano, leaves stripped
1 teaspoon salt
1 teaspoon finely ground black pepper

Heat oil in a large pot. Add rabbit and garlic and sear over high heat. Add red wine, oregano, salt and pepper. Cover and simmer until tender (about 30 minutes for pen-raised rabbit).

Remove rabbit and set aside. Reduce liquid over medium-low heat to about ⅓. Return rabbit to the pot, turn in the sauce and serve.

SERVES: 6

Agnello all'Aceto

Lamb with Vinegar

This southern recipe is reminiscent of Greek cooking.

1 oz (30 g) bacon, sliced
3 lb (1.5 kg) lamb leg, shank end, no fat
2 garlic cloves, cut in a few slivers
6 3-in (8-cm) fresh rosemary sprigs. Strip leaves from 2
3 tablespoons olive oil
½ teaspoon salt
1 teaspoon finely ground black pepper
⅔ cup (5 fl oz/150 ml) red wine vinegar

Cook bacon briefly until fat is transparent. Cut in a few pieces. Insert a narrow knife blade in the lamb leg, lengthwise, piercing it in 4 places. Truss each cut with bacon, garlic and a whole rosemary sprig. Rub leg with olive oil, sprinkle with salt, pepper and the rosemary leaves stripped from sprigs.

Bake in oven preheated to 450°F (230°C) for 10 minutes. Pour vinegar over lamb, reduce heat to 375°F (190°C) and bake 50 more minutes. Serve hot, with pan juices dribbled on top.

SERVES: 6

Braised Rabbit, Lamb with Vinegar

PETER JOHNSON

PETER JOHNSON

Swordfish in Lemon Juice, Baked Fish

Pesce Spada al Limone

Swordfish in Lemon Juice

The fishermen from Bagnara in Calabria specialize in catching these huge fish which are found in the Strait of Messina in early summer. They are harpooned in the same way that they were in the time of the ancient Greeks.

unbleached all purpose (plain) flour for dusting
2 lb (1 kg) swordfish in $\frac{1}{2}$-in (1.5-cm) slices
6 tablespoons olive oil
1 small onion, thinly sliced
$4\frac{1}{2}$ tablespoons lemon juice
1 tablespoon finely chopped parsley
$\frac{3}{4}$ teaspoon salt
$\frac{1}{4}$ teaspoon finely ground black pepper

Flour the fish lightly. Heat the oil in a skillet large enough to accommodate the fish in a single layer. Sauté fish over medium-low heat 3 to 4 minutes per side. Lower heat if fish browns too quickly. (May cook in 2 batches, in 2 different skillets.)

Remove fish, add onion and cook on low heat until tender. Increase to high and brown lightly, add lemon juice and all other ingredients. Turn off heat. Return fish to pan and turn gently in sauce. Arrange on a warmed dish and serve immediately.

SERVES: 6

Pesce al Forno

Baked Fish

This recipe works well with any firm-fleshed fish. A typically southern touch is given by the black olives.

4 red snapper about 12 oz (375 g) each, with head and tail on
4 tablespoons olive oil
4 tablespoons red wine vinegar
$\frac{1}{2}$ teaspoon salt
$\frac{1}{2}$ teaspoon finely ground black pepper
24 black olives, pitted and coarsely chopped

Coat the snapper with oil, vinegar, salt and pepper, inside and out. Stuff with olives. Bake in oven preheated to 425°F (220°C), in a shallow dish or skillet for 20 minutes. Baste a couple of times with pan drippings. Serve hot.

SERVES: 4 to 6

Peperoni e Aringhe

Bell Peppers and Herring

Southerners love roasted bell peppers. In this instance they are combined with smoked herring from the north.

5 large bell peppers (capsicums), any mixture of red, green and yellow
10 oz (315 g) smoked herring, cut in $\frac{1}{3}$-in (1-cm) pieces
1 cup (8 fl oz/250 ml) red wine vinegar
$2\frac{1}{2}$ tablespoons finely chopped parsley
$2\frac{1}{2}$ tablespoons drained capers, squeezed well
$2\frac{1}{2}$ teaspoons lemon juice
5 tablespoons olive oil
$\frac{1}{4}$ teaspoon aniseed
$\frac{1}{4}$ to $\frac{1}{2}$ teaspoon salt
$\frac{3}{4}$ teaspoon finely ground black pepper

Roast the bell peppers on a grill, on medium heat, turning often. When evenly charred remove from heat, cover and cool. Peel, cut in half and discard the core and seeds. Cut in $\frac{1}{2}$-in (1-cm) juliennes.

In the meantime, marinate the herring in the vinegar for 2 hours. Drain the herring. Mix all the ingredients together and serve.

SERVES: 6

Verdure Miste al Forno

Mixed Baked Vegetables

Another simple and sustaining peasant dish, ideal for a vegetarian meal.

10 oz (315 g) eggplant (aubergine)
3 tablespoons breadcrumbs
$\frac{1}{4}$ cup (2 fl oz/60 ml) olive oil
$\frac{3}{4}$ teaspoon black pepper, finely ground
1 lb (500 g) baking potatoes
$1\frac{1}{2}$ tablespoons finely chopped parsley
1 garlic clove, finely chopped
4 tablespoons freshly grated pecorino cheese
1 lb (500 g) tomatoes, sliced
$\frac{1}{2}$ teaspoon salt

Dice the eggplant, soak in water and 2 teaspoons salt for 30 minutes, then drain. Mix the breadcrumbs with 1 tablespoon olive oil and $\frac{1}{4}$ teaspoon pepper. Toss the eggplant with half the remaining oil.

Peel the potatoes and slice crosswise in $\frac{1}{8}$-in (0.5-cm) slices. Cover with water, then drain, leaving some moisture on. Toss the potatoes with the remaining oil. Mix parsley, garlic, pecorino, salt and remaining pepper.

Lightly coat a baking dish, 12 in x 8 in (30 cm x 20 cm) with 2 in (5 cm) high sides, with olive oil. Layer the ingredients in it as follows:
$\frac{1}{2}$ the potatoes, the eggplant, $\frac{1}{2}$ the pecorino mixture, $\frac{1}{2}$ the tomatoes, the remaining potatoes, the remaining pecorino mixture, the remaining

PETER JOHNSON

Clockwise from top: Eggplant Calabria Style, Bell Peppers and Herring, Zucchini in Vinegar, Mixed Baked Vegetables

tomatoes, the breadcrumb mixture. Bake in oven preheated to 375°F (190°C) for 50 to 55 minutes.

SERVES: 6

Melanzane Calabresi

Eggplant Calabria Style

Eggplant is probably the most common vegetable in the region, growing well in dry, hot conditions.

2 1-lb (500-g) eggplants (aubergines); avoid large ones as they have too many seeds
olive oil for deep frying
4 garlic cloves, sliced thinly
1 lb (500 g) tomatoes, ripe but firm, quartered lengthwise, and cut into 1/3-in (1-cm) wedges
2 tablespoons finely chopped parsley
3/4 teaspoon salt
4 anchovy fillets, mashed

Slice the eggplant crosswise 1/3 in (1 cm) thick, soak in water and 4 teaspoons salt for 30 minutes. Drain well.

Sauté the eggplant in 1/3 in (1 cm) olive oil over high heat until pleasantly brown. Do not crowd or puncture while frying. Set on a rack to drain excess oil.

In each of 2 very large skillets place 1/4 cup of the olive oil used to cook the eggplant. Divide the garlic equally between the skillets and heat. Add to each skillet equal amounts of tomatoes and cook over high heat for 1 minute, uncovered, stirring only a couple of times. Turn off heat and transfer contents of one skillet to the other. Add parsley, salt and anchovies and mix well together.

Layer the eggplant slices and the tomato mixture in a serving platter, starting with the eggplant. Serve hot or at room temperature.

SERVES: 6

Zucchine a Scapece

Zucchini in Vinegar

Eaten with home-made bread, this makes a superb meal. Farming people often take a serving with them to the fields for their lunch break.

4 tablespoons olive oil, or as necessary
1 lb (500 g) zucchini (courgettes), cut in 1/2 crosswise, then sliced lengthwise 1/3 in (1 cm) thick
2 garlic cloves, lightly crushed
2 tablespoons red wine vinegar
1/4 teaspoon salt
1/4 teaspoon pepper
1 tablespoon finely chopped parsley

Heat 2 tablespoons olive oil in a skillet. Add a layer of zucchini slices. Cook over medium-low heat a few minutes, until barely tender. Turn a couple of times. Increase heat to high, let zucchini turn a light golden brown, remove from pan. Repeat with remaining zucchini, adding oil as necessary. Set aside.

When all the zucchini are cooked add the garlic to the oil in the skillet and cook over low heat until aromatic. Add vinegar, salt and pepper. Turn off heat, return zucchini to the skillet with the parsley and mix gently. Serve at room temperature.

SERVES: 4

PETER JOHNSON

Almond Cookies

Copete

Almond Cookies

Almond trees are common throughout the south and almonds are used in many dishes, including main courses.

$\frac{3}{4}$ cup (3 oz/90 g) blanched almonds
2 egg whites
$\frac{1}{8}$ teaspoon cream of tartar
$\frac{1}{3}$ cup (3 oz/90 g) sugar
$\frac{1}{2}$ cup (3 oz/90 g) powdered (icing) sugar, well sifted
3 apricot seeds, toasted and ground like the almonds (optional)

Toast the almonds lightly, for 5 to 8 minutes, in oven preheated to 350°F (180°C). Cool. Grind finely. Do not overgrind as it will draw out the oil.

Beat the egg whites until foamy. Add cream of tartar and beat until lightly whipped. Start adding the sugar in a thin stream, beating until stiff and glossy. Beat in the powdered sugar. Fold in the almonds mixed with the apricot seeds, if using them.

Spoon by the heaping tablespoon onto cookie sheets lined with baking paper, keeping mixture mounds well apart. (Traditionally, the mixture should be spooned onto large wafers, like the ones used in making nougat, rather than onto baking paper. If wafers are available, use them.)

Bake in oven preheated to 275°F (140°C) for 45 minutes. Counter cool. *Copete* will have a crunchy and crumbly exterior but be soft and moist on the inside. These cookies may be kept for several weeks, provided they are stored in an airtight container.

MAKES: 18

Pitte Dolci di Pasqua

Sweet Easter Turnovers

Variations of these fruit and nut turnovers are made elsewhere in Italy, but the ingredients that are given here make this an unmistakably southern dish.

Dough:
2 cups (8 oz/250 g) unbleached all purpose (plain) flour
1 tablespoon sugar
$\frac{1}{2}$ cup (4 fl oz/125 ml) olive oil
$\frac{1}{2}$ cup (4 fl oz/125 ml) plus 2 tablespoons Moscato wine
1 teaspoon grated orange rind
$\frac{1}{4}$ teaspoon ground cinnamon
Filling:
$\frac{3}{4}$ cup (4 oz/125 g) dark raisins
2 tablespoons Moscato wine
$\frac{1}{2}$ cup (2 oz/60 g) walnuts, in small pieces
1 oz (30 g) semisweet (plain) chocolate, in small pieces
$\frac{1}{2}$ teaspoon grated lemon rind
2 tablespoons melted honey
powdered (icing) sugar for dusting

For the pastry: Mix flour and sugar then mix with the oil. Heat $\frac{1}{2}$ cup Moscato to just under boiling point. Add it to the flour–oil mixture. Add orange rind and cinnamon and knead for a few minutes. Add, as you keep kneading, the remaining Moscato, up to 2 full tablespoons, or as necessary to obtain a smooth, elastic dough. Set aside, covered.

For the filling: Toss the raisins with the Moscato and leave to marinate for around 3 hours. Drain excess moisture. Mix raisins with all other filling ingredients.

To assemble the *pitte*, roll dough about $\frac{1}{8}$ in (3 mm) thick and lay on lightly floured surface. Cut into 4-in (10-cm) rounds. Divide the filling among the rounds, keeping it away from the edges. Moisten the edges of the rounds lightly with water, fold rounds in half over filling to form a semicircle, press edges together to seal.

Place on cookie sheet lightly coated with oil. Bake in oven preheated to 375°F (190°C) for 8 minutes. Lower to 350°F (180°C) and bake for a further 15 minutes. Dust the turnovers generously with powdered sugar and allow to cool before serving.

MAKES: 16 to 18

Turdilli

Dough Sticks with Honey

One of Puglia's best-known dessert wines is Moscato di Trani, which would be ideal in this recipe. However, any other Moscato or sweet white wine could be used.

2 cups (8 oz/250 g) unbleached all purpose (plain) flour
½ cup (4 fl oz/125 ml) olive oil
½ cup (4 fl oz/125 ml) plus 2 tablespoons Moscato wine
1 teaspoon grated orange rind
¼ teaspoon ground cinnamon
corn oil or similar for frying
½ cup (5 oz/155 g) honey

Mix flour and olive oil. Heat ½ cup Moscato to just under boiling point. Add it to the flour–oil mixture. Add orange rind and cinnamon and knead for a few minutes. Add, as you keep kneading, the remaining Moscato, up to 2 full tablespoons, or as necessary to obtain a smooth, elastic dough than can be easily rolled. Roll dough into pencil-like cylinders. Flour very lightly and cut into 2-in (5-cm) sections. Keep the sticks uncrowded, scattered over a lightly floured surface.

Heat corn oil in a deep pan to just below smoking point. Fry the sticks, uncrowded, over moderate to high heat. Adjust heat so that the dough turns a pleasant golden color in 1½ to 2 minutes. Place fried sticks on paper towels to drain.

Warm the honey in a large pan over a low heat until melted. Add the sticks and stir until coated with honey. Remove the pan from the heat and spread the sticks on platter to cool. Serve cold.

SERVES: 6

Sweet Easter Turnovers, Dough Sticks with Honey

PETER JOHNSON

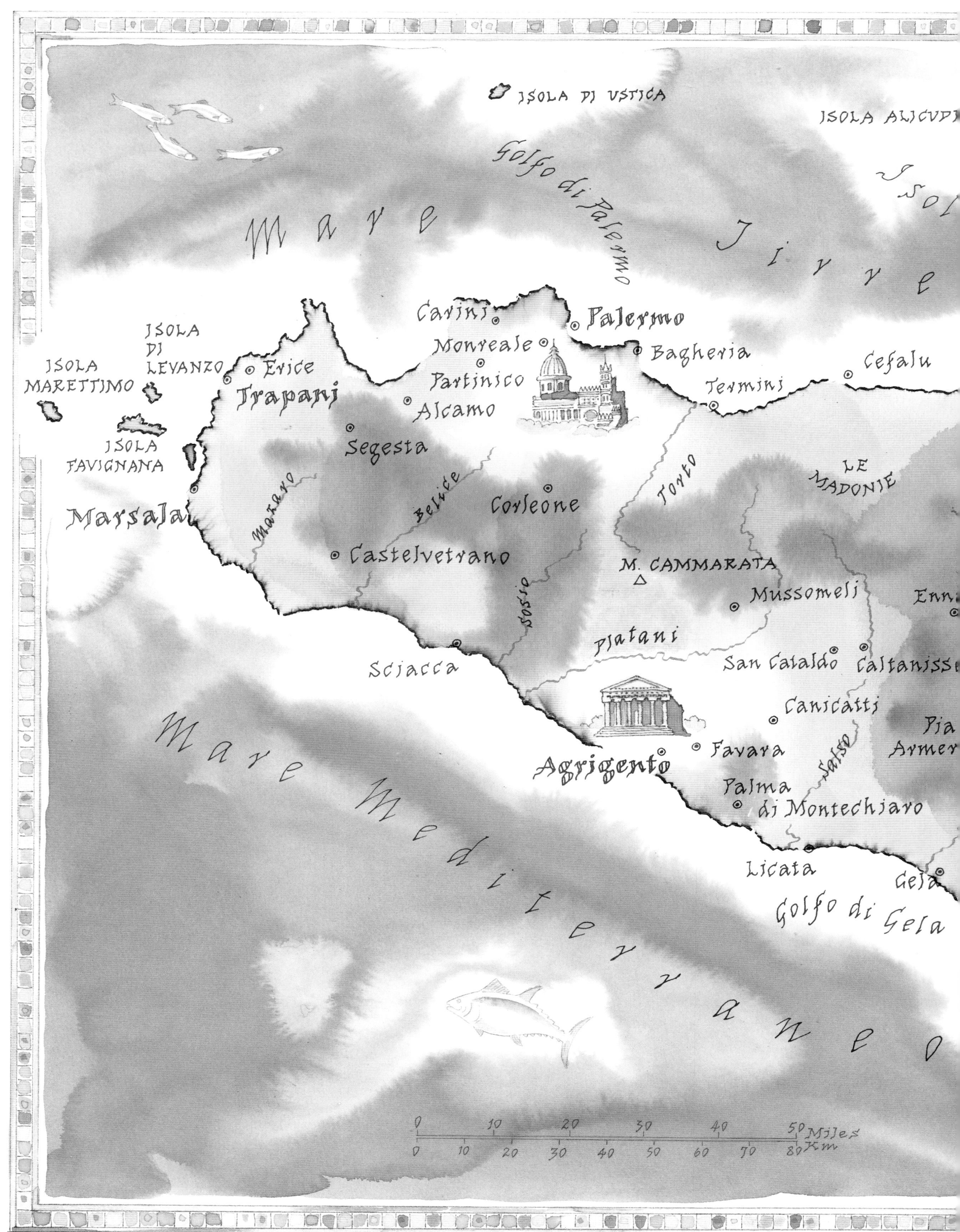

ISOLA DI USTICA
ISOLA ALICUDI
Golfo di Palermo
Mare
Tirre
Isol
ISOLA MARETTIMO
ISOLA DI LEVANZO
ISOLA FAVIGNANA
Carini
Palermo
Monreale
Bagheria
Erice
Trapani
Partinico
Alcamo
Termini
Cefalu
Segesta
Marsala
Mazaro
Belice
Corleone
Torto
LE MADONIE
Castelvetrano
M. CAMMARATA
Sosio
Mussomeli
Enn
Platani
Sciacca
San Cataldo
Caltaniss
Canicatti
Pia
Armer
Agrigento
Favara
Salso
Palma di Montechiaro
Licata
Gela
Golfo di Gela
Mare Mediterraneo
0 10 20 30 40 50 Miles
0 10 20 30 40 50 60 70 80 Km

SICILIA

Vincenzo J. Cincotta

The traveler who crosses the short stretch of sea separating peninsula Italy from Sicilia is greeted by a dazzling spectacle of steep mountain peaks edging to a magical pastel-colored city before plummeting into a transparent Mediterranean.

It is easy to understand why, in the tenth century, an Arab emir had chiselled in an arch on the Zisa Castle of Palermo "...the loveliest possession in the most splendid of the world's kingdoms". Sicilia is the largest island in the Mediterranean and the most sizeable of Italy's twenty regions. Located on a seismic fault, over the centuries it has suffered innumerable devastating earthquakes and volcanic eruptions.

Mount Etna, the largest active volcano in Europe, is undoubtedly the island's most striking feature.

GIULIANO COLLIVA/THE IMAGE BANK

The countryside around Caltanissetta in central Sicilia. The city has a reputation for fine game dishes, particularly partridge, but game is not as plentiful as it once was.

Crossroads between East and West

Broadly triangular in shape, Sicilia is largely mountainous, with one-third of its five million inhabitants concentrated in the coastal regions. The Tyrrhenian coast in the north and the Ionian coast in the east are lushly vegetated and agriculture flourishes, but the south and the plateaux of the interior are harsh, arid, and sparsely populated.

For almost 3000 years the Mediterranean was the epicenter of the Western world and Sicilia its focal point—the crossroads between east and west, north, and south. Between the sixth century BC and 480 BC the Greeks dominated Sicilia, and majestic temples from this golden age can still be seen. The island then fell under Roman control, and in the ninth century the Arabs arrived, making their capital Palermo, which it remains today. Palermo became one of the wealthiest cities in the entire Mediterranean and an Islamic center of learning and culture.

The Arab influence was also felt in agriculture: they established the cultivation of sugarcane, cotton, mulberry trees, date palms, and oranges and introduced sophisticated irrigation techniques.

The Saracens were followed by the Normans, and with them came the influence of the Roman Church and the integration of Sicilia with the European mainstream. The court, established at Palermo, became an intensive center of cross-cultural activity and the economy flourished. Other rulers came and went, Bourbon rule being established in the eighteenth century and remaining until Garibaldi's landing in 1860.

This continuous ethnic and cultural enrichment of the island may well explain the dynamism of the Sicilians. From Archimedes, Aeschylus, and Theocritus to the more recent Nobel laureates Pirandello and Quasimodo, their contribution to Western culture has been constant. It also explains the myriad variety of types one meets—from the fairest blue-eyed blond to the quasi-negroid, with all possible gradations in between—each one very much a Sicilian and sharing a common cultural identity, reinforced over the centuries by a strong Roman Catholic Church.

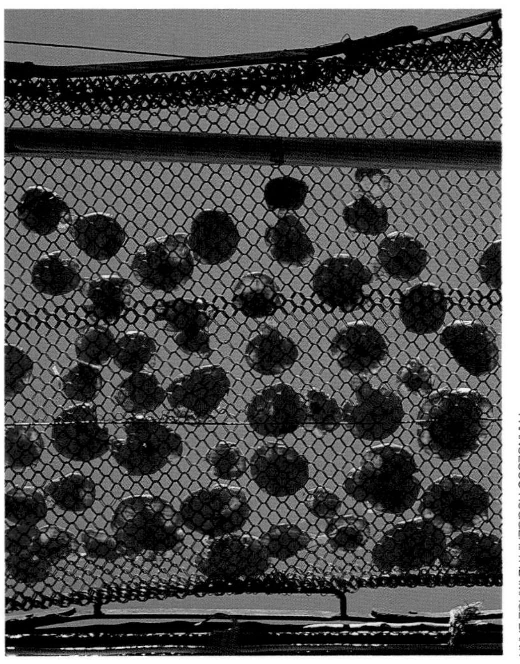

FRANCESCO RUGGERI/THE IMAGE BANK

Tomatoes drying in the strong summer sun. Dried tomatoes are eaten through the winter months until the next crop ripens.

The Roman's Granary

Agriculture is one of the island's principle sources of income. Sicilia has always been a strong producer of winter wheat: the Romans called it the granary of the empire. Other crops include barley, olives, grapes, almonds, pistachios, stone fruit, figs, prickly pears, and, particularly, citrus fruit. Flower cultivation has taken on enormous economic importance in recent years with irrigated, climate-controlled production.

Food for local consumption is available in profusion. In many Sicilian cities the greengrocers take over part of the sidewalk in front of their shops and set up pyramid-like displays of the most varied natural produce, most of it supplied on a daily basis by the local farmers: tomatoes, zucchini, eggplant, artichokes, endive and salad greens, fennel, bell peppers, wild mushrooms, onions, garlic, peas, beans of all kinds, broccoli, cardoons, spinach ... all this not to mention the fruit!

A cart piled high with a generous harvest of broccoli serves as a mobile shop.

MELCHIOR DIGIACOMO/THE IMAGE BANK

Preceding pages: The Greek amphitheater at Segesta, built into a mountain top. Twenty rows of stone seating still remain.

GIULIANO COLLIVA/THE IMAGE BANK

A significant amount of food processing is carried out on the island, and there is sheep and goat grazing and cheese making. Most cheese making is on a family enterprise scale and is for local consumption. Fishing, especially for swordfish, tuna, and sardines, was once of prime importance, but the local fishing for tuna, in particular, has now greatly diminished. Sicilia continues as one of Italy's major olive oil and wine producing regions, both industries now fully mechanized and geared for international markets.

Messina and the East Coast

One's first encounter with Sicilia is usually through Messina—a modern, spacious, pastel, shimmering Mediterranean city. The Messina of today is actually a new city: the old city founded by the Greeks in 730 BC and its twin, Reggio, across the strait, were almost totally destroyed by the earthquake of 1908. The few historic reminders in Messina, such as the Catalan Gothic façade of the cathedral and the Norman-Arabic Church of the Annunciation of the Catalans, are all reconstructions.

The area surrounding Messina has two of the most visited tourist attractions in Europe: the Aeolian Islands just off the coast and Taormina—Winston Churchill's favorite wintering spot. With perhaps the world's most beautiful backdrops—snow-capped Mount Etna—Taormina has a Greco-Roman amphitheater and some handsome Medieval buildings.

No less impressive, but much less frequented, is nearby Tindari. Founded by the Greeks, and destroyed by the Arabs in the ninth century, this is a mountain-top archaeological treasure. Its modern sanctuary to the Madonna makes it a place of pilgrimage for Sicilians, but it is seldom visited by tourists.

Taormina seen through a break in the walls of the ruined Greco-Roman amphitheater. The name Taormina is derived from the Latin taurus, *bull: in ancient times Sicilia was known for its fine cattle.*

KLAUS D. FRANCKE/BILDERBERG

HORIZON/IFA

Europe's largest active volcano, Mount Etna, puts on an awe-inspiring display. It erupts, on average, about once every six years. The rich volcanic soil at its base provides generous crops of olives, grapes, citrus fruits, and figs.

If you are interested in archaeology, not to be missed are the excavations and the various museums on the island of Lipari, which house a large collection of Greek artifacts. Once on Lipari one can easily catch a hydrofoil to nearby Stromboli and see one of the world's most active volcanoes. Do not forget to pick up a bottle of the local Malvasia—a sweet white dessert wine, for years the mainstay of the economy of these islands and nowadays rather difficult to come by.

Out walking in Messina's streets, three things will strike the cuisine-conscious traveler: the displays of local vegetables and fruit; the number of fish shops and markets; and the range of pastry and bread shops—more than 400 for a city of less than a quarter of a million people! The Sicilians have an enviable reputation as pastry cooks.

Early in the morning it is usual to see giant, freshly-caught local swordfish in front of the fish shops on display ready to be sliced and sold. The swordfish, as for thousands of years, are harpooned in the Strait of Messina by local fishermen who work from a *traffinera*, a long skiff with a single tall mast and a crow's-nest for a lookout.

South from Messina is Catania, the island's cultural center, with a superb collection of Baroque buildings, built to replace those parts of the town that were damaged in the earthquake of 1693. The ancient Greek capital, Siracusa, with its historical and archaeological sites and a fine museum, is an important seaport, serving as one of Sicilia's main export outlets. Traveling inland there is Enna, set on a mountain top, a pastoral center where the shepherds make cheese from the milk from their flocks, and where game is plentiful.

Towards Trapani and Palermo

Agrigento, with its Doric temples, is Magna Graecia's best preserved living legacy. Between the city and the sea lies the Valley of the Temples, named after these imposing reminders of its classical past. The city has a folklore festival each year, and in February holds its almond blossom festival.

In the west lies Trapani, famous for its salt flats and for the *mattanza*—a traditional way of trapping tuna. Understandably, the locals have numerous ways of preparing this fish. The town is famous for its Holy Week procession of twenty floats representing the *misteri*, said to rival that of Seville. On a summit overlooking Trapani is the ancient town of Erice, whose *cuscusu* must not be missed. It is made from fine ground wheat, garnished with puréed fish soup, tomatoes, and herbs. In Trapani they serve a very distinctive version of *zuppa di pesce*, containing lobster.

Palermo is a magical city, its most beautiful monuments dating from the period of Arab-Norman synthesis. Not to be missed is the cathedral of Monreale, not far out of town, and the splendid Teatro Massimo, one of the largest opera houses in Europe. In Palermo the visitor will experience the warmest hospitality, and a unique blend of the Arabic and the European.

A Distinctive Regional Cuisine

Culinary traditions vary from one end of the island to the other, but the food is always identifiably Sicilian. In the western region around Palermo and Trapani, the more Arabic part of the island, flavors are stronger, more markedly contrasting, and sweet and salty are sometimes combined. Not long ago the

Following page: Looking down on Palermo, the island's capital and its most colorful city.

BRUCE COLEMAN LTD

Sicilian tourist authorities asked the proprietors of twenty-seven of the island's best known restaurants to name their most famous dish, and topping the list was Palermo's *pasta con le sarde*, pasta with sardines, a pie made with wild fennel, onions, sardines, salted anchovies, pine nuts, sultanas, and macaroni, topped with roasted almonds. This recipe is an exotic elaboration of the traditional pasta *c' 'a anciova* found in one form or another the island over.

A legacy of Norman times remains in the form of salt cod. One little family restaurant in business for years, near the maritime and railroad station in Messina, offers nothing but *pescestocco alla messinese*, dried salt-cured cod with onion, celery, carrot, potatoes, capers, and olives. The dish is eaten with crusty bread and dry white wine.

In the more sophisticated restaurants one is met by an endless display of cold *antipasti*, including perhaps up to ten different types of olives. *Arancine* are stuffed, fried rice balls. *Caponata*, or *caponatina*, broadly speaking, is fried diced eggplant with capers, olives, and celery in a sweet and sour sauce, but there are many regional variations. There will be artichokes galore, seafood salads, marinated vegetables, *"babbaluci"* (snails), salted anchovies—the list goes on and on.

First courses are almost always pasta dishes. Catania's *pasta con le melanzane* is pasta with slices of fried eggplant and a sauce of tomatoes and basil, topped with grated salted ricotta. *Pasta incaciata*, as the name implies, is served with abundant *cacio*, cheese, and is popular throughout Sicilia. A dish lined with fried eggplant is filled with a mixture of macaroni, tomato, grated pecorino, meatballs, *peperoni*, eggplant, hard cooked egg, artichoke hearts, and peas, and baked in the oven. There is an infinite variety of meat and fish sauces for pasta too. In Messina sauces are often made with tomato and swordfish or tuna, and squid is sometimes served with its own ink as sauce.

Main courses commonly feature fish, often grilled and served with *salmoriglio*, a dressing of olive oil, lemon juice, oregano, and parsley, or stewed, *alla ghiotta*, with garlic and tomatoes. *Sciabbacheddu* or *nannatu* are fish fry caught in spring and generally cooked in an omelette. A notable dish is *sarde a beccafico*, being two boned filleted sardines sandwiched with a tasty breadcrumb-based stuffing and fried, named after a bird the dish resembles.

Distinctive meat dishes include *polpettine al limone*, herbed veal rissoles grilled in lemon leaves, *falsomagro*, yearling beef fillet stuffed with egg, salami, mozzarella, and *caciocavallo*, rolled and cooked in a sauce, and *agnello infornato con formaggio*, baked lamb with cheese.

An Island Famous for its Desserts

For coffee and dessert it is best to walk along the main boulevards and stop at a *bar-pasticceria* or *bar-gelateria* and savor the best the world has to offer in terms of desserts—from pastry to marzipan, cookies, candied fruit, sweet liqueur wines, sorbets, and ice creams. This is the land where citrus-flavored ices began. According to legend, when the Arabs occupied Sicilia they found the best antidote to the hot summer sun to be buckets of snow from Mount Etna flavored with lemon juice. And today it is not unusual to see Sicilians clustered around the bar in a café in the early morning having a *granita di limone* with a *"cornetto"*, croissant, for breakfast.

An island specialty is *frutta candita*, fruits such as pears, apricots, peaches, and small blood oranges, cooked in cane sugar until they crystalize. This is the

Marsala

In the west of Sicilia, where the vine-covered hills stretch towards the sea, lies the busy port of Marsala, called *Marsa'Alì* by the Arabs and world renowned for its unique liqueur type wine.

In 1773, John Woodhouse, an Englishman looking for an alternative to Portuguese port and Spanish sherry, made the first Marsala by a process of blending and ageing. The local white wine was blended with distilled alcohol and *mosto cotto*—a syrup made from freshly pressed grape juice slowly boiled and reduced to a thick, dark, very sweet kind of molasses. The wine soon became fashionable and Woodhouse was joined by other Englishmen and, later, by Sicilians in its manufacture.

For a century Marsala was a feature of Italian afternoon teas. Today it is an essential ingredient in a wide range of desserts from *zabaione* to pastries. Around seven and a half million gallons (thirty-four million liters) of the wine are produced annually. The finest and most prestigious, Marsala Vergine, is pale amber in color and very dry to the palate.

Frutti di marturana *are marzipan sweets shaped and colored to look like miniature pieces of fruit. Marzipan, brought originally to the island by the Arabs, is found in all sorts of marvellous confections.*

CHARLES W. FRIEND/SUSAN GRIGGS AGENCY

inimitable candied fruit which is added to ricotta for making the filling for *cannoli* and for *cassata*, which it seems cannot be duplicated outside Sicilia. The *cassata* cake must be tasted, as must the *babà al rum* and the *pignolata*—a miniature honey-soaked fritter molded to look like a pine-cone and covered with dark chocolate. Rice is also used in a number of desserts, such as *gattò dolce di riso*, a rice cake, and *crispelle*, deep-fried rice sticks coated in honey.

Culinary historians attribute Sicilia's unique pastries to two factors: the centuries-old tradition of nuns earning extra income for their convents by preparing, especially for the nobles, elaborate specialties for religious festivals, and to the nobles' desire to have the wonderful pastries more readily available. This led to their bringing to Sicilia, at the turn of the century, a large number of European chefs. When the nobles were no longer able to afford their services these chefs then set up their own pastry shops in Sicilia's main cities, to the people's great benefit.

SICILIAN WINES

Sicilia has always been one of Italy's major wine producing regions. Production today is fully mechanized and industrial controls guarantee wines which hold their own internationally. To achieve this, Sicilian wines have had to pass from being robust, high alcohol, home produced wines to being vintage wines made according to modern techniques. In the past, most Sicilian wine was consumed locally before the next year's production became available. Since it was strong, it was always served with a pitcher of water to be *annacquato*, watered down. For years Sicilian bulk wine has been used to fortify less successful European vintages. Vine cultivation can be seen throughout the island, but it is most intensive in the provinces of Palermo and Trapani, and in the south-eastern corner from Pachino to Vittoria. Traveling through these towns at pressing time there is the strong odor of fermenting must.

In western Sicilia, Casteldaccia and its environs produce the world renowned Corvo wines. The Corvo white is straw-yellow and intense, while the full bodied red is best after two or three years ageing. In the east the best wines are produced from vines grown in the fertile black volcanic soil deposited over the centuries by the eruptions of Mount Etna. Etna white is a pale, generous nutty flavored white, whilst the stronger Etna red is best after at least two years ageing. Even stronger than this red is the straw-yellow Albanello white of Siracusa. Another strong white is the Mamertino from the Messina area. A famous wine of antiquity, it was served to Julius Caeser at a banquet held in honor of his third consulship.

As unique as her hardy reds and whites are, Sicilia's fame rests with her dessert wines, especially Marsala. Malvasia is a golden-yellow dessert wine from the Aeolian Islands. Used locally in pastry making, for centuries the islands produced most of the Malvasia used in Italy for liturgical purposes. Also notable are Sicilia's Muscatels. Besides the golden-yellow Moscato of Noto there is the aromatic Moscato from the island of Pantelleria, between Sicilia and North Africa. Sadly the generous Moscato of Siracusa is now becoming rare.

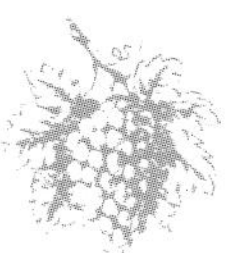

SICILIA WINES

DOC WINES

1. *Alcamo*
2. *Cerasuolo di Vittoria*
3. *Etna*
4. *Faro*
5. *Malvasia delle Lipari*
6. *Marsala*
7. *Moscato di Noto*
8. *Moscato di Pantelleria*
9. *Moscato di Siracusa*

OTHER WINES

Carboj
Corvo
Mamertino
Regaleali
Ribera
Segesta
Settesoli

PETER JOHNSON

RECIPES OF SICILIA

Mimmetta Lo Monte

Spaghetti con Gamberi Marsalesi

Spaghetti with Shrimp Marsala Style

The port of Marsala offers a great variety of fresh fish. Its shrimp are known to be particularly sweet.

$\frac{1}{2}$ cup (4 fl oz/125 ml) olive oil
2 garlic cloves, cut in a few pieces
3 cups canned peeled tomatoes, seeded and chopped finely, juice reserved
$\frac{1}{2}$ cup (4 fl oz/125 ml) packing tomato juice from the can
$\frac{1}{2}$ teaspoon salt
1 lb (500 g) shrimp (prawns) medium-small, headed and shelled
4 oz (125 g) tender tiny peas, parboiled
$\frac{1}{2}$ teaspoon freshly ground black pepper
14 oz (440 g) spaghetti

Cook the oil and the garlic until the garlic starts taking some color. Add the chopped tomato and cook over high heat for a few minutes. Add the reserved tomato juice from seeding, the packing juice and the salt.

Cook uncovered over moderate heat for 10 minutes. Add the shrimp and the peas and cook 3 more minutes. Stir in the pepper.

Cook the spaghetti in plenty of boiling salted water until *al dente*. Drain, toss with the sauce and serve immediately.

SERVES: 6

Olive Bianche Farcite

Stuffed Green Olives

The dissimilar flavors of almonds and olives combine most successfully.

olive oil
20 almonds
2 tablespoons breadcrumbs
12 mint leaves, finely chopped
2 tablespoons red wine vinegar
$\frac{1}{8}$ teaspoon salt (omit if olives are very salty)
$\frac{1}{4}$ teaspoon finely ground black pepper
sprinkle of cayenne pepper (optional)
32 very large green olives, pitted

Heat 2 tablespoons oil in a heavy skillet and stir the almonds in the oil until they start crackling. Cool.

Heat 2 teaspoons oil in a heavy skillet and stir the breadcrumbs in the oil until they are toasted.

Grind the almonds very finely, until they have reached the oily stage. Mix the ground almonds, breadcrumbs, mint, vinegar, salt, pepper, cayenne pepper and stuff the olives with the mixture.

MAKES: 32

Rigatoni con Agglassato

Rigatoni with a Meat Juice Glaze

This is another of the many pasta dishes that, with small variations, are found throughout Italy. This recipe provides a first course of pasta and a main course of braised beef.

$\frac{1}{3}$ cup (3 fl oz/90 ml) olive oil
4 oz (125 g) unsalted butter
1 large onion, finely chopped
2 lb (1 kg) beef eye of round, tied with string, turns every $\frac{1}{2}$ in (1 cm)
$\frac{1}{2}$ teaspoon salt
$\frac{1}{2}$ teaspoon finely ground black pepper
14 oz (440 g) rigatoni *(large ribbed tubular pasta) or similar*
freshly grated Parmesan cheese

In a pot in which the beef will fit snugly, cook oil, butter and onion until onion starts wilting. Add beef and sear. Add water to cover beef half way. Add salt and pepper, cover and simmer $1\frac{1}{2}$ hours, turning often.

Uncover. Increase heat to high and reduce liquid, turning beef constantly, until glaze-like. Remove beef.

Cook the *rigatoni* in plenty of boiling salted water until *al dente*. Drain and toss with the glaze. Serve with Parmesan on the side.

The beef can be used, sliced very thin, as luncheon meat, or it can be served as the main course.

SERVES: 6

Left: Spaghetti with Shrimp Marsala Style, Stuffed Green Olives, Rigatoni with a Meat Juice Glaze

Sformato di Monachine e Ricotta

Ricotta and Little Meat Balls Timbale

Versatile ricotta is served in any number of ways. In this recipe it provides a delicate accompaniment for meat balls, making a substantial dish.

1½ oz (45 g) white bread, crusts removed
1 tablespoon milk
1 small onion, finely chopped
1 tablespoon finely chopped parsley
½ cup (2 oz/60 g) freshly grated Parmesan cheese
½ teaspoon salt
¾ teaspoon finely ground black pepper
4 eggs
12 oz (375 g) very lean ground (minced) beef
½ cup (4 fl oz/125 ml) olive oil
unbleached all purpose (plain) flour to coat meat balls
2 lb (1 kg) ricotta
unsalted butter to coat baking dish

Mix bread and milk well together. Add ½ the onion, the parsley, 2 tablespoons Parmesan, ¼ teaspoon salt, ½ teaspoon pepper, 1 egg and the ground beef. Mix very well, and shape into balls no larger than 1 in (2.5 cm) in diameter. Roll them in flour and set aside.

Heat the oil and the remaining onion until aromatic, using a very wide skillet in which the meat balls can fit in one layer, or divide the oil and onion between 2 large skillets. Add the meat balls and allow to cook over moderate heat for a couple of minutes undisturbed. Then turn very gently with a spatula, taking care not to break the balls. Cook for 6 to 8 minutes, turning occasionally to make sure they brown evenly all over.

Mix ricotta with the remaining 3 eggs, the remaining Parmesan, salt and pepper. Coat an oval baking dish, about 14 in x 10 in (35 cm x 25 cm) with butter and flour, then place the ricotta mixture in a layer on the bottom.

Distribute the meat balls evenly over the ricotta mixture, pressing them in.

Dribble the pan juices evenly over the meat balls. Bake in oven preheated to 375°F (190°C) for about 40 minutes. Serve immediately.

SERVES: 6 TO 8

PETER JOHNSON

Ricotta and Little Meat Balls Timbale

Spiedini di Gamberi Marsalesi

Skewered Shrimp Marsala Style

Shrimps prepared in this way taste even better if they are cooked over an open fire, but the heat must be gentle.

½ cup (2 oz/60 g) breadcrumbs
2 tablespoons freshly grated Parmesan cheese
4 tablespoons freshly grated pecorino or romano cheese
¼ teaspoon salt
¼ teaspoon finely ground black pepper
2 lb (1 kg) medium shrimp (prawns), headed and shelled
olive oil

Mix together the breadcrumbs, the cheese, and the salt and pepper.

Thread the shrimp on skewers by curling each one, tail touching the upper part of the body, and carefully inserting the skewer through it. Keep the shrimp very close together. Coat them with oil, then with breadcrumb mixture.

Grill over low heat on a barbecue, or broil, for about 4 minutes per side. Serve immediately.

SERVES: 6

Tonno a Sfincione

Tuna with Breadcrumb Topping

Tuna is eaten widely in Sicilia, particularly around Palermo, and is considered an opulent meal. This strongly flavored dish is typical of the region.

2½ lb (1.25kg) tuna, in 6 pieces sliced 1 in (2.5 cm) thick
olive oil
3 tablespoons onion, finely chopped
4½ tablespoons tomato paste
6 anchovy fillets, mashed
6 tablespoons lightly packed fresh oregano leaves, or 1 teaspoon dry oregano
3 tablespoons breadcrumbs
3 tablespoons freshly grated Parmesan cheese
½ teaspoon finely ground black pepper
½ teaspoon salt

Coat the tuna slices lightly with oil. Lay them side by side in a shallow baking pan, coated with oil, keeping them uncrowded.

Cook 1½ tablespoons of onion in 6 tablespoons of oil until aromatic. Add the tomato paste and 2 tablespoons water, stir and cook a couple of minutes, allowing the mixture to sizzle. Turn off heat, stir in anchovies, oregano, breadcrumbs, Parmesan, pepper, salt and the remaining onion.

Top the tuna slices with the mixture, then bake 8 minutes in oven preheated to 425°F (220°C). Taste some of the topping. If it is only mildly salty, sprinkle over a little salt.

Decrease heat to 375°F (190°C) and bake for an additional 8 to 10 minutes. Transfer the fish to a warmed dish and serve immediately.

SERVES: 6

Skewered Shrimp Marsala Style, Tuna with Breadcrumb Topping

PETER JOHNSON

PETER JOHNSON

Baked Lamb with Cheese

Agnello Infornato con Formaggio

Baked Lamb with Cheese

Shepherds have probably been eating this combination for centuries, using the most common ingredients available to them.

olive oil
2½ lb (1.25 kg) baking potatoes, peeled and cut in ⅓-in (1-cm) thick rounds
2½ lb (1.25 kg) lean lamb leg meat, cut in 2-in (5-cm) cubes
1 very large onion, sliced in ¼-in (5-mm) thick rings
½ teaspoon salt
¼ teaspoon finely ground black pepper
4 oz (125 g) sharp provolone *cheese, sliced thinly*
12 oz (375 g) tomatoes, in ¼-in (5-mm) thick slices

Heat ¼ in (5 mm) oil in a skillet, and sauté the potato slices, in batches, over medium-high heat. Set aside. Transfer 6 tablespoons of the oil to a large skillet and sear lamb over high heat. Set lamb aside. Sauté the onion in this skillet over medium-high heat until aromatic, then return the lamb, with the released juices. Turn off heat and deglaze pan.

Oil a baking dish. Lay half the potatoes on the bottom, followed by the lamb and the onions, reserving the juices from the skillet. Sprinkle with salt and pepper. Next make a layer of half the cheese, cover with the remaining potatoes, then the tomatoes, and finally the remaining cheese. Dribble pan juices over the top.

Bake 15 minutes in oven preheated to 400°F (200°C). Serve immediately.

SERVES: 6

Filetto allo Zafferano e Mandorle

Beef Fillet with Saffron and Almonds

Saffron and almonds give the beef fillet a most distinctive flavor.

2 tablespoons olive oil
1 oz (30 g) unsalted butter
2 lb (1 kg) beef fillet, very lean, tied with string, turns every ½ in (1 cm)
3 cups (24 fl oz/750 ml) milk
1 cup (8 fl oz/250 ml) beef broth (stock)
¾ cup (4 oz/125 g) blanched almonds, finely ground
⅛ teaspoon ground saffron
½ teaspoon salt
¼ teaspoon freshly ground black pepper

Heat oil and butter in a pot in which the beef will fit quite snugly. Over high heat sear the beef for 5 minutes, turning.

Add all the other ingredients and bring to a boil over high heat. Cook, uncovered, for 10 minutes, turning the fillet frequently, and constantly scraping the bottom of the pot to prevent scorching. Decrease heat to medium and cook a further 5 minutes. The beef will be rare. Remove from the pot, slice and serve hot with sauce on the side.

SERVES: 6

Caponata Catanese

Catanian Sweet and Sour Vegetables

This masterpiece from Catania can be found on the menu in many restaurants throughout the country.

1 lb (500 g) eggplant (aubergine), from which 1-in (2.5-cm) wide skin strip has been removed from stem end to bottom end and around
olive oil
8 oz (250 g) red bell pepper (capsicum), cut in ⅔-in (2-cm) cubes
6 oz (185 g) green bell pepper (capsicum), cut in ⅔-in (2-cm) cubes
1 onion, ¼ finely chopped, the rest cut in ⅔-in (2-cm) cubes
2 oz (60 g) tender celery stalks, leaves included, finely chopped
1 tablespoon capers, well drained and squeezed if preserved in vinegar, very well rinsed if preserved in salt
6 pitted green olives, cut in a few pieces, blanched and drained
2 tablespoons red wine vinegar
¾ teaspoon sugar
6 medium canned peeled tomatoes, seeded and finely chopped
¼ teaspoon salt

Cut eggplant into ¾-in (2-cm) cubes. Cover with water and add 1 teaspoon salt. Weigh down to keep from floating. After 30 minutes drain and dry with paper towels. Deep fry the eggplant in ⅔ in (2 cm) layer of oil, over high heat, until dark gold. Set aside.

Transfer 3 tablespoons of the frying oil to a large skillet. Heat and add peppers, cubed onion and celery. Cook over moderate heat, stirring, for a couple of minutes. Reduce heat to low, cover and cook for 8 minutes. Uncover, increase heat to high and cook, stirring, until vegetables start browning. Add capers, olives, vinegar and sugar. Turn off heat, add eggplant and mix very gently.

Heat 2 tablespoons of the oil used to cook the eggplant in a small pan and sauté the finely chopped onion. Add the tomatoes. Cook over high heat until they sizzle. Stir in salt and add to the vegetable mixture. Serve at room temperature.

SERVES: 6

Beef Fillet with Saffron and Almonds

PETER JOHNSON

Melanzane a Beccafico

Eggplant Rolls

The abundance of eggplant in the south has inspired many forms of preparation. Pine nuts and currants add sweetness to this recipe.

2 1-lb (500-g) eggplants (aubergines), from which 1-in (2.5-cm) wide skin strip has been removed from stem end to bottom end and around
¾ cup (3 oz/90 g) breadcrumbs, plus some to coat pan
4 tablespoons onion, finely chopped, plus 12 to 14 slices 2 in x ¾ in(5 cm x 2 cm)
olive oil
2 tablespoons currants
2 tablespoons pine nuts
4 tablespoons finely chopped parsley
4 tablespoons freshly grated Parmesan cheese
½ teaspoon salt
½ teaspoon finely ground black pepper
4 small bay leaves, each cut in 3 pieces

Cut each eggplant into 6 slices. Cover with water and add 1 teaspoon salt. Weigh down to keep from floating. After about 30 minutes drain and dry with paper towels.

Stir around the breadcrumbs and the finely chopped onion with 2 tablespoons oil in a skillet over moderate heat until breadcrumbs become golden brown. Turn off heat. Stir in the currants, pine nuts, parsley, Parmesan, salt and pepper. Set aside.

Heat ½ in (1 cm) oil in a skillet, sauté the eggplant over high heat until light brown, set on rack to drain.

Spread the filling on the eggplant slices. Roll them and place in a baking pan coated with a little oil and some breadcrumbs. Rolls should fit tightly. Place the onion slices in between them and distribute the bay leaf pieces evenly on top.

Bake for 30 to 40 minutes in oven preheated to 375°F (190°C). Serve hot or at room temperature.

SERVES: 6 (makes 12 rolls)

Eggplant Rolls, Catanian Sweet and Sour Vegetables

PETER JOHNSON

PETER JOHNSON

Queen Cookies

Biscotti Regina

Queen Cookies

These cookies are delightful accompanied by a glass of dessert wine, such as Marsala or Malvasia.

2 cups (8 oz/250 g) bleached all purpose (plain) flour
1/3 cup (3 oz/90 g) sugar
1/2 teaspoon grated lemon rind
3 oz (90 g) unsalted butter, room temperature
2 eggs, white separated from yolk of one, the other beaten as for scrambled eggs
2 tablespoons dry Marsala
2/3 cup (4 oz/125 g) sesame seeds

Mix flour, sugar and lemon rind. Cut in the butter until the mixture resembles coarse crumbs. Add the egg yolk and half the beaten egg. (Discard other half.) Add the Marsala and knead the dough until it is very smooth.

Shape the dough into twenty-four 2-in (5-cm) croquettes. Coat lightly with the reserved egg white and roll in the sesame seeds.

Lay on cookie sheet coated with butter. Bake 50 minutes in oven preheated to 350°F (180°C). Cool.

These cookies may be kept for several weeks as long as they are stored in an airtight container.

MAKES: 24

Gattò Dolce di Riso

Sweet Rice Cake

Gattò is an Italianisation of gâteau. This is a very popular cake, sold in almost all Sicilian bars.

3/4 cup (5 oz/155 g) Arborio rice
1/3 cup (3 oz/90 g) plus 1 tablespoon sugar
3 cups (24 fl oz/750 ml) milk
1 tablespoon orange flower water
1/2 cup(3 oz/90 g) blanched almonds, finely ground
1/8 teaspoon salt
2 eggs
2 egg yolks
1 teaspoon grated lemon rind
1 tablespoon candied citron peel, finely chopped
butter and flour to coat baking dish

Place rice, sugar and milk in a pan, stir well to mix and bring to a boil over low heat. Cook, uncovered, stirring often, until rice becomes soft: heat must be kept so that the milk barely boils.

Add orange flower water, almonds and salt and stir well. Allow to cool a little. Stir in, until well blended, eggs, lemon rind and citron.

Transfer the mixture to a 9-in (23-cm) round baking dish, well coated with butter and flour. Bake 45 minutes in oven preheated to 375°F (190°C). Serve cold.

SERVES: 6 to 8

Dolce delle Monache

Nuns' Dessert

Ricotta is a basic ingredient of Sicilian pastry, traditionally becoming available in spring, and thus used for Easter dishes. Now it is available all year long.

Filling:
6 tablespoons cornstarch (cornflour)
1/4 cup (2 oz/60 g) sugar
3 cups (24 fl oz/750 ml) milk
1 egg yolk
1 cup (10 oz/315 g) orange marmalade
2 oz (60 g) semisweet (plain) chocolate, finely chopped
Shell:
8 oz (250 g) unsalted butter
3/4 cup (6 oz/185 g) sugar
2 lb (1 kg) ricotta, drained of any excess liquid
1 teaspoon vanilla extract (essence)
1 1/2 cups (6 oz/185 g) unbleached all purpose (plain) flour
1 teaspoon baking powder
3 eggs
3 egg yolks

For the filling: Mix cornstarch and sugar. Add a little milk and stir to obtain a smooth paste. Thin it out, adding the remaining milk, little by little at first, while stirring. Stir in the egg yolk. Place over moderate heat and cook, stirring constantly and evenly, until mixture thickens at boiling point. Stir a couple more minutes. Turn off heat and set aside.

For the shell: Beat butter and sugar until very light. Beat in ricotta and vanilla until well mixed. Mix flour with baking powder and beat it into the mixture until well blended. Mix in eggs and yolks just to blend: do not overbeat.

Butter and flour a 10-in (25-cm) spring pan. Pour in 2/3 of the ricotta mixture, pushing some to the sides to cover them. Pour in the filling, dot with the marmalade and sprinkle with the chopped chocolate. Cover with the remaining ricotta.

Bake for 2 hours in oven preheated to 325°F (160°C). Turn out when cooled a little and serve either lukewarm or cold.

SERVES: 8 to 10

Sweet Rice Cake, Nuns' Dessert

PETER JOHNSON

Bocche di Bonifacio
Isola Maddalena
La Maddalena
Isola Caprera
Costa Smeralda
Isola Asinara
Golfo dell'Asinara
Mare Mediterraneo
Mare Tirreno
Liscia
Olbia
Stintino
Castelsardo
Tempio Pausania
Isola Tavolara
Sennori
Porto Torres
Osilo
Lago del Coghinas
Sassari
Posada
Ittiri
Ozieri
Capo Caccia
Alghero
Torralba
Bitti
Bonorva
Bono
Nuoro
Bosa
Sindia
Tirso
Oliena
Dorgali
Golfo di Orosei
Macomer
Grotto dei Buemarino
Mamoiada
Lago Omodeo
Monti del Gennargentu
Tonara
Desulo
Stagno di Cabras
Cabras
Aritzo
Tharros
Oristano
Lago Mulargia
Flumineddu
Golfo di Oristano
Isili
Jerzu
San Gavino
Mandas
Guspini
Monreale
Sanluri
Arbus
Gonnosfanadiga
Flumendosa
Villacidro
Fluminimaggiore
Domusnovas
Sinnai
Iglesias
Decimomannu
Quartu Sant'Elena
Isola di San Pietro
Carbonia
Carloforte
Cagliari
Golfo di Cagliari
San Antioco
Calasetta
Isola di Sant'Antioco
Santa Margherita di Pula
0
10
20
30

SARDEGNA

Gianna Batzella

Halfway between the coasts of Italy and North Africa lies Sardegna, the Mediterranean's second largest island. A mountainous and wild place, it has mild winters but the summers are fierce, the drying maestrale often blowing from the north-west, or the hot, moist scirocco from the south. Most of the rainfall is in fall and spring, and in the scorching months of summer water is always in short supply. For countless centuries shepherds have roamed the mountains and hills with their flocks, their families living harsh, simple lives in the villages.

Although part of Italy for more than 100 years, Sardegna still remains to a large extent independent of Italian culture. The people tend to define their region as "a continent of its own" to emphasize its cultural traditions and to distinguish it from the other "continent", as they call mainland Italy. Even now most islanders speak Italian only occasionally, mainly on formal occasions. Sardinian is not an Italian dialect, but a Romance language, and, of all the languages which developed from Latin, Sardinian resembles it most closely. Ironically, dialects vary so greatly that people from different parts of the island often resort to Italian in order to communicate.

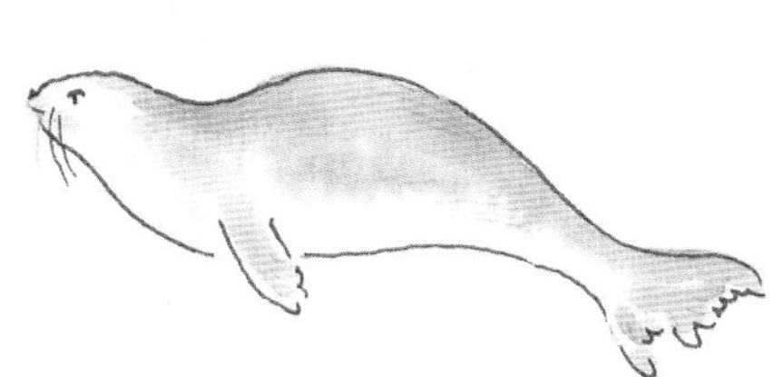

Historians have said that Sardegna looks towards France, Spain, and Africa, turning its back on Italy. This sounds extreme these days, but it does accord with the fairly recent past and with the island's geography. All the major natural harbors, the fertile plains, and the richest areas for fishing and mining are concentrated along the southern, western, and northern coasts, the eastern coast being rocky, dry, and inhospitable. Cultural, political, and linguistic links with the mainland are growing, yet the island is a stronghold of tradition, and its people, suspicious by nature, are wary of change.

Throughout the centuries Sardegna has been invaded, plundered, and colonized. First came the Romans, the Vandals, and the Byzantines, then, in the Middle Ages, the Pisans, the Genovese, and the Catalans. More recently it was the Arabs, the Spaniards, and the Italians. Some brought little more than destruction, all of them exploited the island's resources. But many of these invaders also influenced the local culture and left a lasting legacy in the foods and cooking techniques they introduced.

DEFILIPPIS/FIOREPRESS

Life is harsh for many in Sardegna, but the people are resilient and pride themselves on their independence.

Spanish and Arab Influence

Four hundred years of Spanish domination has had the greatest influence. For instance, the people of Sardegna have the Spanish to thank for their olive oil. Initially the only source of vegetable oil was the wild olive trees which grew throughout the island. This strongly scented oil, *ollestincu*, was replaced by the excellent olive oil from introduced strains of Spanish olive trees, now such an important feature of the landscape and economy. Nowadays *ollestincu* is produced and used in only a few villages, mainly for the preparation of simple soups and stews. In the Middle Ages Spanish traders used to export olive oil to Sardegna. The story goes that two Aragonese brothers used to travel around the island year after year, selling their produce by praising its quality and specifying that it was the "oil of the ... brothers". This is probably why olive oil is *ollu armanu*, from *hermano*, "brother" in Spanish.

Both in Spain and in Sardegna the dishes *tacculas*, blackbirds or thrushes, and *pudda murtada*, chicken with myrtle, can be found. In both cases the birds are boiled, heavily salted and, while still steaming hot, wrapped in myrtle leaves where they remain for at least three days. Another typical Sardegnan dish, *cordula cun pisurci*, *cordula* with peas, was also introduced by the Spanish, the name coming from *cordere,* "lamb" in Spanish. *Cordula* is made from chopped lamb offal (mainly heart, liver, and spleen), seasoned with bay leaves and juniper berries and leaves, all painstakingly wrapped in the lamb's intestine. Usually braised with fresh peas, it can also be cooked on an open fire, and it is then called *trattalia*.

The many spices widely used in Sardinian cooking, particularly cinnamon, nutmeg, and orange flower water, come from the Arab world, probably also via Spain. A direct Arab influence, however, can only be found in Carloforte and Calasetta, on the small islands of San Pietro and San Antioco, off the south-west coast. There delicious *cascà*, or *couscous*, a North African specialty, is still the staple diet for most of the inhabitants. The dish, made from fine ground wheat and chickpeas with meat and vegetables, was copied from the people of Tunisia by Ligurians who were there as slaves of the Saracens. Freed by King Charles Emmanuel III in the late eighteenth century, they settled on these two tiny islands, where their descendants still live, retaining the same language—a Genovese dialect—and the same cultural traditions as their forebears.

A Region of Shepherds and Farmers

Sardegna, unlike Sicilia, was never fully conquered by the Arabs. The island was occupied for just one week, then the Saracens were repelled. However, Arab pirate raids on the coast continued for more than 300 years, terrorizing the people. Hundreds of villages were abandoned and new ones built a few miles inland. As a result, the island became a region of shepherds and farmers, rather than fishermen. Even now the fishing industry is of no great consequence, and is concentrated only in Cagliari, Cabras, Alghero, Carloforte, and Stintino, the last two being important for tuna fishing. So, while the island's cuisine has a few succulent seafood specialties, most traditional dishes are made of meat, pulses, cheeses, and vegetables seasoned with wild herbs. Wild fennel, myrtle, mint, thyme, and bay leaves are the herbs most commonly used.

For lovers of seafood Cagliari, Cabras, and Alghero are probably the places where the best fish can be enjoyed, still cooked according to traditional recipes.

HANS MADEJ/BILDERBERG

Freshly painted fishing boats lie side by side in the shelter of the harbor at Bosa, on the island's west coast.

Cagliari, the island's capital, is on the south coast, near the fertile Campidano plain where wheat is grown, as it was by the Carthaginians and the Romans. The city has some interesting Roman remains, there is a Phoenician necropolis on Tuvixeddu hill, and if you go boating on the Molentargius marsh you will see flocks of pink flamingoes. Cagliari has a delightful fish market, with baskets of fish of every conceivable kind set out in profusion to tempt the customer. A specialty that is well worth sampling in one of the local restaurants is *minestra 'e cocciula*, a garlic flavored clam soup. Cabras, a fishing village on the central western coast, is famous for its *merca*, a thick casserole of fish, usually mullet, flavored with wild herbs which grow near the Cabras marshes.

Alghero, on the north-west coast, is "an island within the island"— colonized by the Catalans in the fourteenth century, its people still speak thirteenth-century Catalan, and the architecture, traditions, and cooking are Catalonian in style. Along with a plentiful supply of fish, lobsters are harvested from the waters off Alghero, as are sponges and coral.

Following pages: A flock of sheep makes its way along a road in the mountainous country not far from Aritzo, led by a young shepherd.

HANS MADEJ/BILDERBERG

SARDEGNA'S FESTIVALS

The great Sardinian religious *sagre*, festivals, are a real feast for the eye. On these occasions precious traditional costumes—often maybe several generations old—are taken out of the *cascias,* hand-carved chests, and worn by those taking part in the celebrations. And, needless to say, each festival means a splendid array of traditional food and wine available in every restaurant and *trattoria,* and also often distributed free by the local tourist associations.

For the Festival of Sant' Efisio, held in Cagliari on 1 May, more than 3000 men, women, and children wearing traditional costumes and jewellery parade along the streets to escort the statue of the saint who saved the city from the plague more than 400 years ago. The procession is an impressive sight, with colorful *traccas,* ox-drawn carts, richly decorated with flowers, hand-woven rugs, wall hangings, and traditional home utensils.

If traveling in Sardegna between Carnevale and Lent, don't miss the sheer splendor of Sa Sartiglia, held in Oristano each year. In this Medieval-style tournament the "knights", riding their horses at high speed, have to collect small metal stars with the points of their swords.

MOUNTAINS AND MACCHIA

Although the rocky, uneven coast and the sheltered beaches are captivating, a trip inland is a must. There are cork forests in the central mountainous regions, and dwarf oaks, chestnuts, ilex, and native pines mingle with granite and basalt rocks to give an eerie lunar landscape. The *macchia mediterranea*, underbrush, has taken the place of forest in many areas, covering much of the island with arbutus, wild roses, fig trees, and myrtle.

In the forests and the *macchia* there are wild boar, and mouflons, forebears of the domestic goat, can still be found in the mountains near Aritzo, Desulo, and Corr'e Boi. Mouflons and deer, their numbers severly depleted, are now protected, and their tasty meat is therefore no longer available. There continues to be an abundance of smaller game, though, such as partridge, quail, and hare, and in the mountain streams there are trout.

The boundaries of privately-owned grazing land are marked either by low, dry-stone walls, *muri a secco*, or by thick prickly pear "fences". Prickly pears are traditionally eaten by shepherds and can be sampled by anyone out in the countryside. They are very tasty, especially after the first fall rains, but are covered in sharp, tiny, almost invisible hairs and should be handled with the utmost care.

TRAVELING INLAND

When touring inland you will see many remarkable archeological sites. Perhaps most mystifying are the *nuraghi*, massive, megalithic stone structures, which may have been dwellings, fortresses or tombs—no-one knows for sure. There are more than 7000 *nuraghi* in Sardegna and they can be seen all over the island, especially in the mountainous central areas. Built at the same time as the *nuraghi*, or even earlier, are the "tombs of the giants", monumental stone sepulchers, and *domus de janas*, "fairies' houses", small circular tombs cut out of the rocks.

Inland is where the best roasts, the tastiest pecorino, the crispest and freshest vegetables can be found. The pace of life has changed the eating habits of city dwellers, and fast food outlets selling pizza, roast chicken, readymade lasagne, and rice croquettes are mushrooming in the larger towns. But in the remote regions, particularly in Barbagia, "civilization" has not yet swept traditions aside. Away from the cities, tasty, wholesome cooking still survives.

Perhaps the island's best known dish is roast suckling pig, *porcheddu* (as it is called in the north), or *porceddu* (in the south). The people of Sardegna are extremely partial to suckling pigs, four to six weeks old, milk fed for all but the last week of their lives, when they are fed grain to add flavor to the meat. The piglet is roasted on an open fire, on metal or aromatic wooden skewers. Roast wild boar, too, used to be another local specialty, but it is becoming rare.

Another favorite roast is lamb, no more than six weeks old, cooked in the same way as the piglets. At Easter, in particular, there is roast lamb on most tables, in the mountains tender kid meat sometimes serving as a replacement.

The old tradition of cooking pork, wild boar, or lamb *a carraxiu* now survives only in the hills, practiced by some of the shepherds. The meat is placed in a hole dug in the ground, lined with twigs and herbs—wild thyme and myrtle being favored. It is then covered with a thick layer of fragrant twigs and leaves and a thin layer of soil. A slow-burning fire is lit on top and after about four hours the meat is ready. This is a real treat, something everybody should try!

HANS MADEJ/BILDERBERG

Tasty sausages hang in the window of this butcher's shop in the Barbagia region, the island's heartland.

In recent years irrigation systems have been established, enabling the islanders to grow quite a variety of vegetables. Artichokes are exported in considerable quantities. Eggplant, cauliflower, zucchini, broad beans, and tomatoes do well, tomatoes often being dried for later use. Citrus fruits are plentiful, as are hazelnuts, chestnuts, walnuts, and almonds.

Breads in Abundance, and Cheeses

Sardegna produces the most amazing variety of breads, bread often taking the place occupied by pasta in the cooking of other parts of Italy. The spiky *coccoi*, soft inside but hard and crunchy on the outside, can be found virtually anywhere. In the south this type of bread, molded into delicate shapes like flowers or feathers, is still baked for traditional country weddings. The variety *coccoi cun ou*, with whole fresh eggs in the dough, used to be baked for Easter, and sent to friends and relatives as a gift.

But by far the best known bread in Sardegna is the flat variety. Essentially a central and northern specialty, it varies considerably from place to place. *La spianata*, a soft version, is typical of Ozieri, and is the closest in shape and texture to some of the breads that are baked in North Africa. In Ogliastra a thickish, crisp flat bread is made, called *pistoccu*. This is so crunchy that many people moisten it with water before eating it. Much thinner and deliciously crisp is *pane carasau*, produced throughout the area. But the thinnest of all is "*carta da musica*", "sheet music". This wafer-thin bread, together with *pane carasau*, is the main ingredient for *pane frattau*, a hearty first course in which the bread is blanched in boiling water, seasoned with tomato sauce and freshly grated pecorino, and then topped with poached eggs.

Sardegna is justly famous for its cheeses, particularly pecorino. Pecorino from Sardegna, unlike other Italian varieties, is always tangy. When it is still fresh it is

Breads of all sorts are baked in the large ovens that are common to most homes in Sardegna. The thinnest and crispiest bread of all is known as "carta da musica", *"sheet music".*

GERT WAGNER/BILDERBERG

DEFILIPPIS/FIOREPRESS

Two men sit chatting on a doorstep, above them a mural of mother Sardegna. Her people consider the island a continent apart, and most speak Sardinian, not Italian.

often eaten grilled; mature, it is generally grated and used as seasoning, either cooked in dishes or sprinkled over them. Many shepherds like to expose semi-mature pecorino to the warm air for several months. The cheese then becomes *casu marzu*, rotten cheese, a slightly moldy, creamy cheese that is spread on bread. *Casu marzu* is so piquant that it can only be eaten in small quantities, and it is usually accompanied by a good many glases of strong red wine. It can also be mixed with a white wine such as Vernaccia, or a dessert wine like Moscato. When prepared in this way, pecorino is known as *cas'e binu*, wine cheese, and is served following the main meal, spread on slices of bread.

Regional Wines

If you are traveling on the east coast, make sure you visit the Grotta del Bue Marino, Grotto of the Sea Ox, near Dorgali. It is here that the only seals left in the Mediterranean can be found. Once in the area, the excellent local wines should be tasted. On the west coast, the area around Oristano produces arguably the most famous Sardinian wine, Vernaccia. This sherry-like wine goes particularly well with seafood. The best Oristano Vernaccias are labeled Oro di Sardegna, Sardinian gold. The island's wines tend to be heavy and strongly colored. Cannonau grapes are grown widely throughout the island, and wines made from them vary considerably in quality. One of the better ones is made in Jerzu, in Ogliastra, a region which gives the wine its name.

When thinking of wine, Oliena is also a name to remember. A number of varieties are made in this small town, near Nuoro. Most families make their own wine each fall, and it is possible, when passing through the town, to buy good quality home-made wine.

Excellent dessert wines like Moscato are produced throughout the island, the best coming from Tempio Pausania and Sorso.

Sweet Seasonal Specialties

As for the island's cakes and cookies, there is a wealth of choice. Many are seasonal specialties. *Pabassinas*, rich chocolate and nut cookies, are still made at the end of October to be ready for 2 November, All Souls' Day. *Pan'e saba*, traditionally eaten at Christmas and Epiphany, is a rich, dark cake made with almonds and *sapa*, sweet wine which has been simmered for hours until syrupy. In the spring *pardulas*, small cakes of fresh cheese or ricotta, flavored with cinnamon and vanilla, are a typical Easter treat. Winter is the time for *gueffus*, *candelaus*, and *durcis de scorza*, little almond-paste cakes, traditionally prepared to mark the end of the almond picking season. And at Carnevale time *fritture* and *zippulas* are fried in virtually every home, even though they also are available in almost all the pastry shops.

There are many other sweets which are well worth trying, many of them made in particular areas using traditional recipes. Almond sweets and cakes—made either from flaked or crushed almonds, or marzipan—are available throughout the island, but the most renowned are certainly the "*sospiros*", "sighs", made in Ozieri in the north, and the *durcis de scorza* of Quartu in the south, not far from Cagliari. *Sebadas* are cheese turnovers, coated in honey, providing a delightful blend of savory and sweet.

The *amaretti*, almond cookies, from Oristano, are light and crunchy and, as people say, not too bitter and not too sweet. To make *amaretti* a special type of bitter almond is grown in selected almond groves, mainly in the Campidano area, and sold throughout the island. Another specialty of Oristano and neighboring towns is *mustazzolus*, large cookies flavored with vanilla and orange flower water. Light and moist, they keep for months if properly stored.

Neglected by tourists until just a few decades ago, Sardegna's coasts are now extremely popular. There is ample choice of accommodation, from simple *pensioni* to elegant resorts like Forte Village in Santa Margherita di Pula on the south coast and exclusive luxury resorts like the Costa Smeralda, in the far north-east. It will be clear, however, from this brief portrait of a remarkable island, that staying in a resort will show the visitor little of Sardegna's character and cooking. Anyone who takes the time to explore, though, will be amply rewarded.

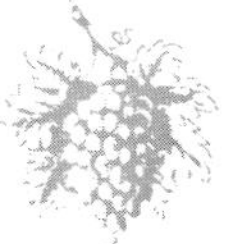

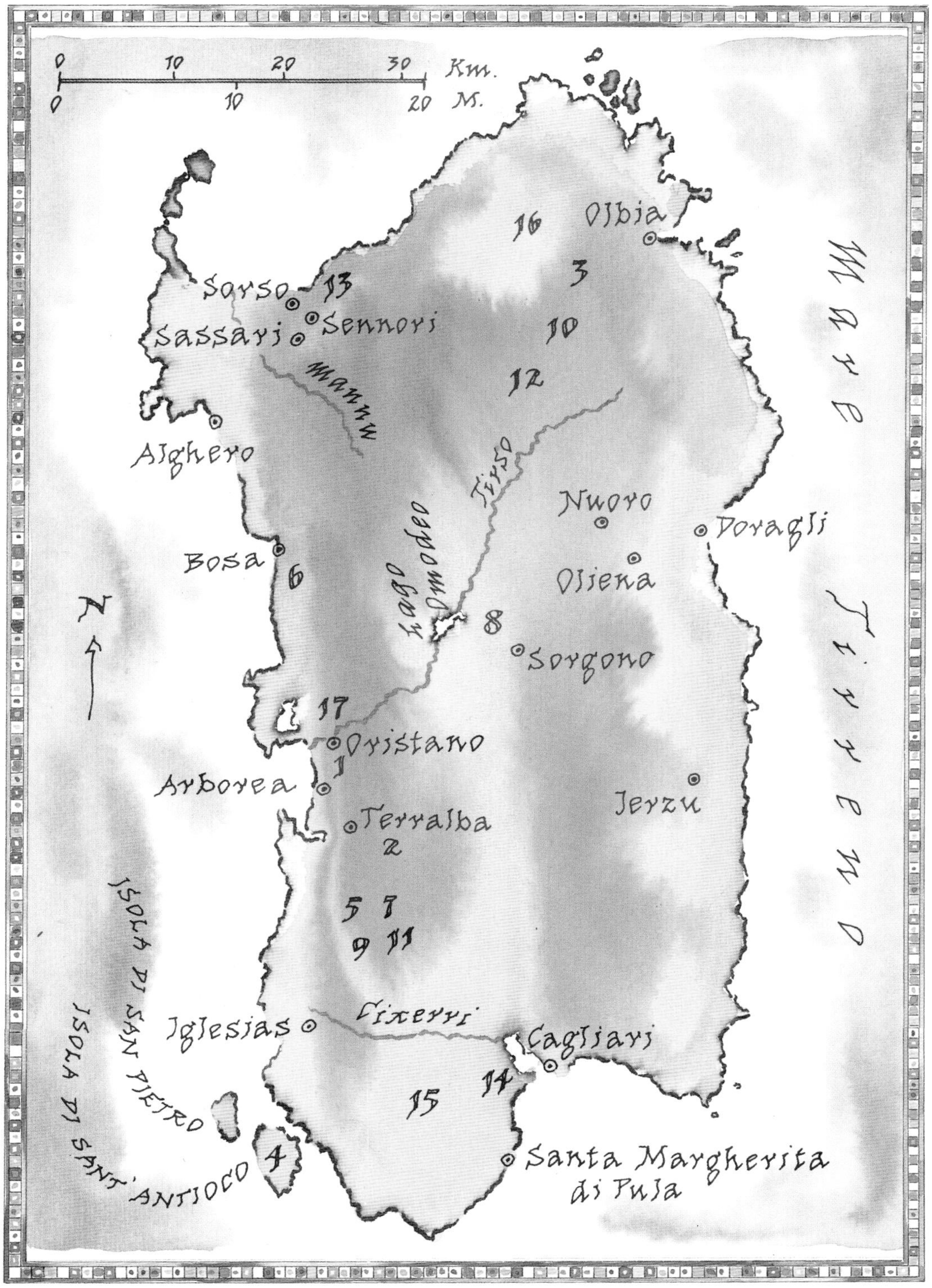

SARDEGNA

DOC WINES

1. *Arborea*
2. *Campidano di Terralba*
3. *Cannonau di Sardegna*
4. *Carignano del Sulcis*
5. *Girò di Cagliari*
6. *Malvasia di Bosa*
7. *Malvasia di Cagliari*
8. *Mandrolisai*
9. *Monica di Cagliari*
10. *Monica di Sardegna*
11. *Moscato di Cagliari*
12. *Moscato di Sardegna*
13. *Moscato di Sorso-Sennori*
14. *Nasco di Cagliari*
15. *Nuragus di Cagliari*
16. *Vermentino di Gallura*
17. *Vernaccia di Oristano*

PETER JOHNSON

RECIPES OF SARDEGNA

Mimmetta Lo Monte

Cascà

Sardinian Couscous

Cascà is derived from the North African specialty *couscous*.

- *2 lb (1 kg) cauliflower in large florets without hard stem*
- *2 cups (12 oz/375 g) chickpeas, soaked in water for 48 hours (change water and rinse at least twice)*
- *½ teaspoon saffron*
- *1½ teaspoons salt*
- *2 cups (12 oz/375 g) slow-cooking cream of wheat (fine ground wheat)—a substitute for the* semolino *used in Sardegna*
- *⅓ cup (3 fl oz/90 ml) olive oil*
- *2 lb (1 kg) very lean boneless leg of lamb, cut in 1½-in (4-cm) chunks*
- *3 large carrots, diced*
- *8 whole spring onions, tough green ends removed*
- *⅛ teaspoon ground nutmeg*
- *½ teaspoon ground cloves*
- *a few parsley sprigs*
- *5 cups (2½ pt/1.25 l)chicken or beef broth (stock) or partridge broth (see* Uccelli Bolliti *recipe)*
- *freshly ground black pepper to taste*

Cook cauliflower in boiling salted water for a few minutes, making sure it does not become soft. Drain well, then set aside.

Cover chickpeas with plenty of water. Bring to a boil, cover and simmer until tender (at least 2 hours). Drain, then set aside.

Mix the saffron with ¼ teaspoon salt. Put between 2 sheets of wax paper and beat with the bottom of a heavy skillet, a large hammer or a rolling pin until finely ground. Mix with the cream of wheat. Place ¼ cup of the mixture in a flat-bottom bowl. Sprinkle with a very little water. Mix with a fork until the water is evenly distributed and the mixture has turned into even crumbs. Add a little more water and mix with fork as before. Stop adding water and mixing when mixture looks like coarse crumbs. Spread crumbs on a cookie sheet. Repeat until you run out of cream of wheat. Allow to dry overnight.

Heat the olive oil in a large pot in which the lamb can be accommodated uncrowded. Add the lamb over high heat. Sear it, cook 5 more minutes over high heat, turning only as necessary to brown evenly. Remove from pot and set aside. Add carrots and onions to the drippings, reduce heat to low, cover and cook 10 to 15 minutes, until carrots are *al dente*. Increase heat to high, add the cauliflower and brown it lightly. Add chickpeas, nutmeg, cloves and parsley. Add 1½ cups of water and the remaining 1¼ teaspoon salt. Reduce heat to low, cover, simmer 10 minutes.

Turn off heat. Add the lamb and any juices lamb might have released. Mix well, trying not to break the cauliflower florets and the onions. Cover.

Bring the broth to a boil. Add the cream of wheat crumbs and stir well to prevent lumps forming. Test after 30 seconds: cream of wheat must be *al dente*. Drain as soon as that stage is reached. Mix with the vegetable–meat mixture and sprinkle with pepper to taste. Serve immediately.

SERVES: 8

Gnocchetti con Agliata

Short Pasta with Garlic Sauce

The *agliata* originated in France and found its way to Liguria and Sardegna.

- *½ cup (4 fl oz/125 ml) olive oil*
- *4 small dried hot red chili peppers*
- *1 cup parsley leaves*
- *2 to 3 garlic cloves*
- *½ teaspoon salt*
- *14 oz (440 g)* gnocchetti *(small, shell-like pasta) or similar*
- *6 tablespoons grated pecorino cheese*

Over low heat, cook ¼ cup oil with the chilies for 8 to 10 minutes. Press down the chilies with a spatula, remove from oil and discard. (If you like hot food, reserve ½ of one.)

In a food processor, purée the remaining ¼ cup oil, parsley, garlic and salt (and the reserved chili, if desired). Add the mixture to the oil in which the chilies were cooked.

Cook the *gnocchetti* in plenty of boiling salted water until *al dente*. Drain and toss with the sauce and the pecorino. Serve immediately.

SERVES: 6

Left: Short Pasta with Garlic Sauce, Sardinian Couscous

Cavolata

Cabbage Soup

A variation of this nourishing soup includes mint leaves.

2 pig's feet, each cut in a few sections
6 tablespoons olive oil
1 onion, finely chopped
2 oz (60 g) pancetta *or rindless bacon, cut in ¼-in (5-mm) cubes*
1½ lb (750 g) cabbage leaves cut in 1 in x ½ in (2 cm x 1 cm) sections
12 oz (375 g) boiling potatoes, diced
2 small bay leaves
1½ teaspoons salt
½ teaspoon finely ground black pepper
6 oz (185 g) ditalini *(short tubular pasta), shells, or similar*
freshly grated pecorino cheese

Cover pig's feet with plenty of water and bring to a boil. Drain and rinse well. Cover again with water and bring to a boil, skimming if necessary. Simmer, covered, until very tender (about 2 hours). Drain. Discard bones. Cut skin and meat into very small pieces.

Place oil in a large pot. Add onion, *pancetta* and chopped pig's feet. Cook over low heat 10 to 15 minutes, stirring often. Add cabbage, potatoes, bay leaves and salt. Barely cover with water and bring to a boil. Simmer, covered, about 1 hour. Remove the bay leaves. The soup will be very thick.

Cook *ditalini* in plenty of boiling salted water until *al dente*. Drain and mix with the soup and the pepper. Serve hot, with pecorino on the side to be added to taste.

SERVES: 6

Fregula in Brodo

Fregula with Broth

This is an original Sardinian creation, not to be confused with *cascà* which is of Arab origin.

¼ to ½ teaspoon saffron stigmas
¼ teaspoon salt, or to taste
1½ cups (8 oz/250 g) slow-cooking cream of wheat (fine ground wheat)—a substitute for the semolino *used in Sardegna*
6 cups (3 pt/1.5 l) partridge broth (stock) (see Uccelli Bolliti *recipe, p. 260)*

Mix the saffron with ¼ teaspoon salt. Place between 2 sheets of wax paper and beat with the bottom of a heavy skillet, a large hammer or a rolling pin until it is finely ground. Mix with the cream of wheat.

Place ¼ cup of the mixture in a flat-bottom bowl and sprinkle with a very little water. Mix with a fork until the water is evenly distributed and the mixture has turned into even crumbs. Add a little more water and mix as before. Stop adding and mixing as soon as mixture looks like coarse crumbs—about the size of a large pin head. Do not expect all crumbs to be exactly alike. Spread crumbs on a cookie sheet. Repeat until you run out of cream of wheat. Allow to dry overnight.

Bring 4 cups of broth to a boil. Add the cream of wheat crumbs. Stir well and cook at a low boil up to 3 minutes, stirring frequently. Taste to see if cooked after just 30 seconds: depending on the size of the crumbs, how dry they are and on the quality of the cream of wheat used, cooking time can vary. As soon as *al dente* turn off heat and add the 2 remaining cups of broth. Stir well and serve immediately. Salt may be added according to taste.

A small amount of Parmesan can be sprinkled on top, although it tends to detract from the very delicate taste.

SERVES: 6

Cabbage Soup, Fregula with Broth

PETER JOHNSON

Coniglio all'Agrodolce

Rabbit in Sweet and Sour Sauce

Of ancient origins, this dish was originally made with hare. Now that game is becoming increasingly scarse, rabbit makes a good substitute.

Sugar is commonly used with wine vinegar in *agrodolce*, but in this recipe the sweetness and additional flavour is provided by prunes.

6 tablespoons olive oil
2 lb (1 kg) clean rabbit pieces, one liver included
1 onion, finely chopped
2 tablespoons capers, well squeezed if in vinegar, well rinsed if in salt
12 green olives, pitted and finely chopped
2 tablespoons red wine vinegar
15 dry pitted prunes
salt to taste

Heat the oil in a large skillet and sear the rabbit pieces, liver excluded. Add onion, 1 tablespoon capers, half the olives and the liver. Cook over high heat, stirring for a minute or two, until the added ingredients begin to brown. Add vinegar, the remaining capers and olives and the prunes.

Stir, then cook, covered, for 20 minutes, leaving lid a crack open. Set heat on low, adjusting it so that there is no build-up of liquid released by the ingredients. Stir occasionally.

Remove the liver, mash it, return it to the pan and stir well. Serve either hot or at room temperature, adding a little salt if necessary.

SERVES: 4

PETER JOHNSON

Rabbit in Sweet and Sour Sauce, Baby Goat Oristano Style, Pot Roasted Beef Fillet

Filetto in Casseruola

Pot Roasted Beef Fillet

There are many versions of *filetto in casseruola* throughout Italy. The juniper berries in this one give it a particularly Sardinian character.

2 lb (1 kg) very lean beef fillet, tied with string, keeping the string turns close together
1 cup (8 fl oz/250 ml) dry white wine
2 teaspoons lemon juice
few small pieces lemon rind
20 juniper berries, crushed
4 small parsley sprigs
¼ teaspoon finely ground black pepper
¼ cup (2 fl oz/60 ml) olive oil
1 tablespoon unsalted butter
4 anchovy fillets, mashed
salt to taste

Marinate the beef for a few hours in the wine, lemon juice, lemon rind, juniper berries, parsley and pepper.

Remove beef from the marinade and sear it in the oil and butter over high heat. Add the marinade and cook over high heat for 15 to 20 minutes, turning often and adding small quantities of water as liquid dries out. At end of cooking period liquid should be the consistency of thick meat juices (thin with water if necessary, or reduce).

Stir the anchovies into the sauce, and add salt to taste. Slice the beef, spoon sauce on top and serve hot.

SERVES: 6

PETER JOHNSON

Boiled Birds

Uccelli Bolliti

Boiled Birds

Hunters flock to Sardegna during the season and spare little. Partridges are particularly sought-after.

4 partridges, approximately 12 oz (375 g) or more each (clean bird weight)
2 large carrots
1 onion
6 parsley sprigs, plus 2 cups lightly packed leaves
6 canned peeled tomatoes, seeded
4 tablespoons capers preserved in vinegar
8 large green olives, pitted
4 tablespoons olive oil
freshly ground black pepper to taste

Place the partridges in a pot in which they will fit tightly. Add water to barely cover them. Bring to a boil, add the carrots, onion, parsley sprigs and tomatoes. Cover, and simmer for 40 minutes.

In a food processor, using the steel blade, very briefly chop the remaining parsley, the capers, olives and olive oil (or cut the solid ingredients rather finely by hand, mixing in the oil at the end). The ingredients should not be puréed. Then mix in 4 tablespoons of the broth.

Remove the partridge from the broth and cut in halves or in sections. Spoon the sauce on top and serve immediately, or refrigerate and serve the following day. Traditionally the dish is served cold, but refrigeration tightens the meat.

To use the broth for other dishes, allow to reduce over a low heat to 6 cups, then strain.

SERVES: 4 to 6

Capretto all'Oristanese

Baby Goat Oristano Style

A straightforward meat dish that will work equally well with lamb if goat is unobtainable.

1/3 cup (3 fl oz/90 ml) olive oil
4 to 5 lb (2 to 2.5 kg) baby goat, bones included, or substitute 1 3/4 lb (875 g) very lean boneless lamb cut into 1-in (2-cm) chunks
10 large canned peeled tomatoes, seeded and finely chopped
1 1/2 teaspoons dried oregano leaves
1/2 teaspoon salt

Heat the oil in a very large skillet and sear the lamb. Add tomatoes, oregano and salt and cook, covered, over medium-low heat for 8 minutes. Keep the heat so that the meat is moist but not watery.

If using baby goat, depending on the parts used (ribs, legs) and their size, the cooking time may need to be somewhat longer and the heat to be a little lower. Serve hot.

Any leftover meat can be used as a filling for *impanadas*, see *Impanadas di Pesce* recipe in the following column.

SERVES: 6

Impanadas di Pesce

Fish Turnovers

Traditionally eel is used for fish *impanadas*. If eel bones do not bother you, in place of salmon fillet use 3/4-in (2-cm) sections of eel.

Filling:
1 1/4 lb (625 g) salmon fillet, cut in 3/4-in (2-cm) cubes (approximately)
3 tablespoons olive oil
2 tablespoons finely chopped parsley
1 garlic clove, finely chopped
1 tablespoon onion, finely chopped
1/4 teaspoon finely ground black pepper
1/2 teaspoon salt

Pastry:
3 cups (12 oz/375 g) unbleached all purpose (plain) flour
4 tablespoons olive oil, or substitute 4 tablespoons melted unsalted butter
¼ teaspoon salt

Marinate the salmon in all the other filling ingredients for 1 to 3 hours.

For the pastry: Make a well in the flour. Pour in the oil, 4 tablespoons room temperature water and salt. Using a fork, stir into the liquid ingredients as much flour as they will absorb. Knead—adding up to 10 more tablespoons of water—until you have made a firm and elastic dough. Wrap in a damp cloth and set to rest in fridge until lightly chilled.

Make the dough into a 2-in (5-cm) diameter roll and slice it in 24 rounds. Roll the rounds out to a diameter of 3 in (7 cm). Place the filling in the middle of 12 of the rounds. Cover with the remaining rounds. Pinch the edges firmly together, twisting the pinched dough a little each time so that the sealed edge looks like a thin rope.

Place the *impanadas*, uncrowded, on a lightly oiled cookie sheet. Bake in oven preheated to 425°F (220°C) for 15 to 18 minutes, until the dough becomes a light golden brown. Serve hot or at room temperature.

SERVES: 4 to 6 (makes 12 *impanadas*)

PETER JOHNSON

Fish Turnovers

Piselli a Tortino

Cake of Peas

Peas are loved by the local people and their use is widespread. This dish can equally well be served as a main course.

2 tablespoons onion, finely chopped
4 tablespoons olive oil
1 lb (500 g) shelled peas, fresh or frozen (if frozen, dip in boiling water for about 30 seconds to defrost)
¼ teaspoon salt
3 eggs, beaten as for scrambled eggs
4 tablespoons freshly grated Parmesan cheese

Cook the onion in olive oil for a couple of minutes over medium-low heat. Add the peas and salt and cook, covered, over low heat, for 8 to 10 minutes. Allow to counter cool a little. Stir in the eggs and cheese.

Butter and flour an 8-in (20-cm) round baking dish and spoon the mixture into it. Bake in oven preheated to 375°F (190°C) for 30 minutes. Serve hot or at room temperature.

SERVES: 6

Fave e Salsiccia

Broad Beans and Sausage

Broad beans and sausages are very much a part of people's everyday diet, and complement each other well.

1¾ lb (875 g) shelled broad beans, fresh or frozen (if frozen, dip in boiling water for a few moments to defrost)
1 lb (500 g) pork sausage, casing pierced in many spots
⅓ cup (3 fl oz/90 ml) olive oil
6 green onions (scallions or spring onions), thinly sliced
½ teaspoon aniseed
20 mint leaves
½ teaspoon salt
¼ teaspoon freshly ground black pepper

If the bean skins are not very tender, remove them, whether you are using fresh or frozen beans. Set aside.

Place the sausage in a pan and cover with water. Bring to a boil and cook for 15 minutes. Drain and cut into ¼-in (5-mm) rounds.

Heat the oil and add onion, aniseed and sausage. Cook for a few minutes, until ingredients start browning. Add beans, mint leaves, salt and pepper. Add ½ cup of water, reduce heat to low, cover and simmer for 15 minutes.

Uncover, increase heat to high and cook for a couple of minutes, or until there is little moisture left. Serve hot.

SERVES: 6

Patate con Maionese

Potatoes with Mayonnaise

Potatoes and mayonnaise go particularly well together. This is the way they are served in Sardegna.

2½ lb (1.25 kg) potatoes
4 egg yolks
½ teaspoon salt
1¼ cups (10 fl oz/310 ml) olive oil
5 teaspoons lemon juice
freshly ground black pepper to taste

Cover potatoes with water. Bring to a boil and cook until cooked but firm—20 to 30 minutes. Peel, cool, then slice into ⅔-in (2-cm) thick rounds.

Place the egg yolks in a small non-metal mixing bowl with the salt. Stir evenly, always in the same direction, for 5 minutes. Add the first ¼ cup oil, a few drops at a time, always stirring the same way. Add the rest of the oil by the ½ tablespoon, stirring after each addition until fully absorbed. When there is only ⅓ of the oil left to be added start alternating its addition with the lemon juice.

Top the potato slices with the mayonnaise and sprinkle with pepper, if you wish. Serve at room temperature or cold. Traditionally the potatoes are cut in ⅔-in (2-cm) cubes and tossed with the mayonnaise, but this presentation might be thought more attractive.

SERVES: 6

Cake of Peas, Broad Beans and Sausage, Potatoes with Mayonnaise

PETER JOHNSON

Pabassinas

Chocolate and Nut Cookies

Pabassinas are sometimes moistened with grape juice before being served.

2 cups (8 oz/250 g) unbleached all purpose (plain) flour
½ cup (4 oz/125 g) sugar
½ teaspoon baking powder
4 oz (125 g) unsalted butter, at room temperature
1 extra large egg
½ cup (2 oz/60 g) walnuts, ground not too finely
½ cup (2 oz/60 g) almonds, ground not too finely
⅓ cup (2 oz/60 g) raisins
3 oz (90 g) semisweet (plain) chocolate

Mix the flour, sugar and baking powder well together, and then roughly mix in the butter. Add the egg, using your fingers to toss and mix the ingredients together. Stop as soon as dough holds together. Quickly cut in nuts and raisins. Shape the dough into a log approximately 6½ in (16 cm) long and 3½ in (9 cm) wide. Cut crosswise into 10 slices. Cut each slice in half.

Butter and flour a cookie sheet. Place the cookies on it, uncrowded. While doing so you may lightly round the edges of the cookies.

Bake in oven preheated to 350°F (180°C) for 20 minutes. Decrease to 325°F (160°C) and bake for a further 10 minutes. Counter cool. Melt chocolate in double boiler. Brush the cookie tops with it.

May be kept for several weeks in an airtight container in a cool place.

MAKES: 20 cookies

Torrone all'Arancia

Orange Nougat

Torrone did not originate in Sardegna but this recipe has a local touch.

2¼ cups (8 oz/250 g) sliced almonds
2 oz (60 g) orange rind (without pith), removed with a potato peeler
½ cup(4 oz/125 g) sugar
1 cup (10 oz/315 g) honey
olive oil

Spread the almonds on a cookie sheet. Place in oven preheated to 250°F (120°C) for 15 to 25 minutes, until barely brown. Keep warm.

Cover the orange rind with plenty of water, bring to a boil, drain, rinse, cover with water again, bring to a boil, drain and rinse. Squeeze, blot out moisture and spread on cookie sheet. Place in oven preheated to 250°F (120°C) for 10 minutes, until dry. Cut in slivers.

Place sugar in a large skillet and stir in 2 tablespoons water. Stir in honey over low heat until dissolved. Add orange rind and stir about 2 minutes. Add almonds and cook, stirring, over medium-low heat for 10 to 12 minutes, until well caramelized.

Transfer the mixture to a surface (preferably marble or formica—*not* wood) well coated with oil. Flatten a little with a spatula. Coat a large knife blade with oil and as soon as the mixture loses a little heat (1 to 2 minutes) shape it with the blade into a 9-in (22-cm) square. If mixture sticks to the knife, wait a few seconds and try again. Press blade down to compact the nougat well. Cut the square into 2 equal rectangles, and then cut across to form 16 bars. Remember, mixture must be cut while warm.

May be kept for several weeks in an airtight container in a cool place.

MAKES: 16 bars

Germinus

Almond Cookies

These very light almond cookies are of Arab origin.

3 egg whites, cold
¾ cup (6 oz/185 g) sugar
1 tablespoon lemon juice
1½ teaspoons grated lemon rind
2¼ cups (8 oz/250 g) slivered, blanched almonds

Beat egg whites until foamy. Add the sugar by the tablespoon, beating between each addition. After last of the sugar has been added, beat until stiff and glossy. Dribble lemon juice in and add rind. Fold in almonds.

Place mixture on cookie sheet lined with baking paper by the heaping tablespoon, uncrowded. Bake in oven preheated to 250°F (120°C) for 1 hour and 10 minutes. Counter cool.

MAKES: 24

Sebadas

Cheese Turnovers

These unusual sweets are found all over the island. A generous dousing with honey before serving is essential.

Filling:
½ lb (250 g) commercial mozzarella, or a comparable fresh mild cheese with a low water content, in ¼-in (5-mm) slices cut in 1-in (2-cm) sections. (Avoid freshly made mozzarella as it has too high a water content)
Pastry:
4 tablespoons melted unsalted butter, or substitute 4 tablespoons olive oil
¼ teaspoon salt
3 cups (12 oz/375 g) unbleached all purpose (plain) flour
corn oil for deep frying
½ cup (5 oz/155 g) honey, heated until dissolved

In a well in the flour place the butter, 4 tablespoons room temperature water and the salt. Using a fork, stir into the liquid ingredients as much flour as they will absorb. Knead—adding up to 10 more tablespoons of water—until you have made a firm and elastic dough. Wrap in a damp cloth and set to rest in fridge until lightly chilled.

Make the dough into a 2-in (5-cm) diameter roll and slice it in 24 rounds. Roll the rounds out to a diameter of 4 in (10 cm). Pile the cheese slices flat, one on top of the other, in the middle of 12 of the rounds. Pinch the edges firmly together, twisting the pinched dough a little each time so that the sealed edge looks like a thin rope.

Heat 1½ in (3 cm) oil in a deep fryer, keeping heat on medium-high to medium. Add the *sebadas* just before the smoking point. Turn each one a few seconds after placing in oil and then keep turning every 10 seconds. Fry until golden—about 1 minute. Set on paper towels to drain. Place on serving dish, trickle hot honey on top and serve hot.

SERVES: 6 (makes 12 turnovers)

Following pages: Cheese Turnovers, Chocolate and Nut Cookies, Orange Nougat, Almond Cookies

PETER JOHNSON

NICOLA SANTORO/SPERANZA

Silhouettes of cypresses in the Tuscan countryside.

ACKNOWLEDGMENTS

A number of people and organizations were of assistance to the publishers in the preparation of this book. Many thanks to the following for photographic props: Corso di Fiori, Chatswood; Appley Hoare Antiques, Woollahra; John Normyle, Paddington; The Bay Tree, Woollahra; Country Floors, Woollahra; Accoutrement, Mosman; Parterre Garden, Woollahra; Hampshire and Lowndes, Double Bay; Villa Italiana, Mosman; Jenny Stuart at Turning the Tables, Mosman; Hale Imports for Pillivuyt, Villeroy and Boch; Ventura for Alessi; Penny's Butchery, Mosman; Porter's Original Limewash; and Metro Marble. Karen Byak, Maureen Simpson, David Furley, Inger Marchant, Susan Whitter, Elizabeth McLeod, Janice Baker, and Peter Johnson kindly lent privately-owned items for photographic propping. Thanks to Susan Whitter and Elizabeth McLeod for food preparation and styling, Robert White for helping with the photography, and Laurine Croasdale and Jane Fraser for valuable editorial and administrative support.

GLOSSARY

ABBACCHIO: Baby lamb slaughtered when between thirty and sixty days old.The meat is pale and tender.

ACETO BALSAMICO: A full-bodied vinegar, dark brown in color, aged for at least ten years. Modena is the home of this versatile preparation, which is used in a wide variety of dishes, both savory and sweet, and also served as a drink.

AFFETTATO: A plate of sliced pork meats, traditionally an *antipasto* but sometimes also served as the main dish at informal lunches. Meats include prosciutto, *mortadella, coppa*, and various types of salami.

ANOLINI: Half-moon shaped stuffed pasta from Emilia-Romagna.

AL FUNGHETTO: A method of cooking vegetables, sautéeing them over a high heat in olive oil, garlic, and parsley. Mushrooms, zucchini, and eggplant are commonly cooked this way.

ALLA PARMIGIANA: Parma-style preparation of vegetables, boiled and then served with melted butter and grated Parmesan cheese. It is also used to describe veal scallops sautéed in butter and then sprinkled with Parmesan.

AMARENE: Fleshy, dark red cherries, with a slightly bitter taste, known as morello cherries. They are generally preserved in alcohol, and used in desserts, particularly ice cream, although they are also sometimes eaten fresh.

AMARETTI: Small, crisp macaroons made with sweet and bitter almonds, available throughout northern Italy.

ACCIUGA: The anchovy, a small fish common in the seas around Italy, widely available preserved in oil or salt. Anchovies have a pungent flavor and are used in many dishes. If using salted ones, thoroughly wash and bone them before use.

ANTIPASTO: The course that precedes the rest of the meal (*pasto* meaning meal). *Antipasti* are more commonly served in restaurants than at home, comprising a selection of dishes to tempt the appetite.

ARBORIO RICE: A plump long-grain rice used in both sweet and savory dishes. It is particularly favored for *risotto*.

BACCALA: Salted, dried cod, in large chunks. The same fish, air-dried but unsalted, is called *stoccafisso*. Both must be soaked for some time before cooking—*baccalà* for twenty-four hours, *stoccafisso* for twice as long—and both can be prepared in the same ways. In the Veneto *stoccafisso* is known as *baccalà*.

BIGOLI: A form of large, home-made spaghetti, made with whole wheat flour. *Bigoli* are a specialty of the Veneto.

BOLLITO MISTO: A specialty of the north consisting of a variety of meats, such as beef, veal, chicken, tongue, and sausage, boiled in water for varying times, depending on how long each piece of meat takes to cook. It is most commonly served with *salsa verde,* a piquant parsley sauce. In Piemonte *bollito misto* is known as *il gran bui* and is served with several different sauces.

BRODETTO: The traditional Mediterranean fish soup, always made with a large assortment of fish, the recipes varying from region to region.

BRUSCHETTA: Served usually before a meal, *bruschetta* is a dish of thick slices of country-style bread, charcoal-grilled then rubbed with garlic and dressed with extra virgin olive oil.

BUCATINI: A type of pasta, resembling thick, hollow spaghetti. *Bucatini* can be used in the place of spaghetti in many recipes.

CACIOCAVALLO: Available throughout the south, this cheese can be eaten fresh or aged. When mature it has a strong flavor and is suitable for grating.

CALAMARI: Squid, known as *calamaretti* if they are small.

COPPA: Pork shoulder, rolled and cured. Ideally it should be equal parts lean meat to fat. It is similar to prosciutto in taste. Coppa is served as part of an *affetato,* and is used to add flavor to sauces and stews.

COTECHINO: A traditional pork sausage from the north, often served with lentils or in a *bollito misto.*

COZZE: Mussels, also known as *mitili.*

CROSTINI: Popular snacks or *antipasti,* consisting of small slices of bread toasted in the oven then covered with any of a large number of tasty spreads. *Crostini alla napoletana* are topped with a slice of mozzarella, a small piece of anchovy, and a slice of tomato and then baked.

CULATELLO: Salted and spiced pork, taken from the top round of the leg, aged for a year or more. This is one of the many fine pork products for which Emilia-Romagna is known.

DI MAGRO: A term that is used to refer to lean meat or to dishes that are meatless.

FARFALLE: Butterfly-shaped pasta, which are usually served with cream sauces.

FARINATA: A thick baked pancake made with chickpea flour, eaten as a snack in Liguria in the bars and at the market.

FETTUCCINE: A pasta similar to *tagliatelle* but a little narrower and thicker.

FONDUTA: A sauce from Piemonte made from melted *fontina* cheese, milk, eggs, and white truffles. It is usually served with toast or grilled polenta.

FONTINA: A semi-soft cow's milk cheese which is used extensively in the north for cooking.

FRITTATA: A thick omelette, similar to a Spanish *tortilla,* made with a variety of ingredients, such as vegetables, cheese, or fish.

FRITTO MISTO: Mixed fry—a dish available throughout Italy. These tasty fried morsels can range from fruit fritters and semolina croquettes in Piemonte to artichokes in Lazio, and seafood, vegetables, and cubes of mozzarella in Campania.

GELATO: Used to refer to an ice cream or a water ice, although the latter should really be called a *sorbetto.*

GNOCCHI: Small dumplings, generally made of potato or semolina, although there are regional variations.

GORGONZOLA: A full-fat, blue-veined cheese, named after the small town just north of Milano where it originated.

GRANA: The generic name for hard, grainy cheeses, the most famous of all being Parmesan.

GRANITA: A drink made from fruit juice or sweet coffee, which has been frozen and then crushed.

IN GUAZZETTO: A style of cooking in which fish, seafood, or frogs are prepared in a white wine based sauce.

IN POTACCIO: A method of cooking common in Marche, in which fish, game, or poultry are braised with tomato, white wine, and rosemary.

IN UMIDO: The braising or stewing method of cooking, a small amount of liquid always remaining in the pan.

LASAGNE: Rectangular sheets of pasta that are cooked and then layered with one of many varieties of sauce and baked in the oven. *Vincisgrassi* is the traditional lasagne from Marche.

LINGUINE: Long, flat, narrow pasta, which can be used in the place of spaghetti.

LUGANEGA: A mild fresh pork sausage, originally made in Basilicata, which is now produced in large quantities in Lombardia and the Veneto.

MASCARPONE: A rich cream cheese which is used in a variety of desserts and sometimes in pasta sauces.

MINESTRA: A thin vegetable soup, often containing rice or the small varieties of pasta especially made for soups.

MINESTRONE: A thick vegetable soup, cooked slowly for at least two hours. There are many different varieties, some containing rice and small tubular pasta. Dried white beans are a common ingredient, particularly during winter.

MOCETTA: At one time mocetta was boned, cured chamois thigh, but as the chamois is now rare, domestic goat is generally used instead. A specialty of Valle d'Aosta.

MORTADELLA: A smooth pork sausage, pink in color, measuring up to 16 in (40 cm) in diameter. It is usually served cold, sliced, as part of an *affetato,* but it is also used in a number of pasta stuffings. The best *mortadella* is considered to come from Bologna.

MOSTARDA DI CREMONA: A mixture of candied fruit, syrup, spices, and mustard, made in Cremona. which is served with boiled meats.

OLIO D'OLIVA: A wide variety of olive oils are produced throughout Italy, choice largely depending on personal taste, although the experts maintain that only certain oils should be used for particular dishes. The highest quality is extra virgin olive oil, which contains less than 1 per cent acidity. Generally, the less cooking a dish is to be given, the higher the quality of oil that should be used.

OLIVE: Green olives are harvested before they are ripe; black ones when they are over-ripe. Methods of processing and preservation vary, the olives being stored in brine or olive oil, to which flavorings are often added, such as lemon, chili, and garlic: there are numerous regional variations. The flavor of black olives is stronger than the green.

PAN DI SPAGNA: Sponge cake, used in dishes such as *zuppa inglese* and *cassata di Sulmona.*

PANCETTA: Cured pork belly, either flat or rolled, used in bases for stews and sauces, and sometimes in recipes in the place of prosciutto.

PANDORO: A light traditional Christmas cake from Verona, now produced commercially throughout the year. Named golden bread because of its color, it is baked in a star-shaped mold and liberally sprinkled with powdered (icing) sugar.

PANETTONE: A dome-shaped yeast cake studded with candied peel and seedless raisins, a specialty of Milano. Now made commercially in huge quantities and sold throughout the world.

PANFORTE: A flat fruit and spice cake from Siena, said to have been carried by the Crusaders because it was so fortifying. Large quantities are made commercially and exported widely.

PAPPARDELLE: Noodles from Toscana, similar to *tagliatelle* but twice as wide.

PARMIGIANO-REGGIANO: Parmesan, a hard cheese from specifically designated regions in Emilia-Romagna, made into massive wheels weighing up to 80 lb (32 kg). No other cheese is matured for so long, the *stravecchio* being aged from between two and three years. Parmesan is used, freshly grated, to season quantities of dishes, but is also served in slivers on salads and in *antipasti,* and eaten as a table cheese.

PECORINO: A ewe's milk cheese made throughout central and southern Italy. The best-known varieties are *toscano, romano, siciliano,* and *sardo* (from Sardegna). These cheeses vary in flavor depending on where they have been produced and the amount of time they have been aged.

PENNE: Dried tubular pasta.

PESTO: A sauce made with basil, Parmesan, garlic, olive oil, and pine nuts, primarily from Liguria, where the sweetest basil is said to grow.

PIZZAIOLA: A tomato, oil, and oregano sauce named after pizza, because it tastes like pizza topping, in which meat and fish are cooked.

POLENTA: A dish made from cornmeal boiled in water, which is quite firm when cooked. A staple in northern Italy, it is served in numerous ways—simply dressed with butter and grated Parmesan; with sauces; as an accompaniment to meat and fish dishes; made into gnocchi.

PORCINI: Boletus mushrooms, which grow wild in many parts of Italy. *Porcini* are widely available in dried form.

PROSCIUTTO: The cured hind leg of a pig and a very popular part of the Italian diet. The three best known prosciutti are those from Parma, San Daniele, and the Veneto. Flavors vary from sweet and delicate to salty and strong. Sliced extremely thinly, it is served as part of an *affetato,* or at the start of a meal with melon or fresh figs. It is also cooked in a wide range of dishes to impart flavor.

PROVOLONE: A cow's milk cheese produced in southern Italy which is kneaded and made into many shapes both large and small–round, oval, and tubular. The small ones are called *provolette,* the medium-size ones *provole,* and the large ones *provolone.* Young *provolone* is quite soft, with a piquant taste. The more mature the cheese, the stronger its flavor becomes.

RADICCHIO: A red leafy vegetable with a pleasantly bitter taste, generally used in salads, but it can be cooked. The Treviso *radicchio,* with long, crisp leaves, has the better flavor, but the rounded variety from Castelfranco is the one more commonly found outside Italy.

RAGU: A rich meat sauce, cooked for at least two hours, used to dress pasta. The word is also sometimes used for fish sauces made with tomato and wine.

RAVIOLI: Stuffed pasta, available throughout Italy with a wide range of fillings, such as meat, fish, vegetables, or ricotta, bound together with eggs and flavored with Parmesan.

RICOTTA: A milk product, made from the whey produced in cheese making. Traditionally made from the whey of ewe's milk, it is now largely made from that of cows. Light and delicately flavored, it is used in many desserts, as a pasta filling, in pies, and in soups, and is also eaten on its own, or with fruit.

RISOTTO: Rice, ideally Arborio rice, cooked in broth (stock) that is added gradually as the grains absorb it. Ingredients of all sorts can be added, from fish to meats, to vegetables.

ROBIOLA: A creamy cheese from Piemonte and Lombardia, which is similar to *taleggio* when aged.

SALSICCIA: Sausage made with coarsely ground pork, a staple throughout Italy. In the north seasoning is generally limited to salt and pepper, whereas in the south chili and various other flavorings are added.

SCAMORZA: A supple white cheese made from whole cow's milk, pear-shaped and tied with string around the top. It is eaten fresh, both as a table cheese and cooked in various dishes. It is sometimes smoked.

SCORZONERA: A black-skinned root vegetable, shaped like a carrot, eaten in northern Italy.

STOCCAFISSO: See BACCALA.

STRACCHINO: A group of cheeses from the north, including *taleggio, robiola,* and *Gorgonzola,* generally made from the warm milk from the morning's milking mixed with the milk of the evening before.

STRACOTTO: Meaning "overcooked", this refers to braising meat for a lengthy period in tomato and wine.

TAGLIATELLE: Egg noodles rolled thin and cut around $^3/_8$ in (1 cm) wide—a specialty of northern and central Italy. *Fettuccine* are Roman-style *tagliatelle.*

TALEGGIO: A soft, delicate cheese that is made in the north. It has a reddish rind that is produced through its being brined while ripening.

TOMA: A cow's milk cheese from the north, eaten fresh in the spring and summer, or mature. *Polenta cunscia* is polenta dressed with *toma.*

TORRONE: A honey and almond based nougat, for which the Cremona area is particularly well known. A range of nougats are made throughout the country, containing such ingredients as candied fruit and chocolate.

TORTELLINI: Stuffed pasta, the gastronomic symbol of Bologna.

TRENETTE: A pasta similar to *tagliatelle,* from Liguria.

ZAMPONE: A boned pig's trotter stuffed with minced pork, rind, and spices, forming a kind of sausage, served as part of a *bollito misto* or with lentils. A traditional *zampone* requires at least four hours cooking, but precooked ones are commonly available from Italian delicatessens.

ZENZERO: Ginger. But in Toscana *zenzero* means chili.

ZUPPA: A thick soup, either vegetable, meat, or fish, poured over toasted bread.

INDEX

Page numbers in *italics* refer to illustrations